ACKNOWLEDGMENT

The authors, editor and publishers are indebted
to Mr. Roderick Ham and The Architectural
Press Ltd. for the use of material and diagrams
from "Theatre Planning" (© Association of
British Theatre Technicians 1972), edited by
Mr. Ham and published by The Architectural
Press.

PLANNING

Buildings for Administration, Entertainment and Recreation

PLANNING, Ninth edition

Other volume titles

Architects Technical Reference Data

Buildings for Habitation, Commerce and Industry

Buildings for Health, Welfare and Religion

Buildings for Education, Culture and Science

PLANNING

Buildings for Administration, Entertainment and Recreation

Edited by
EDWARD D. MILLS, C.B.E., F.R.I.B.A., F.S.I.A.

ROBERT E. KRIEGER PUBLISHING COMPANY
HUNTINGTON, NEW YORK
1976

ENGLAND	Butterworth & Co (Publishers) Ltd
	London: 88 Kingsway, WC2B 6AB
AUSTRALIA	Butterworths Pty Ltd
	Sydney: 586 Pacific Highway, NSW 2067
	Melbourne: 343 Little Collins Street, 3000
	Brisbane: 240 Queen Street, 4000
NEW ZEALAND	Butterworths of New Zealand Ltd
	Wellington: 26–28 Waring Taylor Street, 1
SOUTH AFRICA	Butterworth & Co (South Africa) (Pty) Ltd
	Durban: 152–154 Gale Street
UNITED STATES	**Robert E. Krieger Publishing Co Inc**
	645 New York Avenue, Huntington, NY 11743
	Exclusive Distributor – ISBN 0–88275–426–2

First published in 1936 by Architect & Building News
Second edition 1937
Third edition 1938
Fourth edition 1939
Fifth edition published for Architect & Building News
by Gilbert Wood & Co Ltd 1947
Sixth edition 1949
Seventh edition published for Architect & Building News
by Iliffe & Sons Ltd 1953
Eighth edition published for Architect & Building News
by Iliffe Books Ltd 1959
Ninth edition published by Newnes-Butterworths 1976

© E. D. Mills, 1976

Filmset by Ramsay Typesetting (Crawley) Ltd

Printed in Scotland by Thomson Litho Ltd., East Kilbride

FOREWORD

By Gontran Goulden, O.B.E., T.D., F.R.I.B.A.
Deputy Chairman, The Building Centre Group

The construction industry becomes daily more complicated and to attempt to abstract the relevant information from the mass of literature available is no easy task. It is now almost impossible for one man to know even the main sources of technical information by heart.

For nearly forty years *Planning* has been a leader among the books that list, discuss and illustrate all those vital facts and figures that are not to be found in one place elsewhere. The man on the drawing board, whether a beginner, experienced in general or specialised practice, or about to burst into computerised building design will always need simple basic information of the kind that packs the pages of this entirely new edition of *Planning* which has been expanded and now comprises five volumes.

The whole question of information for the construction industry still awaits a satisfactory solution. It is doubtful even whether it is capable of being solved to meet everyone's demands. At one end of the scale there are those who demand comprehensive lists of manufacturers and products, corrected up to the minute and covering every conceivable detail of each item. Others require research information in the greatest depth with all available sources equally up to date and comprehensive. We know that this problem can be dealt with by computers, at a price. We know too that various attempts and exercises have been and are being made to turn this major undertaking into a financially possible service.

Only time will show whether the user can be trained to realise that time spent in his office on research costs money and that the answer could be available in less time, thereby saving him money. A small proportion of users are prepared to pay for information, most still think it should be free and paid for by the other fellow. Comprehensive information for the industry will require a nationally co-ordinated effort. So far there is little or no sign of this.

In the meantime the need for the right information continues in all branches of the industry. In addition to major outside-the-office sources each one of us has his own particular favourite reference books and catalogues. This personal preference will always be there wherever comprehensive systems develop.

Planning has filled many people's personal information needs for years. With a mass of useful data, and as a guide to the form of construction industry information generally, this new edition should, like its predecessors, prove invaluable and I wish it every success.

Gontran Goulden

CONTENTS

INTRODUCTION

Planning first appeared as a weekly feature in the Architect & Building News and was contributed by two architects under the pseudonym of E. & O.E. In 1936 the first bound volume was published and the authors were subsequently revealed as Roland Pierce and Patrick Cutbush, later to be joined by Anthony Williams. Since that date eight editions have appeared at frequent intervals and the general pattern has changed little over the years. Today, *Planning* is recognised throughout the world as one of the standard reference books for architects. There can be few architects offices in the UK which do not possess and constantly use at least one copy, and in many architects offices in the remote parts of the world a much used copy still holds pride of place on the bookshelf. Architectural students have always found this to be an essential work of reference and many have started their architectural libraries with *Planning* and one or two of the other well known books of reference.

The radical changes which are taking place in the world of building has led to a reappraisal of the place of *Planning* in the technical information field and in the way which the valuable material it contained is presented. New techniques and disciplines are being developed in the building industry and these must be reflected in the technical information available. The building industry is becoming more closely integrated and *Planning* must inevitably reflect this. It has, therefore, been restructured so that it appeals to a wider cross-section of the industry including architects, builders, quantity surveyors, engineers, planners and students. With these considerations in mind, together with the change to metric in the building industry, the publishers Newnes-Butterworth and Building and Contract Journals who have taken over the publishing responsibilities of the Architect & Building News, decided that a completely new approach should be adopted and this volume is one of a series which reflect the new pattern.

The previous edition consisted of three sections; a general section dealing with information applicable to more than one type of building; a section dealing with information applicable to specific building types and metrication information to aid the conversion of imperial units to metric ones. In essence the new edition accepts this broad classification and although the work has been conceived in metric, the conversion material is retained in part.

The volume entitled *Planning—Architects' technical reference data* includes sections dealing with legislation, British Standards, materials etc., as well as basic planning data which concerns all types of building, such as landscaping, car parking, circulation, sanitary requirements, storage requirements etc., together with the metric conversion material originally in the eighth edition. All information contained in earlier editions that is still valid has been retained and a considerable amount of new material has been added. Other volumes deal with specific building types and cover a wide range of subjects, some of these building types have not been dealt with in previous editions.

The unique characteristic of this series of volumes is that it indicates how various types of buildings are planned by supplying information and data which are essential before planning can begin. It does not deal with the aesthetics of design, although in the volumes dealing with particular building types illustration is not only by means of diagrams but by plans and photographs of actual completed buildings, either in part or whole showing the way in which particular problems have been solved.

The endeavour throughout all sections of the new edition has been to provide a ready reference of basic information, or guidance as to where more detailed information can be obtained. One book can never hope to provide all the facts, and inevitably information will be omitted or given in part but it is hoped that readers will find this new method of presentation useful, and that it will carry on the long tradition of *Planning* as an essential publication for all concerned with building.

The volumes dealing with specific building types are subdivided as follows: *Habitation, Commerce and Industry; Health, Welfare and Religion; Administration, Entertainment and Recreation; Education, Culture and Science.* Each building type is covered by the following subsections to ensure uniform treatment and to facilitate ease of reference. These are—Introduction; siting; planning; space requirements; data; accommodation; statutory requirements, legislation and Authorities; examples; bibliography.

Whenever possible diagrams and tables have been used and the bibliography lists the important books and publication that will aid further research. Unlike previous editions, the material for each specialist section has been prepared by architects with a special knowledge and experience in the particular category of building, and the range of building types has been considerably extended. By this means it is hoped that the 9th edition will be even more useful to architects and others than its predecessors.

The sources from which the material for the present edition has been gathered have been many and varied. The Editor greatly appreciates the willing co-operation of the various contributors and a biography of the author is given at the end of each section. Books, periodicals, people and associations have all contributed in a very practical way and because it is impossible to set out a complete list of those concerned, this general acknowledgement is addressed to all who have been associated with the preparation of the book and is an expression of the sincere thanks of both the Editor and publishers.

Finally, special thanks are due to Gontran Goulden who has contributed the foreword in his private and personal capacity. He has been intimately concerned with all aspects of building information in this country and abroad for the past twenty-five years and his continued interest is greatly appreciated.

The Editor would welcome any constructive criticism or comments, as the work will be constantly revised and kept up to date, and every effort will be made to take account of suggestions which may be made, so that they can be applied to future editions.

Edward D. Mills
Editor

Edward D. Mills, *CBE, FRIBA, FSIA, Architect, lecturer and broadcaster, RIBA Alfred Bossom Research Fellow 1953, Churchill Research Fellow, 1969, a member of the RIBA Council from 1955–1962 and from 1963–1969. Senior partner in the architectural practice of Edward D. Mills & Partners, whose works include industrial buildings, schools and research laboratories as well as the Cathedral of St. Andrew, Mbale, Uganda and the National Exhibition Centre, Birmingham.*

Member of the Design Council Farm Buildings Advisory Committee, a member of Uganda Society of Architects and Chairman of the Faculty of Architecture of the British School at Rome. Author of The Modern Factory *(2nd Edition 1959) and* The Modern Church *(1952) published by the Architectural Press;* The New Architecture in Great Britain, *Whitefriars Press (1953);* Factory Building in Great Britain, *Leonard Hill Books (1967);* The Changing Workplace, *George Godwin Ltd. (1972).*

1 TOWN HALLS, CIVIC CENTRES AND MUNICIPAL BUILDINGS

DAVID HUTCHISON, R.I.B.A., A.R.I.A.S., B.A. (Arch), F.F.B., R.I.B.A. Donaldson Medallist.
GRAHAM LOCKE, R.I.B.A., A.R.I.A.S., Dip. Arch. (U.C.L.), Dip. T.P. (Lond.).
NATALIE ROBINSON, D. Arch. (Kingston).
Hutchison Locke and Monk, Chartered Architects

INTRODUCTION

TOWN HALLS

In the strictest sense, a 'Town' (or Civic) Hall is a venue for large scale ceremonial and political assembly, connected with the functions of Local Government. Since the main function is intermittent, economics dictate that such a "Hall" must be capable of dual use, i.e. letting for non-Authority functions, to produce revenue.

In this sense, the Town Hall can provide a focus for the social/cultural life of the community which it serves, and thus help to break down rigid barriers between Local Government and the general public, especially where it is physically associated with the main accommodation.

CIVIC CENTRES AND MUNICIPAL BUILDINGS

These terms describe accommodation for the day-to-day activities of local government, (Town Hall, used in its loosest sense is commonly used to describe this accommodation). In many situations the accommodation will be required to include functional outlets such as libraries, police buildings etc. This discussion is confined to the problems included in provisions for the essential functions of Policy Formation, Execution and Administration. These functions are performed through:

(a) Elected members, in Council, and in Committee with heads of departments, and
(b) Employees—clerical, technical, professional and manual—organised in Departments.

The accommodation concerned is that appropriate for Council and Committee activities, together with Departmental offices and essential support services.

Based on the traditional principle that a service should be rendered by the most local body capable of effective administration, Central Government in Great Britain endows an elected body, related to a defined area, with the duties and powers essential to the local execution of centrally established policies. Today, these functions embrace all elements of the social/economic/political system.

Administrative systems evolved within the functional structure outlined above, together with traditional definition of areas and allocation of functions, have not always proved sufficiently adaptable and flexible, to cope with increases or alterations in the established scope of activities. Thus legislation arising from the results of the Royal Commissions (see bibliography) has been introduced by Central Government, effective from April 1974 (May 1975 in Scotland), to reorganise the basis of Local Authority service. The new structure is illustrated in Table 1.1. The basic services provided by Local Government are illustrated in Table 1.2 where the level of authority to which each function is allocated, is indicated.

Administrative structures to support services have been left to each individual authority, but the majority appear to have made reference to the study group report, commissioned by Central Government, to examine management structures relative to reorganisation. The study group proposed outline management structures, for both members and officers for the various levels of Authority, which could be applied to all situations: the basis of these is illustrated in Table 1.3. The proposed structure is based on the premise, that each Authority is different and that local government (as the outlet for implementation of central policies), needs to be extremely adaptable and flexible, together with the objective that the Authority must not only provide services, but also the physical, cultural and economic framework for the community it serves.

The proposals aim at promoting a sense of corporate image within an Authority by means of

(a) Programme areas at Committee level, in lieu of the established 'Departmental' committees.
(b) Establishment of a matrix system in the organisation of employees, where departments are retained but the development of horizontal systems, between departments in the execution of programmes, breaks down the rigid vertical line responsibility inherent in the traditional department/committee situation.
(c) Co-ordination of resources by the establishment of the

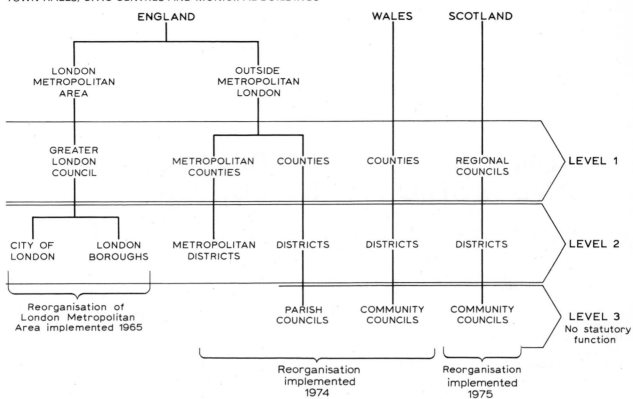

Table 1.1 REORGANISATION OF LOCAL GOVERNMENT

post of Chief Executive: recognition of the significance of organisation and management techniques in the execution of functions.

Wide variations in methods of administration and execution of services are possible within the frameworks proposed, which allow individual Authorities to satisfy prevailing needs, e.g. allocations of functions between programme committees and the structure of departments. Table 1.4 illustrates typical functional departmental groupings for each level of Authority. Departmental structures depend on type of work and scope of total activity within the Authority. The concept of a co-ordinating Director responsible for a number of 'Departmental' functions is only generally applicable where a strong vertical line is appropriate to the functions and where the Director forms the top tier, taking responsibility for activities in each Division of the Directorate, and where the linking of departments as divisions within a Directorate is based on the logical integration of related activities. In authorities with limited function, or small scale the concept of official groupings may be totally inappropriate.

DEPARTMENTAL ACCOMMODATION

In Table 1.3, departments are indicated as providing either a functional or an organisational service. Functional services can be said to be those which provide service to the public. While it is not possible to evaluate exactly how Functional Services will be organised in any particular situation, Table

1.4 indicates that certain departments are commonly found.

(a) FINANCE (Treasurer). This department may also include Valuer and/or Auditor at a small scale, otherwise there may be separate departments. The department is public-orientated, traditionally, subject to intense peaks of visitation at certain times: encounter is formal, requiring physical separation between public and staff. Since the department also deals with internal accounting, it tends to be large and clerical in nature.

(b) DEVELOPMENT/TECHNICAL SERVICES (Engineer, Surveyor, Architect, Planner). At a small scale these may be found in a single department, otherwise they will be operated independently or in various groupings within a directorate. Functions are basically technical and administrative.

(c) PROTECTION (Environmental Health, Weights and Measures etc). All specifically concerned with the administration of legislation, but usually physically separate, owing to the stringent location criteria inherent in the function of Weights and Measures, and the logical linking of Environmental Health with Development Services.
Environmental Health: Accommodation provides a base with administrative back-up, for Inspectors, many of the functions of the old Public Health department having been transferred to the Area Health Authorities.
Weights and measures: In addition to administrative

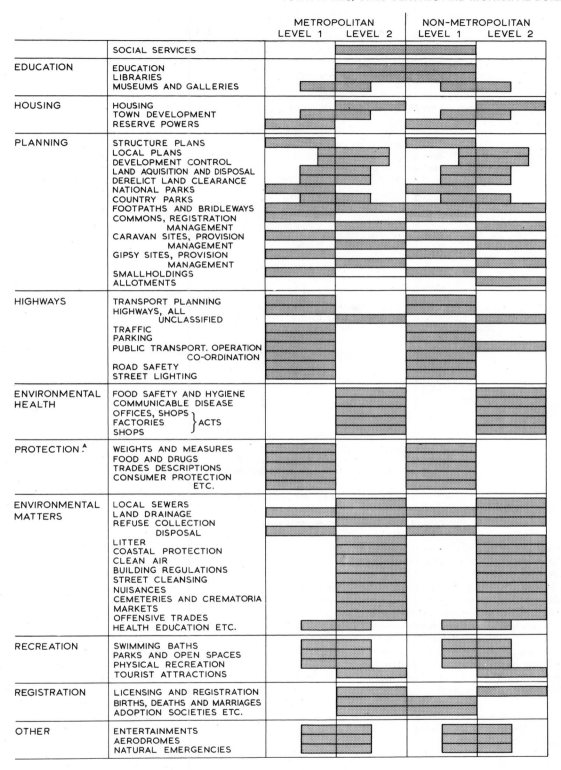

		METROPOLITAN		NON-METROPOLITAN	
		LEVEL 1	LEVEL 2	LEVEL 1	LEVEL 2
	SOCIAL SERVICES				
EDUCATION	EDUCATION				
	LIBRARIES				
	MUSEUMS AND GALLERIES				
HOUSING	HOUSING				
	TOWN DEVELOPMENT				
	RESERVE POWERS				
PLANNING	STRUCTURE PLANS				
	LOCAL PLANS				
	DEVELOPMENT CONTROL				
	LAND AQUISITION AND DISPOSAL				
	DERELICT LAND CLEARANCE				
	NATIONAL PARKS				
	COUNTRY PARKS				
	FOOTPATHS AND BRIDLEWAYS				
	COMMONS, REGISTRATION MANAGEMENT				
	CARAVAN SITES, PROVISION MANAGEMENT				
	GIPSY SITES, PROVISION MANAGEMENT				
	SMALLHOLDINGS				
	ALLOTMENTS				
HIGHWAYS	TRANSPORT PLANNING				
	HIGHWAYS, ALL UNCLASSIFIED				
	TRAFFIC				
	PARKING				
	PUBLIC TRANSPORT. OPERATION CO-ORDINATION				
	ROAD SAFETY				
	STREET LIGHTING				
ENVIRONMENTAL HEALTH	FOOD SAFETY AND HYGIENE				
	COMMUNICABLE DISEASE				
	OFFICES, SHOPS ⎫				
	FACTORIES ⎬ ACTS				
	SHOPS ⎭				
PROTECTION.ᴬ	WEIGHTS AND MEASURES				
	FOOD AND DRUGS				
	TRADES DESCRIPTIONS				
	CONSUMER PROTECTION ETC.				
ENVIRONMENTAL MATTERS	LOCAL SEWERS				
	LAND DRAINAGE				
	REFUSE COLLECTION DISPOSAL				
	LITTER				
	COASTAL PROTECTION				
	CLEAN AIR				
	BUILDING REGULATIONS				
	STREET CLEANSING				
	NUISANCES				
	CEMETERIES AND CREMATORIA				
	MARKETS				
	OFFENSIVE TRADES				
	HEALTH EDUCATION ETC.				
RECREATION	SWIMMING BATHS				
	PARKS AND OPEN SPACES				
	PHYSICAL RECREATION				
	TOURIST ATTRACTIONS				
REGISTRATION	LICENSING AND REGISTRATION				
	BIRTHS, DEATHS AND MARRIAGES				
	ADOPTION SOCIETIES ETC.				
OTHER	ENTERTAINMENTS				
	AERODROMES				
	NATURAL EMERGENCIES				

Table 1.2 ALLOCATION OF FUNCTIONS BETWEEN TYPES OF AUTHORITY

Notes. Allocations in Scotland and Wales are similar to non-Metropolitan.
A. *Police : Fire. Both these are functions of Local Government, and are integrated into communication systems. They are administered from Level 1 in both situations.*

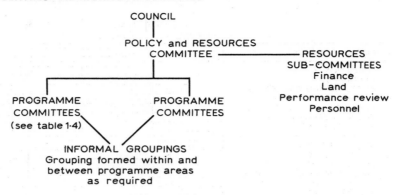

(a) Elected members : committee structure

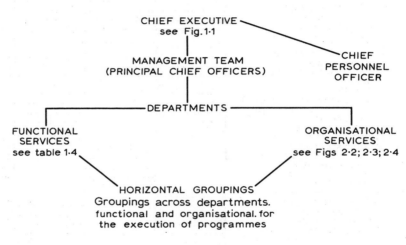

(b) Employees : departmental structure

Table 1.3 BASIC MANAGEMENT STRUCTURES COMMON TO ALL AUTHORITIES

accommodation, storage for specific items and equipment together with laboratory facilities will be required.

(d) PERSONAL (Social Services, Housing, Education, Registration). These are basically administrative, visitor-intensive functions, public visiting being fairly constantly distributed or operated on an appointment system. They are normally treated as independent functions; Registration has distinct requirements relating to the performance of marriages, and Social Services has strong working links with the Area Health Authority system.

Organisational services, offer no service to the public, as such, but are essential to the efficient execution of Authority function, at any level or scale:

(a) CO-ORDINATION: Fig 1.1. (Clerk-Function). The direction of resources is carried out by the Chief Executive. This function is significantly different to that of the original Town or County Clerk in that the organisation hierarchy now acknowledges that this post requires the power of final decision, and responsibility, over the heads of the various departments.

(b) ADMINISTRATION: Fig 1.2. (Secretary/clerk function). In addition to the legal function relative to authorities affairs, activities include Work Study, Organisation and Management and Research and Development. These functions tend to be executed by small groups who may work within *Service Department,* related to a particular piece of work, at a particular time, but who are based within the department and responsible to its Director. In addition it is recommended that the department includes secretarial facilities for elected members. A small library of legislation and the Authority's archives accessible for council and committee members is also required.

(c) PERSONNEL: Fig 1.3. At a large scale, this function will usually be broken down so that officers are located in *Service* departments, but are responsible to a Chief Personnel Officer, leading a small co-ordinating unit, which works closely with the Chief Executive. At the

	PROGRAMME COMMITTEES		DEPARTMENTS: FUNCTIONAL SERVICES	DIRECTORATES WHERE APPROPRIATE
METROPOLITAN	PLANNING and TRANSPORT PUBLIC PROTECTION POLICE (D)	LEVEL 1	FINANCE SURVEYOR PLANNER CONSUMER PROTECTION FIRE OFFICER	
METROPOLITAN	SOCIAL SERVICES EDUCATION RECREATION and AMENITIES HOUSING SERVICES DEVELOPMENT SERVICES ENVIRONMENTAL HEALTH and CONTROL	LEVEL 2 ALTHOUGH APPROPRIATE, DIRECTORATES ARE NOT ALWAYS USED	FINANCE SOCIAL SERVICES EDUCATION ——— LIBRARIES AMENITIES and RECREATION— HOUSING ESTATES and VALUATIONS — PLANNER ARCHITECT ENGINEER ENVIRONMENTAL HEALTH— REGISTRATION	EDUCATION SERVICES TECHNICAL SERVICES
NON-METROPOLITAN	SOCIAL SERVICES EDUCATION AMENITIES and COUNTRYSIDE PLANNING and TRANSPORT PUBLIC PROTECTION POLICE (D)	LEVEL 1 ALTHOUGH APPROPRIATE, DIRECTORATES ARE NOT ALWAYS USED	FINANCE SOCIAL SERVICES EDUCATION ——— LIBRARIES AMENITIES and RECREATION— ESTATES and VALUATIONS— PLANNER ARCHITECT ENGINEER ——— CONSUMER PROTECTION FIRE OFFICER REGISTRATION	EDUCATION SERVICES TECHNICAL SERVICES
NON-METROPOLITAN	HOUSING SERVICES RECREATION and AMENITIES DEVELOPMENT SERVICES ENVIRONMENTAL HEALTH and CONTROL	LEVEL 2 SIZE OF AUTHORITIES VARY	FINANCE (A) HOUSING (A) PLANNING (B) TECHNICAL (B,C) ENVIRONMENTAL HEALTH (A) REGISTRATION	

A. Departments required for any size
B. May be required at small scale
C. Large scale; may be separate departments
D. The Police Committee is the Police Authority which must be integrated into the communications system of an authority.

Table 1.4 MANAGEMENT STRUCTURES FOR VARIOUS TYPES OF AUTHORITY

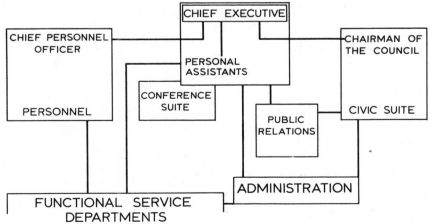

Fig. 1.1. Chief executive

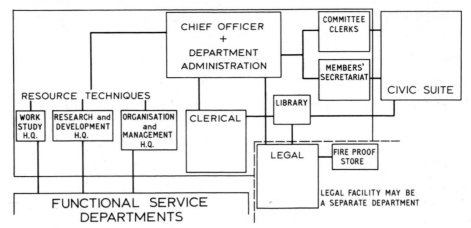

Fig. 1.2.   Administration

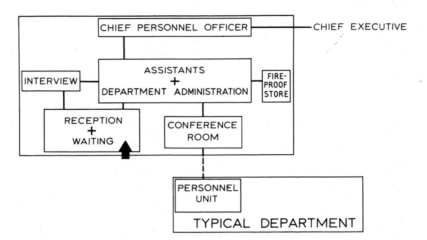

Fig. 1.3.   Personnel

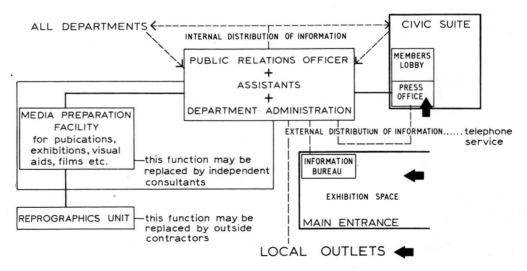

Fig. 1.4.   Public relations

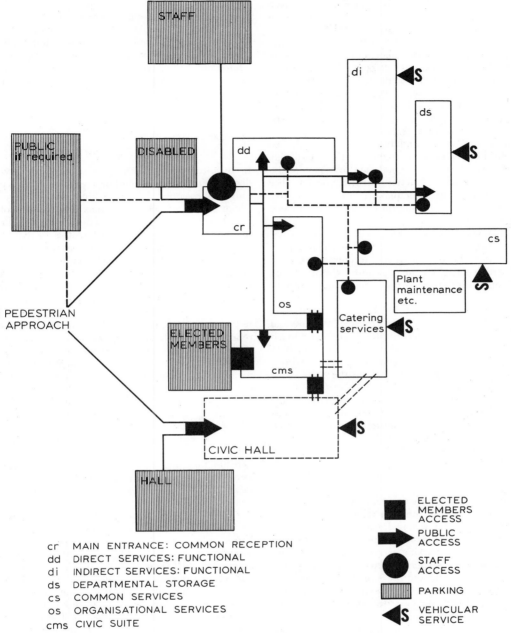

cr MAIN ENTRANCE: COMMON RECEPTION
dd DIRECT SERVICES: FUNCTIONAL
di INDIRECT SERVICES: FUNCTIONAL
ds DEPARTMENTAL STORAGE
cs COMMON SERVICES
os ORGANISATIONAL SERVICES
cms CIVIC SUITE

■ ELECTED MEMBERS ACCESS

➤ PUBLIC ACCESS

● STAFF ACCESS

▦ PARKING

◀S VEHICULAR SERVICE

Fig. 1.5. Access and relationships for elements

small scale only this core unit may be appropriate.

(d) PUBLIC RELATIONS: Fig 1.4. This function provides the source for all information concerning an Authority's activities for consumption by the general public and the press. The function is best organised as a central unit, with local outlets for contact with the general public. The central unit is generally limited in size and concerned with the preparation of information for reproduction, the organisation of exhibitions, and the arrangement of interviews. Contact with the press is facilitated where a permanent Press room is available; this is best located as part of the Civic Suite (see Fig

1.8 'Accommodation'). The main public entrance to the authority's accommodation will usually be required to allow for exhibitions.

SITING

SITE ORGANISATION

The basic requirements are illustrated in Fig 1.5. The accommodation for elected members is traditionally seen as the focus of Local Authority activities but the recent inclination towards corporate image, discourages this approach and suggests that an Authority should be seen as a whole with no particular emphasis in any one area.

The provision of efficient service within an Authority requires employment of management and personnel techniques, (organisational services) together with positive overall co-ordination of resources; the latter is embodied in the post of a Chief Executive, without departmental responsibility. The post forms the basis for the development of the necessary communication and interaction between elected members and employees.

Elected members accommodation will generally be required to be physically integrated with the day-to-day activities within the office accommodation, but should also be capable of independent function outwith normal office hours. In addition the concept of dual use may be applicable to Committee Rooms, depending on the number provided and frequency of use.

Where the Town Hall is provided as part of a Civic Complex, it is likely to be most successful when positively connected to the elected members accommodation, to facilitate its primary use, but the capability of independent function without disturbance to the 'Civic Suite' must be maintained.

Functional services provided by Local Authority are either direct to the community as in Housing, Welfare and Education, or indirect, as in technically orientated departments, i.e. Planning, etc. While visitors are likely in both sectors, public encounter forms a significant part of the direct service, thus such departments should be the most easily accessible to the general public.

The other functions significant to the general public in the provision of service are the collection of revenue and the dissemination of information regarding the Authorities' activities. The former promotes intense peaks of visitors, e.g. rent day (this is now changing with increasingly mechanised methods of payment, e.g. 'Giro' etc). The latter, a relatively new function to many Authorities, is important in the realisation of identified objectives.

Some Authorities will require registration facilities as part of the accommodation. This function requires an entrance distinct from that for the remaining departments and in some cases it will be required to have an identity separate from other functions. Visitors parking is required on a limited scale in connection with the performance of marriages.

Certain departments will require storage facilities with vehicular access, and garage accommodation. In some cases this must be integral with the department, but otherwise a separate facility is acceptable.

General accommodation, supporting the complex will include:

(a) Caretaking and cleaning facilities, including refuse and incineration.
(b) Plant space, maintenance stores and workshop with vehicular access, telephone equipment and operators' room.
(c) Catering, rest and first aid facilities. Accommodation may be required in some cases for trade union or professional representation organisations.

Common services, such as Computer Suite, Central Supply Department and Reprographic Unit may be required. Small scale Authorities may take advantage of their existence within a larger scale Authority in the vicinity. Each requires direct vehicular access, for collection and unloading, together with the facility for bulk storage for paper goods and equipment. Other criteria relative to location are high floor loadings, structural fire precautions and intense servicing requirements.

CENTRALISATION

In the provision of direct service an Authority is usually dealing with the least mobile members of the community, thus it is essential that these functions are brought to the Client in the form of local outlets. The location of these will not always coincide for all functions. This will also improve the flexibility of an Authority, relative to those changes in central government policy requiring quick reaction.

This concept, already well established relative to libraries, implies that the headquarters (management and administration) function of a department is centralised together with any indirect service function, with local offices, in contact with the public, under an Area Manager taking day-to-day responsibility for activities. The successful working of this relies on the intelligent application of telecommunications to allow immediate access to information.

Technical services, organisational functions and elected members' accommodation will gain advantage from centralisation, relative to the community. Decentralisation may be applied to revenue collection, but this is liable to alter with changing patterns of payment: it is obviously essential with regard to public relations.

The concept is applicable to both levels of Authority. The location of Level One local offices with Level Two centralised functions will reinforce the image of local government as a whole, be most convenient to the public, and allow the local office to take advantage of the Level Two common services, see Fig 1.6.

The requirement for flexibility, inherent in Local Authority function, suggests that expansion must be allowed for in any complex. This is obviously constrained by the selection of a site (see 'location and access' below) and the policy adopted by the Client, with regard to expansion of accommodation. The organic approach to form, which allows additions to be made without destruction of the visual integrity of a building and allows it to continue to be seen as one unit, has generally been adopted over the last decade. However, policies of form, detailing, design life/cost ratio etc. established in the original scheme have not always been adhered to by Local Authorities, when expansion or physical adaption becomes necessary. It has been argued that the original accommodation should be architecturally self-contained and any expansion take the form of new buildings visually independent from the original.

The movement towards corporate image, and the acceptance of visual image (from buildings to graphics) as a significant factor in its attainment, already displayed in certain Authorities occupying or preparing to occupy new building complexes, suggests that Authorities would now be willing to continue established policies in the execution of expansion or adaptation of premises.

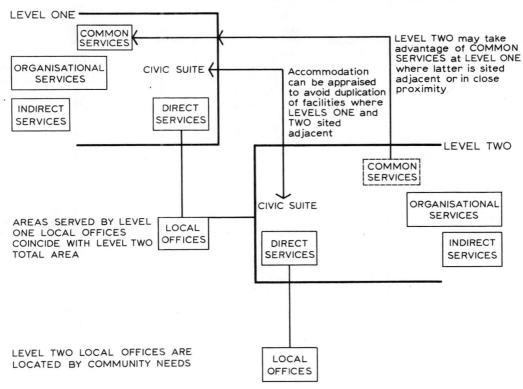

Fig. 1.6. Centralisation

LOCATION AND ACCESS

The ideal location for accommodation is undoubtedly at the physical centre of activity of the community it serves. Such sites are likely to be urban and this may restrict the required accommodation provision and relationships, and preclude expansion. The scale of provision likely may also require careful handling of building forms and texture to achieve appropriate visual integration.

A more 'rural' site, often using a park, has advantage in this respect. However, access requires a positive effort on the part of the general public in visiting. The decentralisation of *direct* services, will tend to alleviate this problem, but obviously the integration potential arising from constant awareness of the total Authority service is lost.

Vehicular access and parking will be required relative to elected members accommodation, together with a percentage allowance relative to the office accommodation, dependent on site location and local planning policy. Site location relative to local transport systems will also determine any requirement for parking by the general public.

Immediate pedestrian access to the accommodation, should ideally be channelled through one point in the interests of security, with other potential access points, made necessary by need for service, means of escape, or independent operation, restricted. Access must allow for wheelchair users, and close approach by invalid vehicles.

PLANNING

GENERAL

The problems in provision of Town Halls and elected members accommodation are essentially technical, concerning the provision of the environment appropriate for known activities. The basic problems in the design of offices are:

(a) Flexibility to allow quick reactions to changes in the management of functions, or extensions or compressions of the functions themselves, and

(b) Communications, to increase effective contact within and between departments.

Maximum flexibility and face to face contact are promoted by the absence of physical divisions between or within departments; this must be equated with the following criteria:

(a) Many departments will require special facilities, relative to function, which will place abnormal (relative to office accommodation) loads on structure, services and fire separation, security etc. e.g. paper stores, strong rooms, machine rooms, laboratories etc. While such accommodation must be relatively inflexible to satisfy functional needs, advantage can be gained if a degree of interchangeability is available.

(b) Unlike commercial offices, encounter with the public is a significant factor in most departments. Thus internal scale and clear orientation in layout are important.

(c) Basic work types vary between departments tending to be either technical, clerical or administrative; each requires different degrees of privacy, interaction potential or work supervision.

(d) Within each department, local authority function dictates that certain tasks (including encounter with the public, and formal meetings) require visual and/or aural isolation. The percentage area of isolation relative to overall floor area necessary will vary from department to department.

(e) Hierarchy and reflection of status have always been important aspects in Local Government management systems. While current thinking discourages the continuation of this, it can still be argued that the real need for flexibility and communications occurs below the management level of a department, as the need for expression of leadership and the confidentiality and privacy of the work involved in leadership are paramount and liable to infrequent adaptation.

FLEXIBILITY

The satisfaction of the requirement for flexibility, implies the adoption of a structure independent of any internal divisions, apart from 'core' units relating to departments providing for 'special' activities which, together with a system of providing enclosure within the shell, can be adapted to immediate needs without disruption of work, services etc. and without detriment to intended circulation and orientation systems.

Examples completed over the last five years, show a fairly consistent approach to the provision of office accommodation. although the buildings are very different; see examples 1 to 4. at the end of this section. This approach basically accepts the traditional linear solution, a 'central' corridor with limited depth work areas utilising Permanent Supplementary Artificial Lighting (PSALI), perimeter dependent for services. The opportunity for adaptability is created with independent partitions, related to a structural grid discipline. These tend to be blockwork owing to the difficulty and expense of achieving the required sound attenuation from more flexible systems.

These solutions were formulated prior to the recommendations regarding management structures, resulting from the re-organisation proposals, and also before increasing interest in the application of landscaping principles to office accommodation (Bürolandschaft). Such solutions allow either the adoption of total cellular division related to the central corridor or the use of the total floor area as one space, or combinations of the two, according to work type.

The advantage of locating all members of staff in a single open space are generally agreed to be better working conditions, increased flexibility and opportunity for interaction, and a reduction in capital outlay, (relative to placing the same staff in a traditional lineal block) arising from the potential of optimum plan form. These advantages are gained by the application of a rigid acoustically-based

discipline relative to minimum floor areas and ceiling heights, environmental services, finishes etc. The concept can still be applied where a limited degree of perimeter enclosure is required, e.g. for executives, but the introduction of parititioning will offset the cost advantage. However, the ability for an organisation to adapt it's detail planning to immediate circumstances is extremely valuable in terms of the management strategies recently proposed for Local Authorities.

The discipline involved is now recognised as being detrimental to the visual environment of the space, producing large vistas and monotonous lighting levels, with little awareness of diurnal change, and a significant loss of spatial identity relative to the individual workplace. In addition, the scale necessary for the application of the concept, is likely to form a barrier in the function of public encounter.

Recent solutions now under construction, acknowledge some of those problems, and propose positive measures to break down internal scale and vistas, using changes in floor level, ceiling modelling and strategic location of core areas housing special services, see Examples 5 and 6.

A more recent solution appears to provide a satisfactory answer to all the above criticisms identified but only by dispensing with the rigid disciplines, and therefore the economies of Bürolandschaft; see Example 7.

COMMUNICATIONS

Communications concern:

(a) interaction between people,
(b) information storage and retrieval systems.

The former is promoted where there are no visual barriers between people, as the ideal form of contact is 'face-to-face' and is promoted by visual awareness of proximity. In certain situations this contact is inadequate or impractical, and telecommunications based back-up systems will be required, e.g. internal telephones, telephone conference facilities, videophones, staff locations systems etc.

Within a department, contact is promoted by limitation of the degree of division to that absolutely necessary, according to work type. Between departments, a 'live interface' obtained by allowing departments to be visually integrated is significant; it also improves flexibility.

This is difficult to achieve in traditional lineal forms, where area per floor tends to relate to average department size (horizontal travel is preferred to vertical) and department edges coincide with major circulation zones. Recent solutions, based on office landscape principles, overcome this, by means of non-lineal planning with horizontal junctions between departmental spaces; see Examples 5 and 6. Others deliberately place departments on two floors, allowing the vertical circulation to be integrated into the department, resulting in potentially good contact between different departments on the same floor, see Examples 1 and 7.

Information production, storage and retrieval, are paper based, and involve secretarial and filing systems. Day to day, secretarial and typing functions are most efficiently executed within the various working groups in a department, continual involvement in the group promoting productivity, quality, and job satisfaction.

The use of a central typing pool and dictating system, economic on paper relative to dispersed, direct contact facilities, is only appropriate in the production of repetitive work, and precludes the involvement essential to efficiency. Report typing, a considerable factor, in Local Authority activities, is a specialised task and is best dealt with, as part of a publishing and printing function, within a Reprographics Unit.

Filing may be dispersed related to working groups, or centralised. The latter, providing general access and simple supervision seems preferable and is probably essential to the visual environment where open office areas are utilised. When applied at a larger scale, access becomes a problem which must be solved by mechanisation.

Physical systems rely on bulk storage of information, with a document conveyance system, requiring spatial allowance within the structure (this may also be required relative to the distribution and collection of mail in a large organisation). The use of facsimile transmission instead of physical conveyance, demands less space, and is time saving. Mechanised systems, such as computer storage, with access via teleprinters, visual display etc, are a logical extension of centralisation: wire transmission allows rapid information retrieval. These systems are essential where Authority activities are dispersed between headquarters and a number of local offices, and are justified by the now common use of computer systems in the fiscal activities of an Authority.

SPACE REQUIREMENTS

EMPLOYEES ACCOMMODATION

Space requirements per employee, excluding executive functions (although these are affected by work type: a Chief Technical Officer dealing with drawings may require more space than a Chief Education Officer), depend on task, use of machinery and equipment, degree of privacy necessary and storage requirements. Work carried out in each department is largely administrative, clerical or technical, thus space standards relative to each department will vary, over and above the minimum.

The requirement for adaptability implies the adoption of an area ratio between work types, which acknowledges working pattern tendencies, e.g. groups and status. This, expressed in modular form can provide the basis for the various grid disciplines necessary, e.g. construction, services, workplace structure. The establishment of this ratio, may be properly said to be the task of Organisation and Management experts, either from within the Authority or employed as consultants to the Authority, and as such this information should form part of the brief to the design team.

Sanitary and washing facilities must be provided for employees. These are most economic as permanent standardised accommodation, strongly related to major horizontal and vertical circulation patterns, convenient for use of visitors. Traditionally, the status of Heads of Departments is reflected by private 'Cloakrooms' *en suite* with their offices; this is discouraged in more recent approaches to the problem.

The function of public encounter requires up-grading of these provisions, together with appropriate allowances in circulation, for visitors and including the disabled is best accommodated by up-grading the staff provision, on a percentage basis. This increase will also help to counteract the problems of 'overload at peak times', resulting from the rigid timetabling of use, often found when only statutory minimum requirements are applied to Local Government Office Accommodation.

ELECTED MEMBERS ACCOMMODATION

Accommodation has to be provided for:

(a) Leisure and informal meetings for members and their guests in a Member's Suite.
(b) Members' work including private study, public interview and offices for those whose position requires privacy.
(c) Meetings between members and officers in Committee.
(d) Formal Meeting, for a specified number of persons in Council.
(e) Public access to Council Proceedings.

Members Suite. The main rooms should allow a variety of space, from open to visually private, but should be capable of use as one space. A bar and pantry, should be easily accessible within the Suite but not dominant. Clothes storage and sanitary washing facilities, for both sexes, must be provided in conjunction with the suite, but should also be easily accessible from Council Chamber and Committee rooms. Clothes storage requires locker or wardrobes and sanitary accommodation should be provided at the rate of 1 w.c. per 5 females and 1 w.c. and 1 urinal per 10 males. Allowance should be made for at least one third of the Council being comprised of females.

Reading room. This provides for members' private study, and may be integrated into the Member's Suite, but should be associated with the library facilities in the administration function of *organisational services*.

Working/Interview rooms. These may be required for elected members' discussions with members of the general public.

Chairman's Suite. Combined office/reception function. This room relates particularly to the council chamber and also to the Chief Executive's suite in addition to the elected members' accommodation. It requires a cloakroom and sanitary and washing facilities *en suite*; an additional room may be required for the Chairman's Private Secretary. Similar accommodation may also be required for the Leader and Leader of the Opposition, in Council.

Committee rooms. The size of any particular Committee and the frequency of assembly, is unpredictable and liable to frequent change. Traditionally, the flexibility required of this accommodation is acknowledged by the provision of several rooms, the layout capable of accommodating as many as 50 persons, with others for medium and small groups. An alternative, feasible today, as a result of technological improvements in the Sound Attenuation of flexible wall systems, allows the creation of rooms as required; the employment of this approach must be considered with

(a) The cost of operation of such a system, (employment of labour).
(b) The potential advantages of dual use, outwith the

primary function, from permanent accommodation such as a large 'conference room' equipped with projection facilities.

Council Chamber. This element provides the setting for formal debate and policy making. It should be located so as to obviate external noise sources, and constructional precautions are necessary, relative to exclusion of noise from immediately adjacent areas and service elements. The debating function requires the maintenance of reality in large-scale discussion; this is mainly achieved by considerations of plan form, requiring a compromise between directional emphasis to the 'Chair' and visual awareness 'across' the Chamber of speakers addressing the Chair.

Variations on a semi-circle or horseshoe are the most successful in this respect. The division of seating into two groups facing, across a central well is not successful in that it divides the Council into parties, and encourages members to address each other rather than the Chair.

Public access. Council proceedings are open to the press and the general public. Physical disturbance of proceedings is avoided where public/press seats are provided overlooking the Chamber, with access and circulation separate to that for Elected Members, preferably direct from outside in an apparent position within the constraints imposed by the need for security. It is generally considered essential that the Press are allowed within the Chamber so that reporters can easily identify speakers and reactions to events; members of the press have access to the Members Lobby and a Press Room for Press Releases, with telephones, may be required.

Traditionally the general public are accommodated in a gallery, or raised seating area towards the rear of the Chamber either shared with, or separate from, the press. Alternatively, the public may be excluded from the Chamber itself, and accommodated in a viewing gallery, separated by a glazed screen and provided with a sound relay system. The latter approach may be appropriate in the circumstances where a large public attendance for Council meetings is experienced; the public are observers of the debate, and physical separation will reduce the risk of disruption of proceedings. At the present time, public attendance for 'Town' councils is greater than that for 'County' assemblies, but the realisation of the intentions of Local Government Reorganisation, in terms of public involvement will alter this situation and attendances may show marked increases at both levels. Such situations will warrant attention to the provision of means of escape, sanitation etc., appropriate to public assembly.

TOWN HALLS

Besides the primary function of the building, activities taking place in Town Halls include a wide range of leisure and cultural pursuits. A single hall cannot cater satisfactorily for the whole range, many of which are incompatible. The criteria of selection of compatible functions are fully covered in the DOE Design Bulletin No. 28 'Multi-purpose Halls' (HMSO, 1972) but, generally, the best variety of use can be obtained from a Hall with a flat floor. The addition of bleacher seating will then provide the appropriate arrangement for cinema/lecture/drama activities; this may be provided in conjunction with a permanent raked gallery.

The civic function of the hall will require a raised platform, together with easy access from both foyer and platform ends. Cinema/lecture activities will require a projection room, while those pertaining to drama/concerts etc. may require considerable provisions in accommodation 'backstage'. The latter may include dressing rooms, storage and staff facilities, special equipment for scenery, lighting etc. and, possibly, an orchestra pit.

DATA

As mentioned previously, data for Town Halls will depend to a large extent on the proposed leisure function of the building in addition to the adminstrative function. For data on specific functions the reader is referred as follows:

Lecture Halls, etc (Sections 2 and 3 in *Planning: Buildings for Education, Culture and Science*)

Sports, etc (Section 6 in this volume and also Section 9 'Community Centres and Youth Clubs' in *Planning: Buildings for Health, Welfare and Religion*)

Concert Halls and Theatres (Sections 2 and 3 in this volume)

DEPARTMENTAL ACCOMMODATION

Data for functional and organisational office accommodation is generally as for offices. Revenue collection requirements, including writing and waiting facilities and data for the provision of strong rooms are generally as for banks. (Data on both offices and banks will be found in the appropriate section in the volume *Planning: Buildings for Habitation, Commerce and Industry*).

Accommodation is also required for those services common to all departments. Among the most important of these is the provision for a Computer Centre. (See Section 7 'Computer Centres' in *Planning: Buildings for Education, Culture and Science*.)

ELECTED MEMBERS ACCOMMODATION

The function of an elected member demands considerable time spent, formally and informally within the Authority accommodation. Thus it should be comfortably furnished, and every opportunity for observance of the outside environment should be exploited.

Committee rooms. These are essentially Conference Rooms: to allow seating both sides of a table, the minimum useable width is 4.5m. Such rooms require low noise transmission from external sources and sound deadening relative to internal movement. Natural light is an advantage and all rooms must be accessible without disturbance to Committee Rooms adjacent.

Council chamber. This is usually arranged as follows:

(a) Dais to accommodate the Chairman, Vice-Chairman and Chief Executive, which should be at the opposing end of the Chamber to the access points to avoid disturbance from circulation during proceedings. A lectern allowing 'presentation' by Committee Chair-

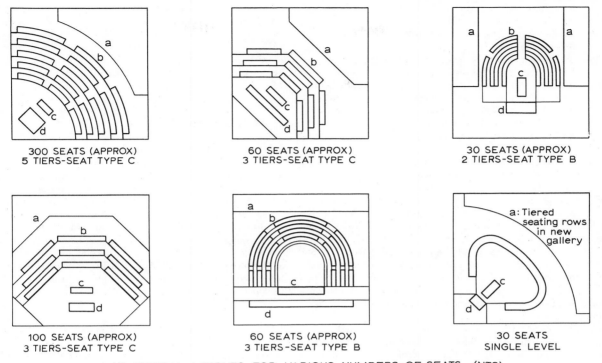

300 SEATS (APPROX)
5 TIERS-SEAT TYPE C

60 SEATS (APPROX)
3 TIERS-SEAT TYPE C

30 SEATS (APPROX)
2 TIERS-SEAT TYPE B

100 SEATS (APPROX)
3 TIERS-SEAT TYPE C

60 SEATS (APPROX)
3 TIERS-SEAT TYPE B

a: Tiered seating rows in new gallery

30 SEATS
SINGLE LEVEL

(i) TYPICAL LAYOUTS FOR VARIOUS NUMBERS OF SEATS, (NTS)

a = GALLERY, PRESS AND PUBLIC   b = ORDINARY MEMBERS   c = OFFICALS   d = CHAIRMAN ETC.

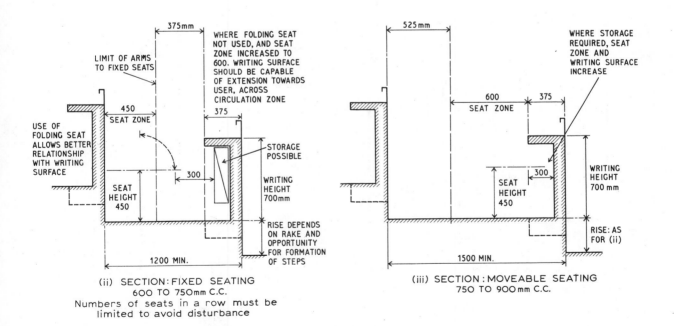

(ii) SECTION: FIXED SEATING
600 TO 750mm C.C.
Numbers of seats in a row must be limited to avoid disturbance

(iii) SECTION: MOVEABLE SEATING
750 TO 900mm C.C.

Fig. 1.7.   Council chamber: seating

men, and seating for Chief Officers behind and flanking the dias may also be required.

(b) Table, facing the dais, for officers recording the proceedings.

(c) Tiered seating rows, with desk space for each seat, facing the dais, for ordinary council members. A maximum of six seats (preferably four) in continuous rows; no seat being more than three seats away from a gangway. Proper allowances for circulation will avoid disruption from members entering and leaving during the proceedings, see Fig. 1.7.

Need for reality implies the avoidance of sound amplification systems, and the use of the sectional shape of the chamber and applied finishes to control acoustics. The volume per person should be limited to $3m^3$; seating should be arranged on a steep rake so each tier has uninterrupted sound and sight lines. Seating should be treated so as to allow equal absorbancy whether the Chamber is empty or full. The maximum ceiling height should be 7.5m to take advantage of the reflections available from an appropriate profile, while the upper part of walls should be absorbent and the lower reflective. Large scales of assembly may require the incorporation of speech reinforcement systems in addition to the above.

Limited views, allowing awareness of time through daylight change, will be beneficial; windows should be located across the axis of the Chamber to avoid glare. Artificial illumination should be based on general flooding, capable of being dimmed, with local sources for writing/reading tasks.

A gallery should provide adequate sound and sight lines. This is most easily achieved where it is wide and shallow in depth, incorporating two or three rows of tiered seating. It should be treated as acoustically dead with carpet, upholstered seating and sound absorbent linings to ceilings and walls.

ACCOMMODATION

ELECTED MEMBERS ACCOMMODATION

Fig 1.8 indicates typical accommodation requirements for this function. These elements are normally physically linked by a lobby or concourse, which concentrates the circulation between elements encouraging informal meeting and allowing assembly, prior to meetings, and waiting for elected members and officers. This is usually required to be distinct from major circulation for the rest of the accommodation, but the latter is preferred as the means of access. Where a ceremonial balcony is required it is convenient to relate it to this concourse.

DEPARTMENTAL ACCOMMODATION: FUNCTIONAL SERVICES

Figures 1.9 to 1.14 and the following notes illustrate basic requirements and relationships for departments or groups of

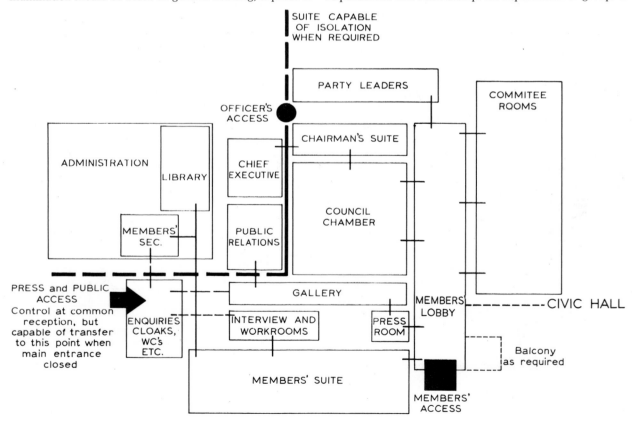

Fig. 1.8. Elected members' accommodation

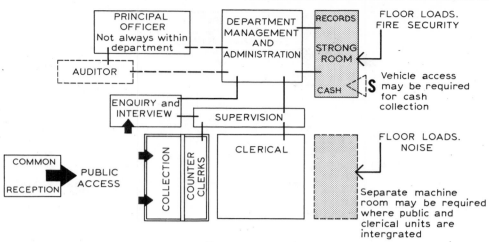

Fig. 1.9.   Finance

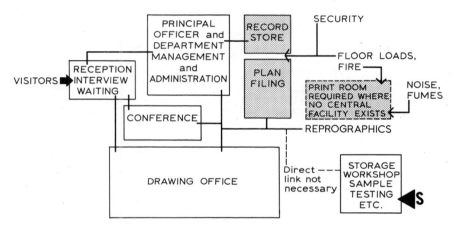

Fig. 1.10.   Development/technical services

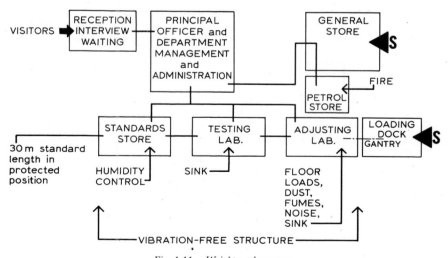

Fig. 1.11.   Weights and measures

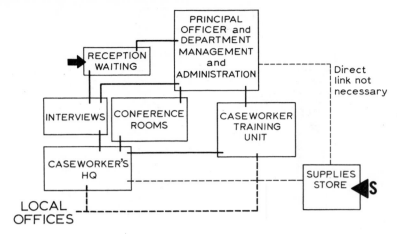

Fig. 1.12.   Social services

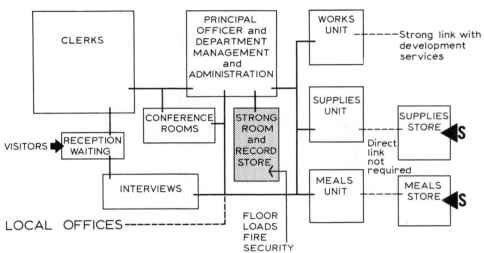

Fig. 1.13.   Education services

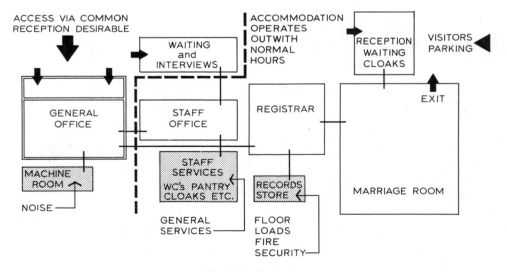

Fig. 1.14.   Registration

departments, commonly found, which have specific requirements over those for normal office accommodation.

Finance (Fig 1.9). Direct access or immediate access via the common reception point is desirable. The collection functions may be part of the general office space, but use of local machinery relative to the clerical function may require separation. The department requires strong rooms, for cash and records; these are preferred as part of the department accommodation but where separate, a 'book' lift is required for movement of paper.

Development/Technical Services (Fig 1.10). These functions require storage for drawings (including documents submitted), and printing facilities (these may be centralised and housed with a reprographics unit). Accommodation with vehicular access may also be required for certain facets of these functions, e.g. sample testing, visual aid preparations, materials and equipment storage, including models and exhibition equipment, which need not be physically associated with the departmental accommodation.

Weights and Measures (Fig 1.11). Functions of storage of heavy weights, samples, petrol etc, dictate the need for immediate vehicular level access, and a gantry and loading dock may be required in connection with the delivery of such items. Laboratories, for measurement and adjustment may require a constant degree of atmospheric adjustment, relative to normal office use, while the Standards Store will definitely require this adjustment. The storage of petrol requires compartmentalisation, in terms of fireproofing and flame spread, together with appropriate precautions in the electrical installation.

Social Services (Fig 1.12). Location at a major predestrian level is essential for this department due to the limited capabilities of many clients. The annoyance factor produced by even a limited number of children, in a waiting situation, should be taken into account. Facilities are required for interviews, conferences, and case-worker training. Goods reception and storage may be separate from the main accommodation. Where a Probation Unit is involved, it must be capable of independent operation, as it is likely to be required to be open outwith normal working hours.

Education (Fig 1.13). This function may also require storage for registry, teachers records, visual aids, with a film library and workshop facilities.

Registration (Fig 1.14). The marriage function, requires distinct separation from that of births and deaths, to allow privacy necessary for the latter functions. Staff accommodation includes offices and a strong room for record storage. The marriage function may require several marriage rooms, ideally arranged to allow use as one space, with waiting room(s), capable of accommodating large parties. The marriage room should connect with the Registrar's room, and have separate entrance, and exit. The births and deaths functions require registration rooms with associated waiting rooms independent of the marriage facilities, as the latter may be required to operate outside normal working hours.

STATUTORY REQUIREMENTS, AUTHORITIES AND LEGISLATION

GENERAL

Town and Country Planning Act, 1971. HMSO.

Town & Country Planning (Scotland) Act, 1972. HMSO.

Statutory Instrument 1972 No. 317 'Building Regulations 1972' HMSO. Covers all aspects of construction.

Statutory Instrument 1973 No. 1276. 'The Building (First Amendment) Regulations 1973. HMSO. Revision of above, and addition of Part EE, Means of Escape, in respect of Offices, Shops and Flats over two storeys. Deemed to satisfy Clause i.e. applicable to Office Accommodation where British Standard CP 3 Chapter IV: Part 3: 1968 Office Buildings is complied with.

The Building Standards (Scotland) (Consolidation) Regulations 1971.

Offices, Shops and Railway Premises Act, 1963. HMSO.

Sanitary Conveniences Regulations, 1964. HMSO.

Washing Facilities Regulations, 1964. HMSO.

Chronically Sick and Disabled Persons Act, 1970. HMSO.

In the provision of any building to which the public are admitted, the needs of visitors who are disabled must be met as far as is practicable and reasonable. Reference should be made to the Government Circulars associated with this act:

MOHLG, Circular 33/68; 'Design of public conveniences with facilities for the Disabled', HMSO.
DHSS Circular 12/70; 'The Chronically Sick and Disabled Persons Act 1970', HMSO.

The design implications of this legislation are contained in:

British Standard CP 96: Part I. 'Access for the disabled to Buildings: General Recommendations'.
'Designing for the Disabled', Selwyn Goldsmith, Royal Institute of British Architects 1967.

All the above-mentioned functions are administered by Local Authorities. In addition, aspects of security, both life and property, in a particular situation will require reference to:

(a) The Local Fire Service for advice on means of escape, smoke control, passive defence systems etc.
(b) The Client's Insurance Company, who may have no specific requirements relative to planning, at the present time, but who will need to be positively involved at the detail design stage. In future, Insurance Companies may pay close attention to aspects of security involved in the organisation of movement of staff and particularly visitors around the accommodation.

ADDITIONAL REQUIREMENTS FOR CIVIC CENTRES AND MUNICIPAL BUILDINGS

The provision of the Council Chamber, as a place of public assembly, may require reference to Local Authority regulations governing such forms of assembly, see GLC Regulations below.

The requirements for the storage of petroleum, as considered for the Weights and Measures Department, are embodied in the Petroleum (Consolidation) Act 1928 (HMSO) administered by Local Government.

ADDITIONAL REQUIREMENTS FOR TOWN HALLS

The application of the Offices, Shops and Railway Premises Act, will depend on management policies associated with this accommodation. Operations may be administered from the hall itself, particularly where it is isolated from the Authority's main accommodation.

Greater London Council: Places of Public Entertainment: Technical Regulations.

These have been adopted by many other Local Authorities; they provide a minimum standard for the provision of means of escape, lighting, seating, sanitation etc., for places of permanent, large scale public assembly.

The licensing of premises for various forms of entertainment is required, and is a function of Local Government. The following Acts apply:

The Licensing Act, 1964.
The Gaming Act, 1968.
Statutory Instrument 1955 No. 1129 'Cinematograph (Safety) Regulations 1955'.
Theatres Act, 1968.

Expert guidance of policies for the provision of multi-purpose Halls is available from professional bodies such as:

The Institute of Municipal Entertainment Managers.
The Theatres' Advisory Council.

EXAMPLES

Several examples of completed multi-purpose Town Halls are given as Appendices in DOE Design Bulletin No. 28 'Multi-purpose Halls' HMSO 1972. These show a variety of approaches on the part of Local Authorities, to the provision and operation of such accommodation. The examples given are:

North Romford Community Centre
Town Hall, Sittingbourne
The Maltings, Ely.
The Pavilion, Hemel Hempstead.

A significant portion of Design Bulletin 28 is devoted to a demonstration project of a multi-purpose hall by a Local Authority, in collaboration with the Department of the Environment. This project, Bedworth, now complete is fully described and illustrated in 'Multi-Purpose Halls', *Building* (30.11.73). This building is also compared with another recently completed example at Elstree.

Few buildings in this category have been completed since the last war, initially as a result of lack of finance, and latterly owing to the impending re-organisation resulting from lengthy Central Government investigations. The following examples represent a cross section of recent completions and proposals in chronological order.

1. Bedford County Hall   Completed 1969
Client: County Council's Organisation and Management Unit.
Architect: Bedford County Architect's Department
Architect's Journal, 23 (30.12.70)
Flat urban site in renewal area. Accommodation comprises; Council suite; departmental accommodation; central library and library headquarters.
A curved linear office block, eight storeys, with allowance for expansion of present needs. The Council Suite forms upper storey of a two storey podium, with a self-contained entrance from the members' car park at ground level. The main entrance is at the axis of the podium and office block, with reception at first floor level adjacent the refectory. The library accommodation is physically separated from that for officers and elected members, but visually integrated. The library, office block and podium forming a U-shape, surrounding a courtyard, terminated by the River Ouse to the North. Extensive employees'/visitors' car parking to the South forms a barrier between the development and the main access road.

2. Paisley Civic Centre   Phase I completed 1969
                           Phase II completed 1972
                           Phase III completed 1971
Client: Paisley Town Council and Renfrew County Council.
Architect: Hutchison, Locke and Monk (Winners of two stage competition)
Architects' Journal (7.11.73)
Urban site in renewal area, dominated by Paisley Abbey to West. Accommodation consists of: Phase I, Police buildings including repetitive offices, Court House, Registry, Social Services and Children's Departments. Phase II, County Council administrative offices. Phase III, Town Council administrative offices. Phase IV, Council Suites; banqueting facilities (construction deferred).
A series of linear, traditionally arranged office blocks of various heights and as foils to the vertical emphasis of Paisley Abbey with vertical service cores at each end, arranged on a podium containing functions with individual requirements and visitor intensive departments. The civic suites and banqueting facilities will be set on pilotis at first floor level between Town and County Buildings on an axis with the Abbey as the central focus of the development. Parking for members and employees only is below podium level and roofed to form a series of pedestrian areas at pedestrian access level.

3. Hove Town Hall and Civic Centre   Completed 1973
Client: Hove Borough Council
Architects: Wells-Thorpe and Partners
Building (19.4.74)
Urban site, centre of commercial/shopping area. Accommodation comprises 1200 seat multi-purpose hall and ancill-

aries; council suite and administrative offices.
Accommodation is integrated into surroundings by height restriction and horizontal emphasis on highly articulated plan form. The main entrance links the two functionally different parts of the building, traditional linear offices, arranged around a courtyard and the council suite and public facilities including the multi-purpose hall. Multi-storey car park opposite is linked to centre by subway giving access to basement foyer.

4. Sunderland Civic Centre   Completed 1970
Client: Borough of Sunderland
Architects: Spence, Bonnington and Collins
Architects' Journal (18.11.70) and *Architectural Review* (March 1971)
Urban perimeter site on sloping ground (previously wasteland). Accommodation comprises, council suite, administrative office with Council Halls as a later phase.
Complex planned on a hexagonal discipline, based on a grid of equilateral triangles, linear offices at a maximum of four storeys form the perimeters to two hexagonal courtyards, with the main entrance at the intersection of the figure of eight thus formed. The council suite is housed in a hexagonal block, attached to and within the discipline of the offices. The Civic Halls will be added in the same manner. This accommodation is based on a podium whose geometry unifies the complex is and which contains multi-level car parking, including allowances for visitors.

5. Reading Civic Hall   Completed 1974
Client: Reading District Council
Architect: Robert Matthew, Johnson-Marshall and Partners
Architects' Journal (17.1.71)
Urban, central, site. The development forms a comprehensive improvement for the central area, and includes a shopping centre. Accommodation comprises council suite, and administrative offices.
Planned to a hexagonal discipline, based on a equilateral triangle grid with all elements integrated into a single building on a deck over car parking. Elected members accommodation, multi-purpose hall and banking hall, all at pedestrian level, with open planned office areas above as a spiral of hexagons around a central core.

6. Hillingdon Civic Centre   Under construction
Client: London Borough of Hillingdon
Architect: Robert Matthew Johnson-Marshall and Partners
Architectural Review (March 1972)
Urban site in renewal area, related to proposed new road.
Accommodation comprises, council suite, administrative offices, banqueting hall, Registry with Civic Hall as later phase.
Planned as a series of linked buildings, based on a hexagonal discipline minimising scale and allowing strong articulation of external walls and roofs to echo images of surrounding residential forms. Smaller elements, such as civic suite, registry etc. are also located to minimise the bulk of the office accommodation. Office space is planned as a square form to provide for open planning around a central core.

7. Northampton Civic Centre   Commenced 1973
Client: Northamptonshire County Council
Architect: Cross, Dixon, Gold, Jones and Sampson.
   Winning solution of two-stage competition.
Architects' Journal (31.11.73); Presentation of competition 2nd Stage entries, and *Design Magazine* (January 1974)
Flat rural site. Accommodation comprises council suite; administrative offices and central library.
Planned as total entity, a pyramid with main entrance and library at ground floor, five floors open office space. Staff rooms and elected members accommodation on sixth and seventh floors respectively and council chamber at apex. Extensive car parking adjacent building.

ACKNOWLEDGEMENT

The authors would like to acknowledge the help given by the following:

Mr D. L. J. Horne, Chief Executive, Surrey Health Borough Council.

Mr Campbell, Chief Executive, Broxbourne Borough Council.

Mr Lederer and Mr Gifford of 'Inbucon' (Management Consultants) in discussion on the realisation of the aims of the reorganisation of Local Government in terms of building.

BIBLIOGRAPHY

Local Government in Britain, Central Office of Information in Britain. Reference Pamphlet 1 HMSO.
Royal Commission on Local Government in England. Report Command 4040, HMSO (1969) (Summarised in *Local Government Reform* Command 4039, HMSO)
Royal Commission on Local Government in Scotland. Report Command 4150, HMSO (1969) (Summarised in *Scotland: Local Government Reform* HMSO.)
Local Government in England: Proposals for Reorganisation. Command 4584, HMSO (1971)
Reform of Local Government in Scotland. Command 4583, HMSO (1971)
The Reform of Local Government in Wales. Consultative Document, HMSO (1971)
The New Local Authorities: Management and Structure, HMSO
'Local Government Reorganisation' *Architects' Journal*.
   Part 1: Responsibilities of New Authorities (3.4.74);
   Part 2: The Water Act, 1973, (10.4.74)

David Hutchison and Graham Locke *attended University College, London from 1955 to 1960, where they obtained a 1st Class Honours Degree and a Diploma in Architecture respectively. They both qualified as RIBA Associates in 1962. Graham Locke obtained a Diploma in Town Planning, at University College, London, in 1964.*
   The Partnership was founded in 1963 to submit an entry for the two-stage competition for Paisley Civic Centre, and after success in gaining the first premium, the Practice was launched in 1964 when commissioned to carry out the winning design; various further commissions of a civic nature have followed.

Natalie Robinson *is a Senior Architect with the practice, having joined in 1967, and played a considerable part in developing the designs for the Civic Centre in Paisley.*

2 CONCERT HALLS, OPERA HOUSES AND AUDITORIA

MICHAEL BARRON
Sandy Brown Associates

The design of concert halls and auditoria has many aspects common with other rooms of entertainment. Requirements for gangways, exits etc. are dealt with under Theatres (Section 3). Similarly the organisation of audience seating and the maintenance of sight-lines is covered again under Theatres.

The peculiar considerations for auditoria relate almost wholly to acoustic considerations; these can be readily divided into two categories: provision of a suitably quiet environment and provision of suitable listening conditions relative to the performers.

CONCERT HALLS AND AUDITORIA

NOISE LEVELS AND SOUND INSULATION

The tolerable noise level in a music auditorium is one of the lowest for a human environment. For the majority of sites this imposes severe insulation requirements which generally precludes the use of windows and doors leading directly from the auditorium to the exterior.

An accurate measurement of present site sound levels and an estimate of future levels should be made. Particular attention should be paid to the possibility of aeroplane flight paths being altered and providing a future noise problem. In urban environments, double construction walls and ceilings are generally required for optimum standards. This may economically be achieved by surrounding the auditorium with a zone of rooms. Doors into the auditorium from the foyer should be double wherever possible; as well as giving a higher sound insulation, the reduced probability of both doors being open greatly reduces the risk of accidental intrusion. The space between double doors should contain substantial acoustical absorbent. Figure 2.1 shows sound insulation measures used in the Royal Festival Hall, London which as well as incorporating insulation against sound, incorporates isolation from ground vibration in the form of column supports with intervening floors.

The recommended level of intruding noise and of air-conditioning noise is frequently stated in terms of an NC rating, though special criteria are also encountered.

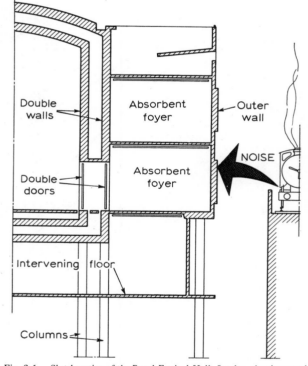

Fig. 2.1. Sketch section of the Royal Festival Hall, London, showing sound insulation measures (after Parkin and Humphreys)

The following are typical criteria:

Concert halls	NC 10–15
Opera houses	NC 20
Music rooms (e.g. school auditoria)	NC 25

Fig 2.2 illustrates the relevant NC curves and special criteria for concert hall and opera houses (after Parkin and Humphreys). In each case the curves indicate the maximum permissible octave band level.

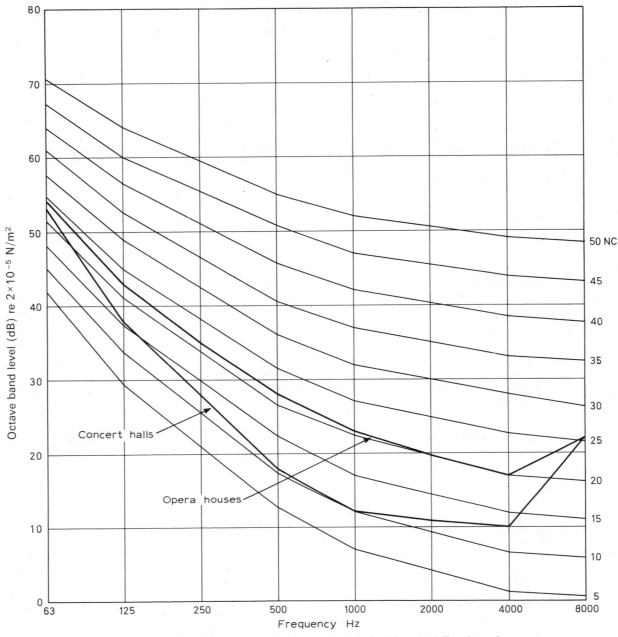

Fig. 2.2. Recommended maximum permissible octave band noise levels in concert halls and opera houses

ACOUSTICAL DESIGN OF MUSIC AUDITORIA

Due to the subjective nature and acoustically complex situation in an auditorium, there are still many areas of disagreement among acousticians regarding the most important considerations for good acoustics. The criteria in the following paragraphs are based, of necessity, on current general thinking. For specific advice it is normal practice to employ an acoustical consultant for auditoria. After a brief description of the behaviour of sound in auditoria, the criteria for direct sound, reverberation time, diffusion and avoiding faults are discussed. This is followed by more controversial criteria relating to early sound and a general discussion of suitable hall shapes.

BEHAVIOUR OF SOUND IN AUDITORIA

The direct sound from a musical instrument or performer becomes rapidly attenuated as it spreads out in space. When sound is produced in an enclosure, reflections off the walls etc. supplement the direct sound in such a way as not only to

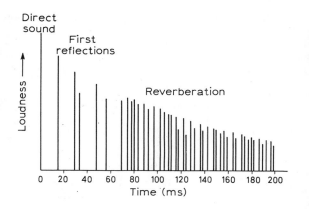

Fig. 2.3.   Time history of sound received by a listener in a concert hall

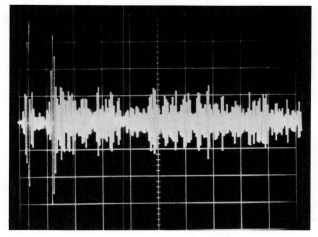

Fig. 2.4.   Echogram recorded in a concert hall (Horizontal time scale: 10 ms per division)

offset the attenuation of the direct sound, but also to create a desirable addition to the sensation of the direct sound. In fact, at the rear of a concert hall the energy contained in the direct sound is typically only one twentieth of the total sound energy reaching a listener. The problem of auditorium acoustics is essentially to manipulate this additional reflected energy to provide pleasurable auditory sensations for the human hearing system.

Figure 2.3 illustrates the time history of sound received by a listener in an auditorium. After the direct sound, the listener receives a series of early reflections from the side walls, ceiling etc. These reflections become more frequent but less intense until the sound can be considered to decay at a uniform rate, a process known as *reverberation*. A time history, or echogram, similar to Fig. 2.3, can be produced by using an impulsive sound source (e.g. a pistol shot or an electric spark) as shown in Fig. 2.4.

This picture of sound in an auditorium is however a grossly simplified one, and ignores the wave nature of sound. The wave nature of sound explains, for instance, why sound can 'bend' round corners, and the mechanism of resonance, which is basic to the function of wind instruments. The wave behaviour of sound critically depends on the frequency, or more precisely on the wavelength. (Wavelength = Speed of sound/Frequency).

The important frequencies in auditoria are from 50 Hz (or c/s) to 15 000 Hz which have corresponding wavelengths from 7 m to 22 mm. The importance of wavelength can be seen when we consider the reflection of sound off a flat surface, say a 0·5 m square. If the wavelength of the sound is much less than 0·5 m there will be a pronounced reflection from the surface, but at low frequencies where the wavelength is much larger than 0·5 m the sound wave behaves virtually as if the obstruction were not there.

The reverberation in a room can, according to wave acoustics, be considered like resonant behaviour. These room resonances are generally called *normal modes*. At high frequencies the normal mode frequencies are very close together, however at bass frequencies they can be sufficiently far apart that when a single note is sounded between two normal mode frequencies, there is a pitch change in the reverberation when the note is cut off. This behaviour is only likely to be evident in the smallest auditoria, and is unlikely to be a problem in the average auditorium.

DIRECT SOUND

An unobstructed passage of sound between the player(s) and the listener is desirable for concert hall listening. This criterion is satisfied if sight lines to the performers are maintained, such that there is a clearance of at least 75 mm, but preferably 100 mm between the sight lines of adjacent rows. This results in an ideal shape for stalls seating which is a curving rake. Simplifying this rake to a straight one should not be done at the expense of the sight line criterion. (Design for correct sight lines is included in Section 3.)

In auditoria in which a flat floor is required for other reasons, the performers should be placed on a platform to maintain sight lines as much as possible. This expedient is not however wholly satisfactory for large orchestral groups since sound from the rear performers tends to be shielded by front ones, even where risers are used for these rear performers.

The direct sound also suffers attenuation in the bass frequencies as it passes over the audience. It appears that this deficiency is generally compensated in halls, but it does have implications in terms of minimum ceiling height (see later).

REVERBERATION TIME

When a sound source in an enclosure is turned off, it will generally decay a certain number of decibels in each unit of time.

The reverberation time is defined as the time in seconds for the sound to decay 60 dB, which is roughly the time in seconds for a loud sound to become inaudible. Figure 2.5 shows an idealised decay, a straight line decay such as this is called *linear*.

Actual decay curves show modulations around a straight line, as shown in Fig. 2.6(a). A linear decay will not occur unless the sound flow is uniform in all directions. Fig. 2.6(b) shows a form of decay that can occur in a non-uniform situation, which is considered undesirable.

Since the work of W. C. Sabine around 1900, reverberation time has been considered as the single most important physical quantity defining the acoustics of an auditorium. In real life, the reverberation time varies from about 0·5 sec in

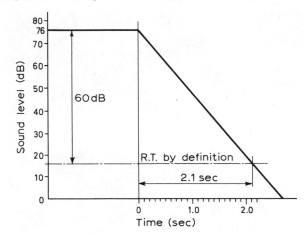

Fig. 2.5. *Idealised linear reverberant decay*

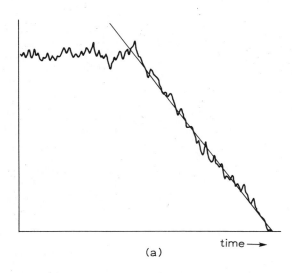

(a)

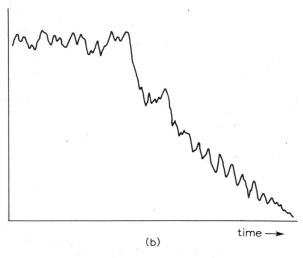

(b)

Fig. 2.6. *Actual reverberant decays. (a) Linear decay, (b) Irregular decay*

domestic living rooms to 3 to 6 sec or more in churches and cathedrals. The optimum reverberation time is a function of programme and room volume. Recommended mid-frequency (500–1000 Hz) reverberation times (in sec) for different programmes are as follows:

Organ music	2·5
Romantic classical music	1·8–2·2
Early classical music	1·5–1·7
Opera	1·2–1·6
Chamber music	1·4
Speech—theatre	1·0

For multi-purpose auditoria used predominantly for musical performance the reverberation times shown in Fig 2.7 are recommended.

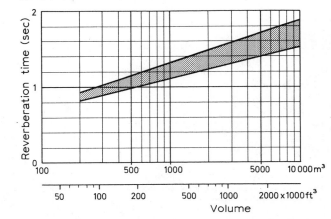

Fig. 2.7. *Recommended reverberation time as a function of hall volume*

Where a hall is for a predominant function, the reverberation time should be selected on the basis of programme; otherwise selection on the basis of volume is recommended. In many situations both approaches will give the same value, since programmes requiring shorter reverberation times are generally performed in smaller environments.

In any case this choice of reverberation time should be given serious consideration. A long reverberation time is associated with a sense of fullness of tone, but at the expense of definition and clarity. A particularly difficult compromise is required for an auditorium suitable both for speech and music. Choosing an intermediate reverberation time produces an acoustic which is too dry for music and detrimental to intelligibility for speech. Variable acoustics have recently become popular, but available systems have yet to be fully proven.

The reverberation time (RT) can be up to 50 % higher at bass frequencies, as shown in Fig 2.8 based on an optimum mid-frequency value of 2 sec.

A rise in reverberation time in the bass is considered to contribute to a sense of acoustical warmth. A large bass rise in RT is popular in the USA, but European halls generally have a more flat reverberation time characteristic.

Auditoria for use with speech as well as music should in particular not be designed with too high a bass frequency reverberation time. The reverberation time at high frequencies (associated with a sense of acoustical 'brilliance') generally decreases at higher frequencies due to air absorp-

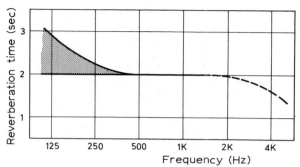

Fig. 2.8. Recommended reverberation time frequency characteristic based on a mid-frequency RT of 2 seconds

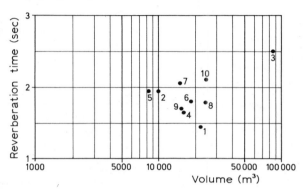

Fig. 2.9.   The volume and reverberation times of 10 concert halls
  1. *Royal Festival Hall, London*
  2. *Queen Elizabeth Hall, London*
  3. *Royal Albert Hall, London*
  4. *Usher Hall, Edinburgh*
  5. *The Maltings, Snape, Suffolk*
  6. *Boston Symphony Hall, U.S.A.*
  7. *Grosser Musikvereinsaal, Vienna*
  8. *Philharmonic Hall, New York*
  9. *Beethoven Halle, Bonn, Germany*
 10. *Concert Hall, Sydney Opera House*

tion, a factor beyond the control of the designer.

Figure 2.9 shows the volumes and mid-frequency reverberation times (occupied) of 5 British concert halls and 5 other famous concert halls.

PREDICTION OF REVERBERATION TIME

The reverberation time of a room can be calculated from the Sabine equation, which relates the reverberation time to the room volume and amount of acoustical absorption:

$$\text{Reverberation time (RT—sec)} = \frac{0 \cdot 16 \, V}{A}$$

where V is the room volume (m^3) and A is the acoustical absorption (m^2). If these latter two quantities are measured in ft^3 and ft^2, the constant becomes 0·05. The acoustical absorption of a surface is the product of its area and its absorption coefficient (the fraction of incident sound it absorbs). The total absorption in the room is simply the sum of the acoustical absorption of the various surfaces.

In concert halls and auditoria the majority of absorption is produced by the audience, and even if no additional absorbent is added a large volume is required to achieve a

sufficiently long reverberation time. Since additional volume is seldom required due to other acoustic or non-acoustic considerations it is general practice not to include any more acoustical treatment than is strictly necessary, at least for mid-frequencies. As the audience is the most significant absorbent surface, a simple estimate (due to Kosten) of the required volume for an auditorium may be made using the following equivalent absorption coefficients at mid-frequencies:

  α_{eq} (Occupied)   1·07
  α_{eq} (Unoccupied)   0·82

If S_A is the area occupied by audience seating and orchestra (in m^2), including aisle areas up to 1 m in width

$$\text{RT} = \frac{0 \cdot 16 \, V}{S_A \, \alpha_{eq}}$$

For example, if a concert hall is required to seat 2500 with an area of 500 × 900 mm per seat with an aisle area (1 m width) of 400 m^2 and an orchestra of 100 players occupying 1·1 m^2 each, then $S_A = 1635$ m^2. For a mid-frequency reverberation time of 2 seconds, a volume of

$$21{,}900 \text{ m}^2 \; \frac{(= 2 \times 1635 \times 1 \cdot 07)}{0 \cdot 16} \text{ is required.}$$

In many auditoria the whole floor is covered with either audience seating, narrow aisles or orchestra and S_A in an auditorium without a balcony can be taken as the floor area. In this case the reverberation time requirement leads directly to a specification for the height of the auditorium namely h = 6·7 × RT (m). Thus for a single floor hall for speech, with a design RT of 1 second, we expect a mean ceiling height of approximately 6·7 m (22 ft).

As shown in the figures for α_{eq} the absorption coefficient of unoccupied seating is lower than occupied. These figures assume upholstered seating; it is strongly recommended to use such seating to minimise the change in acoustical conditions with and without audience.

For more precise calculation of reverberation time, Table 2.1 contains absorption coefficients of commonly encountered surfaces. (It should be noted that the absorption of the audience is based on the *area* occupied by the audience rather than the *number* of the audience, which has given erroneous results in the past.) The area of the audience and orchestra is inclusive of aisles up to 1·1 m wide. Absorption figures for other surfaces are to be found in references 1 and 4.

Table 2.1 ABSORPTION COEFFICIENTS OF SURFACES IN AUDITORIA

Frequency (Hz)	63	125	250	500	1000	2000	4000
Audience and orchestra	0·25	0·39	0·57	0·80	0·94	0·92	0·87
Upholstered seats, unoccupied	0·08	0·19	0·37	0·56	0·67	0·61	0·59
Leather covered, thinly upholstered seats, unoccupied	—	0·12	—	0·28	0·34	0·34	0·31
Plaster or thick wood	0·21	0·19	0·14	0·09	0·06	0·06	0·05
Plaster on concrete	0·16	0·12	0·09	0·07	0·05	0·05	0·04
Concrete	0·05	0·02	0·02	0·02	0·04	0·05	0·04
Thin wood panelling	—	0·42	0·21	0·10	0·08	0·06	0·06
Curtain (velour, draped)	0·05	0·06	0·31	0·44	0·80	0·75	0·65

Table 2.2

Material	Area (m²)	63		125		250		500		1000		2000	
	Sα	Sα	Sα	Sα	Sα	Sα	Sα	Sα	Sα	Sα	Sα	Sα	Sα
Audience	1041·0	0·25	260·3	0·39	406·0	0·57	593·4	0·80	832·8	0·94	978·5	0·92	957·7
Thin wood panelling	512·8	0·42	215·4	0·42	215·4	0·21	107·7	0·10	51·3	0·08	41·0	0·06	30·8
Stone	1756·3	0·01	17·6	0·01	17·6	0·01	17·6	0·01	17·6	0·02	35·1	0·02	35·1
Wooden coffered ceiling & plastered balcony soffit	1041·0	0·21	218·6	0·19	197·8	0·14	145·7	0·09	93·7	0·06	62·5	0·06	62·5
Total (= A)			711·9		836·8		864·4		995·4		1117·1		1086·1
$RT = \dfrac{0·16\,V}{A}$ ($V = 13\,840\,\mathrm{m^3}$)			3·1		2·7		2.6		2·2		2·0		2·0

It can be seen that audience areas absorb less sound at bass frequencies. Bass absorption was frequently present in traditional constructions in the form of fibrous plaster panels, or wooden panels over an air space or suspended ceilings. In modern constructions solid walls and ceilings are frequently used so that additional bass absorption is necessary to achieve the flatter RT characteristics favoured in Europe. This can be achieved by using wood panelling, but alternatives exist in the form of membrane absorbers (e.g. using roofing felt) or Helmholz resonators (as employed in the Queen Elizabeth Hall, London). At 4 kHz additional absorption is present due to air absorption, which typically reduces the reverberation time by about 20 % at this frequency.

A sample calculation of the reverberation time of a typical traditional concert hall is given in Table 2.2. The hall has dimensions of length, width and height of 45·0 × 19·1 × 16·1 m. The floor is totally covered with either audience or orchestral seating (and aisle areas which for Table 2.1 are to be included). In addition there is a balcony extending 9·5 m into the hall running across the total width of the hall. The underside is plastered. There is a wood panelling round 80 % of the perimeter to a height of 5 m, the remainder of the walls are stone and the ceiling is coffered wood.

To summarise the general procedure for design of correct reverberation time: the approximate volume requirement can be determined on the basis of Kosten's method. Once the hall design is established, the mid-frequency reverberation time should be calculated. If any significant areas of absorbent have been included, e.g. extensive curtains, an increase in volume may be required to maintain the correct reverberation time. The value at 125 Hz should then be calculated and if it is too large relative to the mid-frequency value some bass absorbent should be introduced. The reverberation time at other frequencies should then be checked. Calculations should be made to the nearest 0·1 sec, which is probably the smallest detectable difference. In any case inaccuracies in the prediction of at least this order frequently occur, particularly at bass frequencies.

Building a hall with slightly larger volume than is predicted as necessary is a recommended safety precaution since, introducing absorption can be done very simply, whilst removing it is frequently impossible. However, excessive volume with large areas of absorption to reduce the RT is acoustically detrimental in other ways.

DIFFUSION

Diffusing surfaces, which 'break up' the sound on reflection, are frequently used in concert halls and auditoria. Such surfaces are required to achieve a reverberant sound which travels uniformly in all directions, to create a state of diffusion. Diffusing surfaces are also used to eliminate echoes and flutter echoes.

For a diffusing surface to be effective at all frequencies, surface projections of the order of 0·3–0·6 m are necessary. Fig. 2.10(a) shows an example of the plaster decoration frequently found in traditional halls, which provides a good diffusion except at lowest frequencies. Fig. 2.10(b) shows a highly diffusing surface. Diffusing surfaces should be solidly built, say of at least 25 mm of wood or plaster.

There is a general concensus that a highly diffusing ceiling is desirable, since tonal degradation results from a strong discrete overhead reflection. The coffered ceiling, frequently found in traditional buildings, is considered good in this respect.

The provision of diffusion on side walls is probably not so critical, though light surface decoration is desirable to avoid the possibility of false localisation of the sound source, as can occur, for instance, with brass instruments at high frequencies when they are highly directional. The use of panels at different orientations would be suitable in this respect, though too regular a pattern for a diffusing surface is not recommended, since this can result in strange frequency effects.

The necessary degree of diffusion is largely a matter of experience and empiricism. The use of diffusing surfaces is a safe expedient, but too much use of diffusing surfaces may create problems of uniformity in the largest halls.

EARLY REFLECTIONS

The importance of early reflections has been appreciated for some time. Whilst precise physical quantities relating to early reflections remain to be established, two considerations appear to be significant for the overall acoustic impression.

(a) *The ratio of early to reverberant energy.* The early reflections arriving soon after the direct sound contribute to the

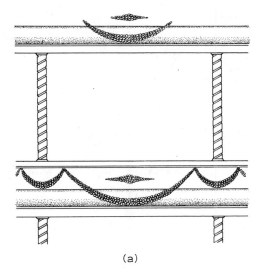

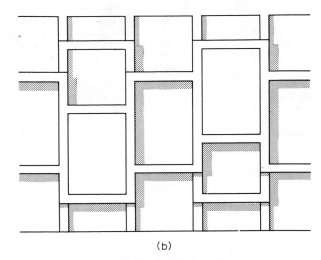

(a)

(b)

Fig. 2.10.   Diffusion in auditoria (a) Light diffusion on a traditional balcony front. (b) Heavily diffusing surface

direct sound and maintain the 'clarity' of the music even when the direct sound is weak. For instance, by having a large number of early reflections off surfaces adjacent to the orchestra, the clarity of music can be increased at the expense of fullness of tone. Or conversely by using dispersive surfaces adjacent to the orchestra the sense of being surrounded by the sound at the expense of clarity can be increased. Recent results suggest that the correct balance between early and late sound is critical, though the situation appears to be self-regulating in smaller halls. The use of reflected surfaces suspended above the orchestra and profiled ceiling shapes to direct sound to the rear of the hall to effect the balance will both be discussed below.

Designing for the correct balance of early to reverberant sound is basically a matter of experience, though scale models can be of use to quantify the situation at the design stage.

(b) *Early lateral reflections.* There is growing evidence that early lateral reflections from the side walls contribute a sense of envelopment which is a characteristic of halls with the best reputations. Not only is it important that these reflections arrive early enough (less than 8 ms after the direct sound) but also that the angle from which they arrive is sufficiently large relative to the direct sound. Fig. 2.11 shows how a fan-shaped hall is bad in this respect whilst a reverse-splay shape is particularly good. Reflections at angles of much less than 20° can be considered as frontal rather than lateral.

Source

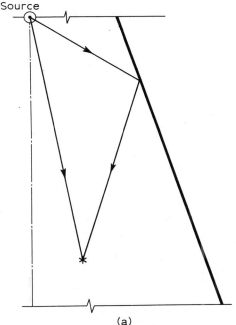

Source

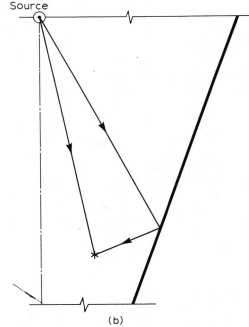

(a)

(b)

Fig. 2.11.   Lateral reflection situation in (a) a fan shape hall and (b) a reverse splay shape

Further since bass frequencies are strongly associated with this envelopment effect, cornice reflections off the ceiling and side walls should not be obscured (the reason for this being the sound passing over audience seating suffers bass attenuation).

At the design stage reflections should be determined geometrically, though account should be taken of the fact that a diffuse surface will widen the area of reflection. As a design principle all seats should receive some early lateral sound, and generally the more early lateral sound the better. Only in the narrowest halls is there some risk that the sense of envelopment might appear excessive to some.

ACOUSTICAL DEFECTS

(a) *Echoes.* Reflections off large plane surfaces risk being heard as echoes, that is discrete delayed repetitions of the direct sound. An echo is more obvious the later (at least more than 35 ms after the direct sound), the more intense, and the more 'exposed' it is relative to the reverberant sound. In a well-designed hall with adequate diffusion the surfaces most likely to create an audible echo are at the rear of the hall. This defect can be eliminated either by making the reflecting surface diffusing or absorbent, or in some situations suitable reorientation of the offending surface.

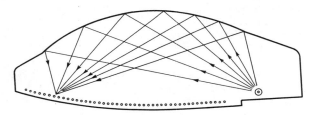

Fig. 2.12. Poor ceiling design causing focusing and a troublesome echo

Particularly troublesome echoes can result from reflection off concave curved surfaces (see Fig. 2.12) or a series of plane surfaces giving equivalent reflections. Even if the focal point is not at the position of the audience, acoustical non-uniformity will result, and such surfaces should be avoided in auditoria. The traditional domed ceiling in opera houses is probably their most serious acoustical defect.

(b) *Flutter echoes.* If a sound is made between two parallel surfaces, the regular reflections between the two surfaces are heard as a highly metallic ring. This is known as a 'flutter echo'. It is only likely to be noticeable when the performer is between two parallel surfaces, a situation which must therefore be avoided.

Elimination of flutter echoes require a small amount of diffusing treatment on the offending surfaces, inclination of as little as 5° of one surface relative to the other, or application of a little absorbent.

DESIRABLE PLAN SHAPES FOR CONCERT HALLS

Given the volume requirement based on reverberation time discussed previously, the limiting dimension for a concert hall is the maximum distance between the orchestra and the

furthest listener, about 40 m. However consideration of early reflection requirements imposes restrictions in terms of required reflecting surfaces which make designing a concert hall for an occupancy of more than 2500 exceedingly difficult if uniformly good acoustical conditions are to be produced. An occupancy of 3000 can be considered the upper limit for good acoustics.

There is no established optimum for a concert hall, and different considerations apply for different sizes. Design shapes much depend on the priorities placed on the various acoustical considerations, which still differ between acousticians. It is only possible to give a rough guide by listing the virtues and vices of simple shapes which are shown in Fig 2.13.

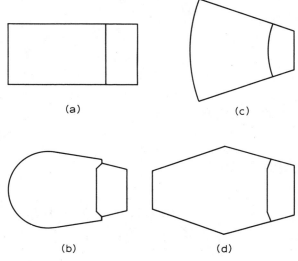

Fig. 2.13. Sketch plans of a concert hall

(a) *Rectangular shape.* This shape has the best tradition for excellent acoustics (e.g. Boston Symphony Hall, Leipzig Gewandhaus (no longer standing) and the Musikvereinsaal, Vienna). All these have high ceilings (15–18 m) relative to their width (19–23 m). To accommodate larger audiences, balconies are employed, which in the older halls generally extended round the whole length of the side walls. The virtues of this shape are a high degree of uniformity and an inherently good balance of early and late energy. The small width is responsible for a substantial amount of early lateral sound, enhanced by the additional contribution of multiple reflections between the side walls.

For larger halls the auditorium width is likely to be too wide for the stage itself. One solution to this problem is to narrow the sides at the orchestra level but maintain full width at the higher levels (e.g. Royal Festival Hall, London and De Doelen, Rotterdam). Alternative solutions involve a basic fan-shape, which will be discussed later. Halls with a width much in excess of 32 m are unlikely to be satisfactory from the point of view of early lateral reflections. Further, a ceiling height much below 12 m is not to be recommended due to the audience attenuation effect.

The rectangular shape is probably ideal for smaller halls (e.g. the Maltings, Snape), and can readily accommodate about 1500 persons without degradation of quality. Some earlier halls managed to accommodate larger numbers with a narrow format, but this is frequently at the expense of good sight lines.

(b) *Horse-shoe shape.* This shape, which has proved to be particularly suitable for opera, does not share these advantages for concert hall usage. Achieving a sufficiently long reverberation time is unlikely to be possible with the conventional opera proportions. The particular virtue of this shape in minimising performer-listener distances is however not a high priority in a concert hall. The use of concave curved surfaces is also not recommended unless made highly diffusing or acoustically absorbent as in an opera house where these surfaces would normally be concealed by audience seating.

(c) *Fan shape.* The fan shape has the advantage of containing the maximum number of people in a given angle for a specified maximum source-receiver distance. This characteristic is attractive for economic reasons as well as enabling the hall to fulfil multi-purpose requirements. It does however have certain acoustical shortcomings which have given this shape a poor acoustical reputation. It has the inherent characteristic that the side walls barely contribute in providing reflections so that these halls tend to have non-uniform acoustics, with poor conditions in the centre of the seating area. The lateral reflection situation is also particularly poor (see above), which probably accounts for the lack of intimacy associated with this plan shape.

A significant improvement in the lateral reflection situation and the degree of uniformity is achieved by giving a stepped form to the side walls. This approach overcomes the problem of providing a narrow orchestral area in a wider hall (e.g. the Queen Elizabeth Hall, London).

If a hall is to have a fan shape the angle at the apex of the fan should be made as small as possible. A 90° apex angle can be considered an absolute maximum; an angle in excess of 25° is not recommended. If the rear wall is curved, it should, preferably be made highly diffusive or, at the risk of non-uniformity, absorbent.

(d) *Elongated hexagonal shape.* A compromise concert hall form, which if properly designed may overcome the acoustical limitations of the fan shape, whilst permitting a larger audience than the rectangular shape, is the elongated hexagon. It is not possible to give recommendations concerning dimensions, other than for the angle of fan, for which the considerations under (c) above also apply. This hall shape has not a long tradition behind it, but it is interesting that two recently built halls (De Doelan, Rotterdam and Sydney Opera House Concert Hall) have included the tendency to modify the rectangular shape in this direction.

CEILING PROFILES AND ORCHESTRAL REFLECTORS

As concert halls have increased in size to accommodate larger audiences, so there has been concern that listeners at the rear receive inadequate sound. Since the ear adds the early reflection energy to the direct sound energy for its assessment of clarity, there has been a tendency to profile ceiling shapes to ensure that strong early reflections from the ceiling are present at all seats.

A similar rationale has been used to establish the need for suspended reflectors above and in front of the orchestra (e.g. Royal Festival Hall, London). Fig. 2.14 illustrates the reflec-

tion behaviour for such a hall.

This design procedure was popular up till about 1960, particularly in England. However it has since been established that strong ceiling reflections produce an unpleasant tone coloration, whilst the need to direct sound specifically to the rear of the halls appears to be less critical with a suitably designed plan shape. Halls designed since 1960 have frequently employed a basically horizontal diffusing ceiling.

The use of orchestral reflectors may well be justified for providing reflections for the orchestra, particularly when the ceiling is otherwise high. Their use in providing early reflections for the audience appears limited. For example, the movable reflector in the Queen Elizabeth Hall, London, is seldom used in its 'reflecting' position with regard to the audience.

BALCONY DESIGN

In a large concert hall, the incorporation of balconies frequently becomes inevitable. The requirement for adequate sight lines dictates a steep seating rake for balconies. The overhang relative to the seating contained below the balcony should not be excessive. Figure 2.15 shows the principal dimensions. For optimum design *D* should not exceed *H*, and the height at the rear should not be less than 3 m. The soffit may also be shaped to reflect direct sound onto listeners towards the rear, below the balcony.

THE DESIGN PROBLEM FOR CONCERT HALLS

Acoustical requirements place severe restrictions on the design of concert halls, particularly those seating more than 2000 people. Some halls which accommodate larger numbers do so at the expense of poor listening positions, such as audience seating deep under balconies, or to the rear or side of the orchestra. It may however be considered worthwhile to include such seating but to charge low prices for them.

It must be evident from the above discussion on hall shape that it is difficult to quantify acoustic requirements in terms of hall shapes. This is because there is no direct relation between the acoustically relevant quantities and hall shape. This has led to the building of acoustical models, to enable

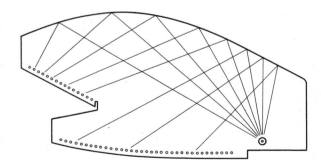

Fig. 2.14. Ceiling profile to concentrate reflected sound on the remote balcony seating

halls to be tested with regard to their acoustics in a way that can only be vaguely estimated in drawings. Model scales of 1:8 or 1:10 are generally used. Model techniques are still in their infancy, but are likely to be used on most large scale projects in the future.

STAGE DESIGN (ORCHESTRAL)

The following minimum requirements are based on the findings of Parkin & Humphreys:

1. For violin players and the smaller wind instruments an area of at least 1×0.6m is required; slightly more is necessary for bassoons and horns.
2. A tier at least 1.05m deep is required for all string and wind players including, cellos and double basses; players however prefer at least 1.2 m.
3. A tier 1.8 m deep is necessary for percussion.
4. Tier risers should not be more than 0.45m, to enable instruments to be carried up them.
5. A concert grand piano has dimensions 2.75×1.6m in plan.

As a general rule about $1\,m^2$ should be allocated to each player with additional space of 3.8×1.8m per grand piano and about $20\,m^2$ for a full percussion section. In this way a large orchestra of 100 players requires about $130\,m^2$ to be comfortably seated.

The platform should be neither too deep nor too wide, otherwise the time delay between sounds from different instruments is too large to maintain balance. Maximum dimensions for satisfactory balance are width 18 m and depth 12 m. Where choir seating is included, the maximum depth from the stage front to the rear choir should be limited to 13.5 m. For smaller platforms the depth should be reduced more than the width.

The use of a stepped platform has become general in larger auditoria. This enables the weaker instruments, the woodwind, violas and 'cellos, to be placed such that they are not screened by other instruments. In practice however, platforms frequently have a large flat front section to accommodate a piano and two or three tiers at the back. Since the tiers are generally used for the brass and percussion sections, which do not require exposure, it is difficult for conductors to maintain good balance with this arrangement. Either a platform which is fully stepped or a system of movable tiers would appear to be the best compromise.

The platform floor is made of wood on a wooden frame; this is essential for 'cellos and double basses, which radiate some of their sound from the platform. There is still no general agreement on design of the stage enclosure. The musicians require to be able to hear each other; an enclosure round three sides of the orchestra is desirable for uniform conditions.

The musicians also probably appreciate a diffusing enclosure, though this may mitigate against possible reinforcement of the direct sound at the rear of the hall by strong reflection off the stage enclosure surfaces. The use of suspended reflecting surfaces to further assist the ability of musicians to hear each other is a subject of controversy. Practice in recently built halls suggests that a full canopy over the orchestra is not necessary. With a sufficient degree of

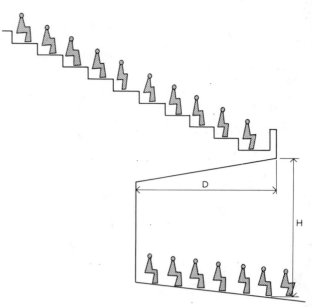

Fig. 2.15.   Recommended balcony proportions for a concert hall

orchestra enclosure, a reflector is probably not necessary unless the ceiling is excessively high.

OPERA HOUSES

The design of opera houses follows the same principles as concert halls but with two important differences. Firstly, that there are two sound sources to consider and, secondly, that there is a more stringent visual requirement. Just as concert halls generally include compromises for different musical styles, so opera houses are generally built for a range of operatic styles, from intimate Italian opera, through grand opera to Wagnerian opera. Some houses exist which are specifically suitable for a particular style, but most modern buildings require a compromise to be made.

REVERBERATION TIME FOR OPERA

The reverberation time should be between 1.2 sec for Italian opera up to 2.0 sec for Wagner, though 1.6 sec is probably a maximum value for other forms of opera. If the opera house is also to be used for speech (theatre), a short reverberation time is recommended.

For calculation, no standard absorption coefficient exists for the proscenium opening—a value between 0.5 and 0.8 seems reasonable for a well draped stage.

DESIRABLE SHAPES FOR OPERA HOUSES

The limiting length between the stage front and the rear seating is about 30 m for satisfactory opera. (For theatre the figure is 20 m.) This makes designing a hall for an audience 1000–1200 relatively easy, but in excess of 1500 very difficult.

With this serious length limitation the possible shapes are the fan shape, the horseshoe shape or a modern variant of it. For the fan shape exactly the same comments apply as were listed for concert halls. This shape is not recommended. The horseshoe shape or its modern variant becomes the recommended shape. In detail there remain problems of uniform acoustics and provision of lateral sound.

It is almost inevitable that, in plan, some degree of fan is required beyond the proscenium. This angle of fan should be the minimum possible; the splay should not be continued further than necessary. Using vertical panels inclined at a smaller angle to the longitudinal axis than the basic fan is also preferable to the simple fan shape. These measures contribute both to producing uniformity and suitable lateral reflections. Figure 2.16 illustrates the areas receiving lateral reflections for a source 6m from the proscenium in the new Metropolitan Opera House, Lincoln Centre, New York.

BALCONY DESIGN IN OPERA HOUSES

The balconies in opera houses require very careful design if adequate sight lines are to be maintained. For acoustical purposes the degree of overhang should be limited to D being less than $2H$, see Figure 2.17, though less overhang is desirable if possible. A good criterion is that a significant proportion of the total ceiling area should be visible from all seats. Designing the soffit to reflect direct sound to the rear seating positions is probably recommended.

Two basic forms of balcony design are possible, the sledge form, in which individual 'boxes' are cantilevered out from the side walls, and the continuous balcony. The choice

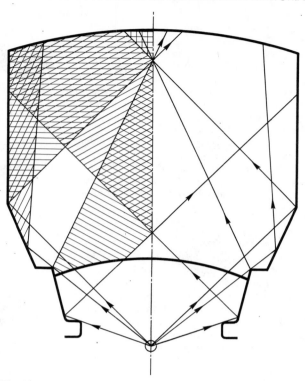

Fig. 2.16.   The lateral reflection situation for the stalls (in plan) of the Metropolitan Opera House, Lincoln Centre, New York. Shaded areas in the left half of the audience receive lateral reflections for a source position on stage.

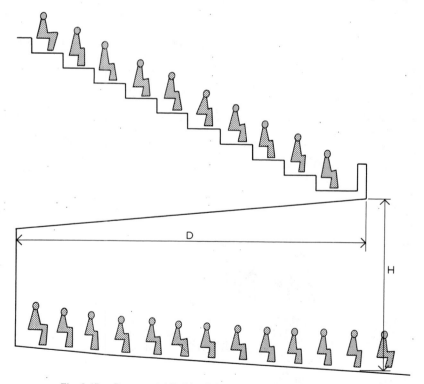

Fig. 2.17.   Recommended limiting balcony proportions for an opera house

between these is likely to be dominated by architectural and sight line considerations.

ACOUSTICAL BALANCE IN OPERA HOUSES

A significant problem in opera houses is to obtain a suitable balance between the sound from the singers on the stage and the orchestra in the pit. To a certain extent this depends on pit design. Surfaces in the vicinity of the proscenium should be orientated so as to provide useful reflections in the auditorium for the singers voices.

The ceiling surface should be roughly continuous, as seen from the stage, and contain some diffusion. Suspended reflectors are unlikely to be applicable to opera houses.

PROSCENIUM DIMENSIONS

Proscenium width and height is a function of the required acting area and maintenance of sight lines. The proscenium width roughly defines a square acting area behind it. Typically proscenium widths between 10 and 18 m are used, though 14 m would be general for grand opera, smaller widths being used for smaller sized productions. Proscenium height up to 9 m is general for grand opera.

There is much to be said for incorporating a movable proscenium, both in width and height and position relative to the stage front. To maintain optimum acoustical conditions surfaces adjacent to the proscenium which provides useful reflections should be moveable as well.

PIT DESIGN

Floor area should be calculated on the basis of at least $1·1 m^2$ per orchestral player. For grand opera space for 100 players is normally required, special arrangements normally being made to accommodate up to 20 additional players that would be used for Wagner operas. The stage usually overhangs the pit (V in Fig. 2.18). The top of the (solid) orchestral rail is generally in line with the stage, a distance D above the stalls floor.

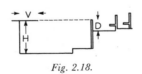

Fig. 2.18.

Typical dimensions are:
V 1–2 m
D 1 m
H 2·5–3·5 m

As a general rule, the width of the pit should be less than four times the depth (along the longitudinal axis). To accommodate the orchestra in the splay in plan beyond the proscenium a cranked orchestra rail is frequently used.

As mentioned above, the balance between the orchestra and the singers depends in part on suitable pit design. Extending the orchestra rail as a cover over the front of the orchestra has only been used successfully in Wagner's Bayreuth Festspielhaus which was specifically designed for the requirements of Wagnerian opera, to produce a sense of remoteness and a high degree of blend in the orchestral sound. A stage overhang is recommended in all but the smallest orchestral pits, since the loudest instruments can be placed under this area. To enable optimum conditions to be achieved for different operatic requirements and orchestra sizes it is strongly recommended to include the possibility of raising or lowering the orchestra floor. Bass frequency absorption is frequently included on the pit walls to limit bass-frequency reverberation.

SMALL AUDITORIA

The design of small auditoria with satisfactory acoustics is much simpler than their larger counterparts. Providing certain requirements are met, satisfactory acoustics can be generally guaranteed.

The reverberation time should be chosen as indicated above. This will largely determine the height of the roof, which should be high enough to produce a ceiling reflection at an angle of elevation of at least 15° in the rear seating positions. Wherever possible, seating should be raked, but in all situations a raised stage relative to the floor should be used.

A rectangular shape in plan, or a variant of it, is probably the optimum shape for smaller halls. A narrow, long hall with a ratio of length to width of about 2:1 is a very rough optimum dimension ratio though this is not thought to be critical. The ceiling should be lightly diffusing, but should not contain deep transverse beams, since this results in areas not receiving ceiling reflections (see Fig. 2.19).

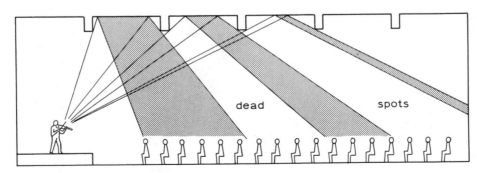

Fig. 2.19. The ceiling reflection situation in a hall with deep transverse beams below the ceiling. Only shaded areas receive ceiling reflections, with dead spots in between.

The requirements for stage design are similar to those for larger halls, though the use of risers becomes less critical in smaller halls, in which balance and blend of the orchestra tends not to be a problem. If the stage area is bounded by parallel surfaces, these should be made diffusing to avoid flutter echoes. There is no case for having a lower ceiling over the orchestra than in the hall; too low a ceiling will result in coloration and balance problems for the players.

When musical performances are to be conducted on a stage with a proscenium curtain, a screen, preferably diffusing, should be placed behind the players. This can be moveable but should be of solid construction, at least 12 mm thick wood or plaster.

CONCERT HALLS

Royal Festival Hall, London

Volume   21 900 m³
Audience seating   3000
Reverberation time (500/1000 Hz) = 1·5 secs.
Uses: Symphony and choral concerts.

This hall is noted for its high degree of clarity, due in part to the orchestral reflector. The short bass frequency reverberation time has been extended by a specially designed electronic system, known as 'assisted resonance'.

Queen Elizabeth Hall, London

Volume   10 000 m³
Audience seating   1106
Reverberation time   2·0 sec.

Uses: Small orchestral and chamber concerts.

Grosser Musikvereinsaal, Vienna, Austria

Volume   15 000 m³
Audience seating   1680
Reverberation time   2·05 sec.
Uses: Symphony concerts

This hall has a world wide reputation for its good acoustics.

Neues Festspielhaus, Salzburg, Austria

Volume   14 000 m³
Audience capacity   2158
Reverberation time   1·45 sec.
Uses: Opera, Concerts, Drama.

Note the unusually wide proscenium. An orchestral shell is used for concerts, as shown here.

Staatstheater, Kassel, Germany

Volume   6500 m³
Audience seating   953
Reverberation time   0·9 sec.
Uses: Opera (40–50 %), drama and ballet

OPERA HOUSES

Festspielhaus, Bayreuth, Germany

Volume   10 300 m³
Audience capacity   1800
Reverberation time   1·55 sec
Uses: Wagner opera

Note the unique pit design with canopy.

War Memorial Opera House, San Francisco, U.S.A.

Volume   20 900 m³
Audience capacity   3252
Reverberation time   1·6 sec
Uses: Concerts, Opera

A traditional design opera house. The upper balcony extends too far for stasfactory listening.

BIBLIOGRAPHY

1. Parkin, P. H. and Humphreys, H. R. *Acoustics, Noise and Buildings (Revised)*, Faber and Faber Ltd. London. (1969).
2. Beranek, L. L., *Music, Acoustic and Architecture*, John Wiley and Sons Inc., New York. (1962).
3. Furrer, W., *Room and Building Acoustics and Noise Abatement*, Butterworths, London. (1964).
4. Evans, E. J. and Bazley, E. N., *Sound Absorbing Materials*, HMSO. (1960).
5. Aloi, R., *Teatri e Auditori*, Hoepli, Milan. (1972).

Barron, Michael, *M.A., Ph.D., has been employed with Sandy Brown Associates since 1973. Graduated from Cambridge he took up research into the subjective aspects of concert hall acoustics at Southampton University and the University of Western Australia, Perth. He has maintained his special interest in auditorium acoustics and worked with Sandy Brown Associates on, among other projects, the Edinburgh Opera House scheme and its one-eighth scale acoustical model. He has since taken up a research post at the Dept. of Architecture, Cambridge University, studying acoustical models.*

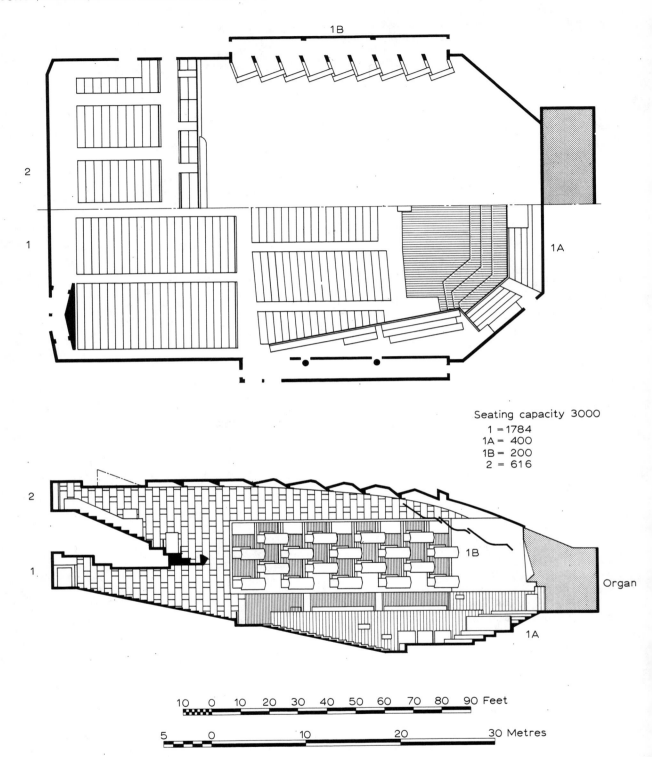

Seating capacity 3000
1 = 1784
1A = 400
1B = 200
2 = 616

Fig. 2.20. Plan and section of the Royal Festival Hall, London. Designed by the GLC's Department of Architecture and Civic Design. Architects Sir Robert Mathew and Sir Leslie Martin (reprinted by permission from 'Music, Acoustics and Architecture' (L. L. Beranek) published by John Wiley & Sons Inc.)

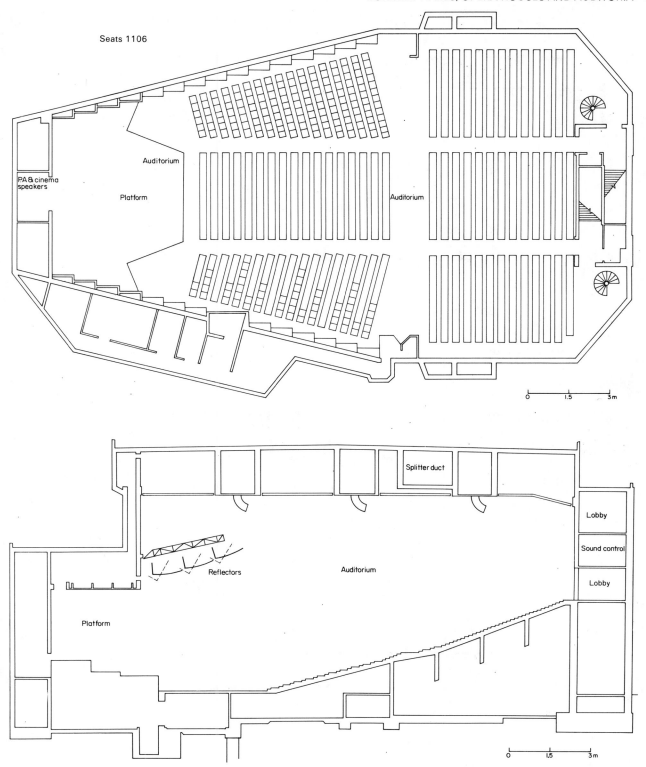

Seats 1106

Fig. 2.21. Plan and section of Queen Elizabeth Hall, London. Designed by Architects Department, GLC

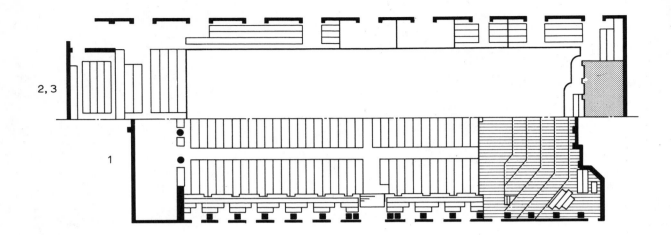

Seating capacity 1680
1 = 1032
2 = 548
3 = 100 + 320 standing

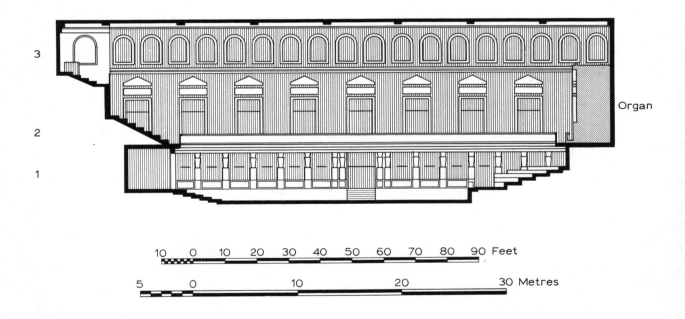

Fig. 2.22.   The Grosser Musikvereinsaal, Vienna, Austria

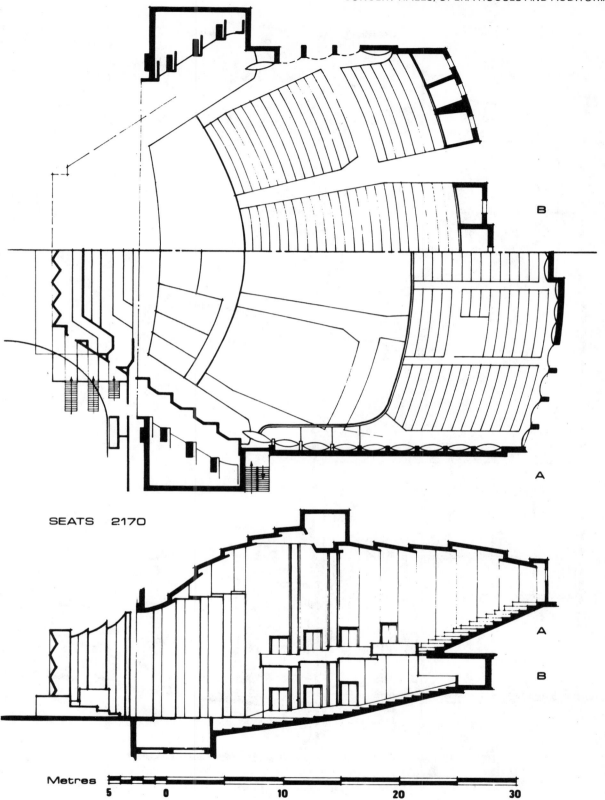

SEATS 2170

Metres

5   0   10   20   30

Fig. 2.23.   The large concert hall of the Salzburg Festspielhaus, Austria

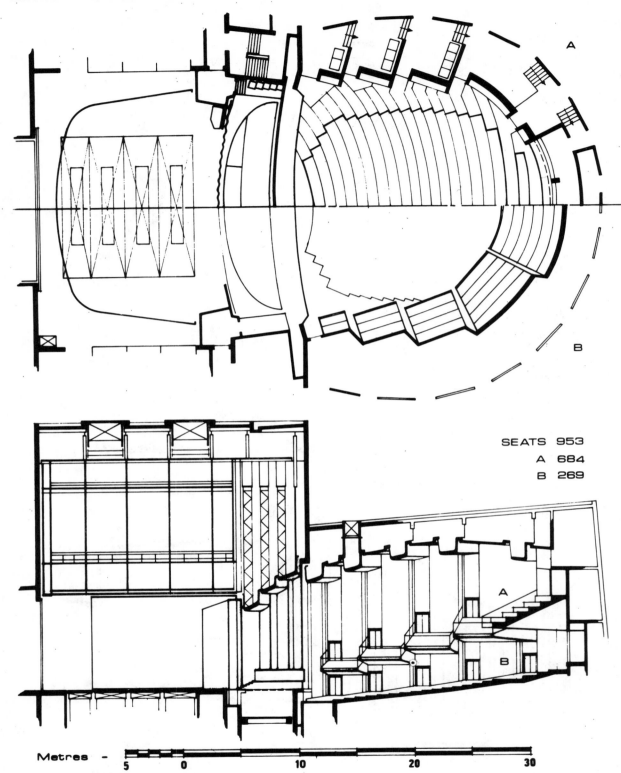

SEATS 953
A 684
B 269

Metres

5   0   10   20   30

Fig. 2.24.   The Staatstheater, Kassel, Germany

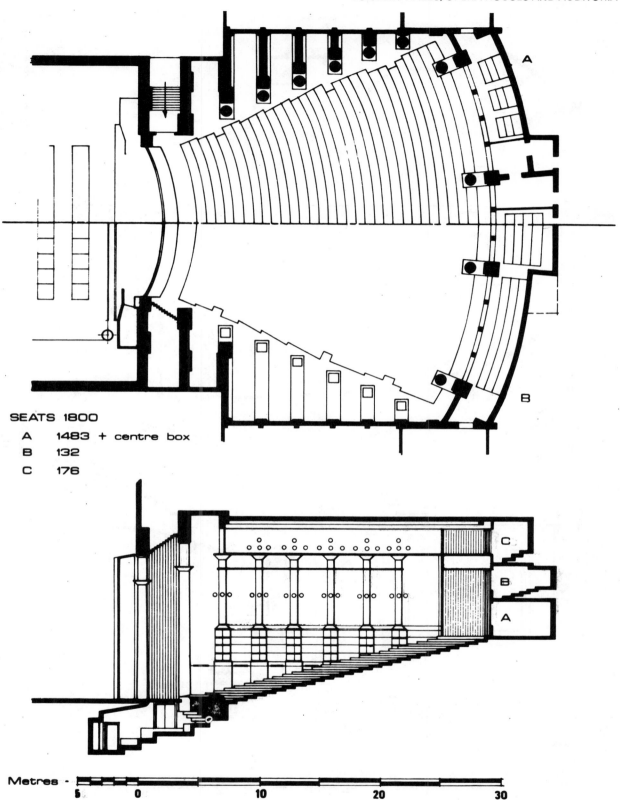

SEATS 1800

A   1483 + centre box
B   132
C   176

Metres -

5   0   10   20   30

Fig. 2.25.   The Bayreuth Festspielhaus, Germany

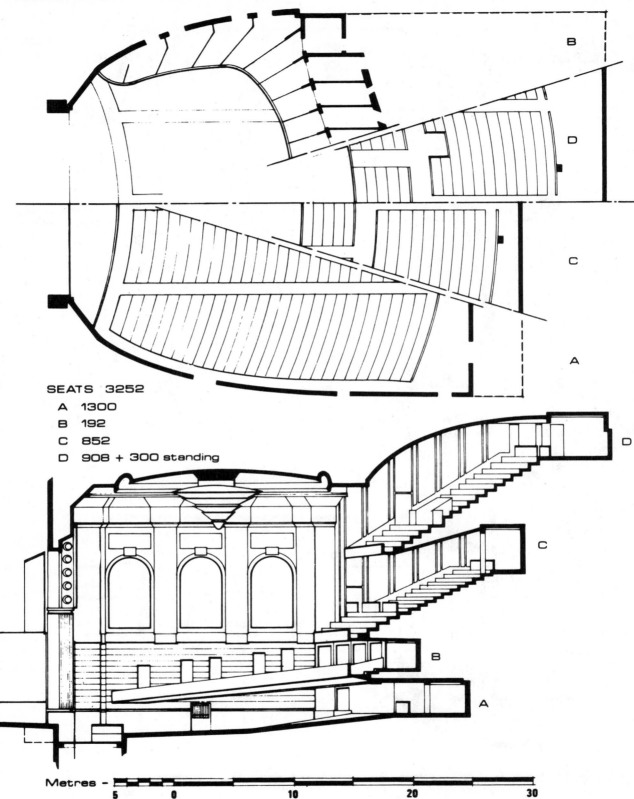

SEATS 3252

A 1300
B 192
C 852
D 908 + 300 standing

Metres -

5   0   10   20   30

Fig. 2.26.   The San Francisco War Memorial Opera House

3 THEATRES

PETER G. HUGHES, A.A. Dipl., F.R.I.B.A.
Percy Thomas Partnership
and
MALCOLM LOVIBOND, B. Arch., Dip. TP, F.R.I.B.A., M.R.T.P.I.

INTRODUCTION

Over the past twenty-five years, the theatre in Britain has undergone considerable change. Outside London, the commercial theatre has suffered a drastic decline and, of the 130 private enterprise theatres in the Provinces before the war, only about 30 were still in use in 1970. Even in London, where the principal commercial theatres far outnumber the principal subsidised theatres, they are barely holding their own. The building of any new West End commercial theatre would therefore be most unlikely and, in the Provinces, new commercial theatre building would be out of the question.

On the other hand, during the quarter of a century since the Arts Council was founded, there has been a most encouraging increase in the number of subsidised, non-profit-making theatres, especially outside London. Since 1958—when the 'Housing the Arts' programme was launched by the Arts Council—the number of repertory companies in the Provinces has more than doubled and over 30 new theatres have been built. Many Local Authorities have provided accommodation for both touring companies and their own repertory companies by taking over failing commercial theatres for this purpose, carrying out improvements and extensions as necessary; and a few have even undertaken the management of them with great success. But there are also an increasing number of Local Authorities who have decided to build and support new theatres to house their local repertory companies and they have clearly become the principal sponsors of theatre building in Britain today. Indeed, the Arts Council's report in 1970 on 'The Theatre Today in England and Wales' made it clear that the future of the theatre outside London will be mainly determined by the Local Authorities.

The Universities are another major breeding ground for British theatrical development and many have constructed purpose-built theatres, not only for their own use within Drama Departments and for student productions, but also for use by professional touring and repertory companies.

The major national subsidised companies in London—National Theatre, Royal Shakespeare Company, English Stage Company and Mermaid Theatre—all have theatre buildings extant or under construction and therefore the scope for new theatre building in Britain would seem to depend mainly on the sponsorship of Local Authorities and, to some extent, the Universities.

FUTURE PROSPECTS

The theatre in Britiain will undoubtedly undergo further changes in the future, with present trends moving towards greater community involvement. Already many small local repertory companies have not only been presenting a wide range of productions to appeal to as many sections of the community as possible, but they have also put on dramatic documentaries of local issues, taken 'theatre' out to the people in the streets and involved themselves in the education of school children. The theatres have increasingly become the centres for a variety of community activities, including amateur dramatics, amateur operatics, children's concerts, film matinees, meetings and conferences.

All new theatres will continue to depend heavily on subsidies from public funds mainly through the Arts Council and Local Authorities, and 'service to the community' will clearly be the central justification for this expenditure. It seems reasonable to assume therefore that most theatres in the future will be located and planned to meet the cultural and practical needs of the community, rather than any esoteric or commercial purpose, and that they are likely to be seen as integral parts of the town centre, possibly linked to other facilities in community arts centres.

BASIC BRIEF

When designing a theatre, the architect is faced with a wide range of complex problems and it is absolutely necessary, at the outset, for him to clarify the brief with his client in some depth. It is particularly important to agree the size, type and cost of the theatre.

The design solution in any particular case will depend on many factors, such as the management and artistic policy, seating capacity, the scales and types of performances envisaged and their pattern of use, the form of audience/performer relationship, the extent of production facilities (scenery, property and costume making) to be provided, the management structure and the degree of audience comfort. The emphasis placed on these factors will vary in each case and, coupled with the unique characteristics of individual sites, it is rarely possible for any two theatres to be completely alike.

With his professional colleagues in the design team, especially the theatre consultant, the architect should therefore ensure that the developing brief does not call for conflicting requirements. These can only produce unsatisfactory compromises, and the architect should be aware of the degrees of adaptability made possible by the different solutions outlined and the main principles involved in the sub-section on planning.

SEATING CAPACITY

The number of seats to be provided will depend mainly on the policy and vigour of the management, but also on the number of people within the catchment area of the theatre, their comfort and the types of production to be presented. For example, a repertory company in a large city or conurbation might well be able to fill a 700 seat theatre for a two or three week run if it enjoys a wide and popular reputation; but this would be practically impossible in a small town with a local company, where a much smaller capacity of say 300 seats, filled for each performance, would be the best that

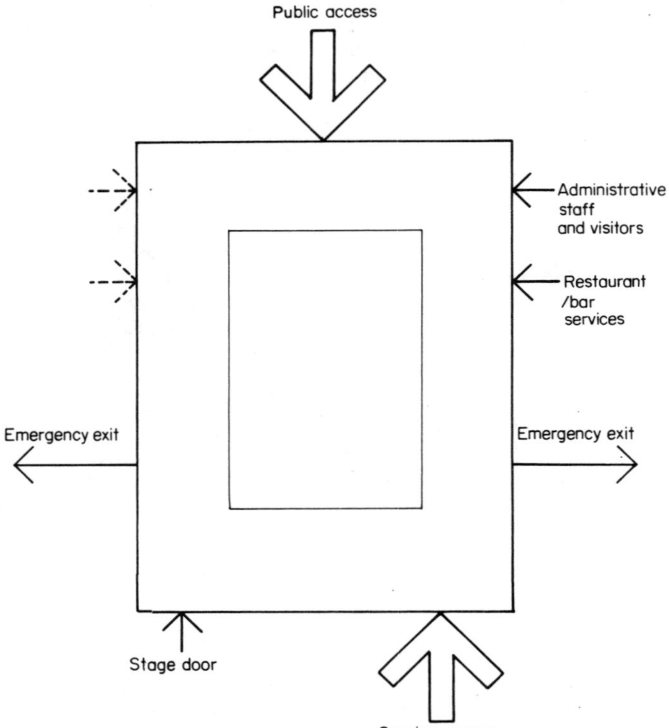

Fig. 3.1. Access to the theatre

could be expected. Amateur opera invariably attracts bigger audiences than amateur drama because of the much larger numbers of people involved, but this consideration should not unduly distort the brief for a building whose main function is drama.

To provide a rough basis for the definition of size, the Association of British Theatre Technicians has suggested the following categories:

Very large	1500 or more seats
Large	900–1500 seats
Medium	500–900 seats
Small	Under 500 seats

Most new Local Authority and University theatres fall into the medium and small categories.

TYPES OF PRODUCTION

The normal function of most theatres today is the performance of plays with a cast of up to 12, but occasionally a large cast of up to 20. The brief, however, might call for other types of production (either as the main function of the theatre or as occasional events) for which adequate provision should be made in the building. The main purpose of the theatre should not be compromised by attempting to accommodate another incompatible use, but the following types of production might well be considered at the briefing stage.

Drama
Large-scale drama
Grand opera; full-scale ballet; musicals; pantomime.
Chamber opera; chamber ballet; music hall and variety; cabaret; plays with music.
Concerts.

The main problem likely to arise from the occasional use of a theatre for large-scale drama, grand opera, ballet or concert music is the provision of sufficient accommodation, both on and off stage, for comparative large numbers of people. A greater stage depth than normally needed for drama would be required, together with more changing facilities, although a rehearsal room or similar space could be used temporarily for changing.

In addition, the brief might envisage the building being used for projecting films, lectures, meetings and children's performances and future possibilities in this respect should be considered.

REPERTOIRE AND REPERTORY

It is useful to note the difference between these two terms. Repertoire theatres are used by companies (e.g. National Theatre and Royal Shakespeare Company) which maintain a reperoire of several productions that might be changed frequently, possibly daily. They require adequate storage for all the sets in the repertoire and good handling facilities.

Repertory theatres present new productions at two or three weekly intervals, rarely reviving a production at a later date.

FURTHER INFORMATION

The main purpose of this section is to provide the basic data for those engaged on the design of theatres. Good theatre design, however, involves a great deal more than the mere use of basic data and the designer will need to develop a thorough understanding of the problems and possibilities of the particular project in hand.

For more detailed technical information on all aspects of theatre design—particularly stage lighting and sound control—the designer is advised to contact the Association of British Theatre Technicians, 9 Fitzroy Square, London W19 6AE, and, for information on the appointment of theatre consultants, the Society of Theatre Consultants at the same address.

SITING

LOCATION

Most theatres require close contact with the general public and will normally be located at the centres of population. If built in the town centre, theatregoers can either use the public transport systems or the existing car parks during the evening.

University theatres also benefit from contact with the public, especially if they are designed to house professional productions, but their location will more often be determined by their function within the campus for teaching, student productions and their contribution to University social and cultural life.

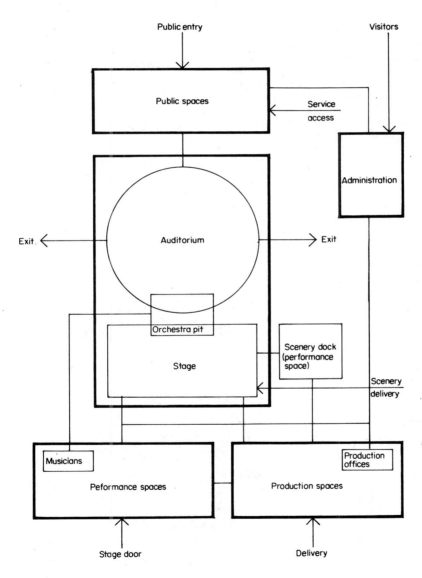

Fig. 3.2. Relationship between groups of spaces

THEATRES

The choice of site for a theatre will also depend upon:
(a) The availability and cost of land.
(b) The type, size and pattern of use of the theatre.
(c) Accessibility for public, service vehicles and staff.

ACCESS

Public access to the theatre needs to be conveniently located in relation to car parks, easily seen and recognisable as the entrance by strangers. It should be designed to allow cars to draw up to set down and pick up patrons under cover, especially disabled and aged persons.

The main service access will normally be located on the opposite side of the building. It should allow large pantechnicons or furniture vans to deliver scenery straight onto the stage level and should be carefully screened from the public access. Parking space for 2–3 pantechnicons will usually be required.

Other accesses will include a 'stage door' (performers entrance), entrance to administrative offices for staff and visitors, service accesses to restaurant and/or bars, and a special disabled persons entrance if steps are required from entrance foyer to auditorium. It will also be necessary to plan for additional points of egress from opposite sides of the building to deal adequately with fire escape.

Ideally, the site should therefore be accessible from all sides (see Fig. 3.1), but where this is not possible, some additional space for internal site circulation should be allowed.

CAR PARKING

The need to provide car parking for the public will often depend on the proximity and capacity of municipal car parks, the availability of public transport and Local Authority policy, but it will usually be necessary to provide car parking for administrative staff and performers within the theatre site, exclusively for theatre use. A reasonable provision would be one car space to two permanent members of staff, with additional spaces for visitors.

ORIENTATION

Orientation does not play a significant role in the siting of a theatre, except for some of the ancillary accommodation such as the offices and workshops.

NOISE

As far as possible, theatres should be sited away from sources of serious external noise, such as railways and airline routes, although some notable theatres have been designed to overcome such noise problems.

PLANNING

COMPONENT PARTS OF THE THEATRE

The main spaces provided in a typical theatre can be grouped under five headings:

(a) Auditorium/stage (including orchestra pit).   House
(b) Public spaces.   Front of house
(c) Performance spaces (including scenery dock).
(d) Administrative spaces.   } Backstage
(e) Production spaces.

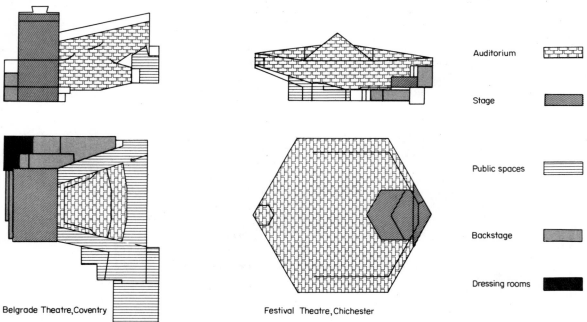

Auditorium

Stage

Public spaces

Backstage

Dressing rooms

Belgrade Theatre, Coventry

Festival Theatre, Chichester

Fig. 3.3. Examples of planning arrangements (see also facing page)

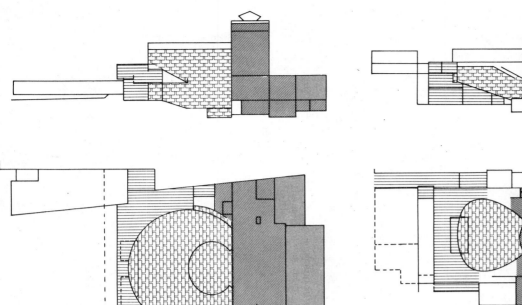

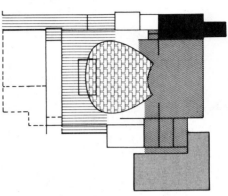

Playhouse, Nottingham

Thorndike Theatre, Leatherhead

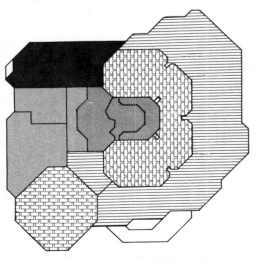

The Crucible Theatre, Sheffield

The normal relationship between these groups of accommodation is shown in Fig 3.2, but the architect should also bear in mind the need for service spaces—plant rooms and service routes—for which allowance should be made from the outset in the planning of the theatre.

EXAMPLES OF PLANNING ARRANGEMENTS

The dispositions of groups of spaces for the following theatres are illustrated in Fig 3.3:

Belgrade Theatre, Coventry (1958)
Festival Theatre, Chichester (1962)
Playhouse, Nottingham (1963)
Thorndike Theatre, Leatherhead (1969)
The Crucible Theatre, Sheffield (1971)

AUDITORIUM/STAGE RELATIONSHIPS

The relationship between the actor and his audience is the basis of 'theatre'. The auditorium/stage relationship is there-

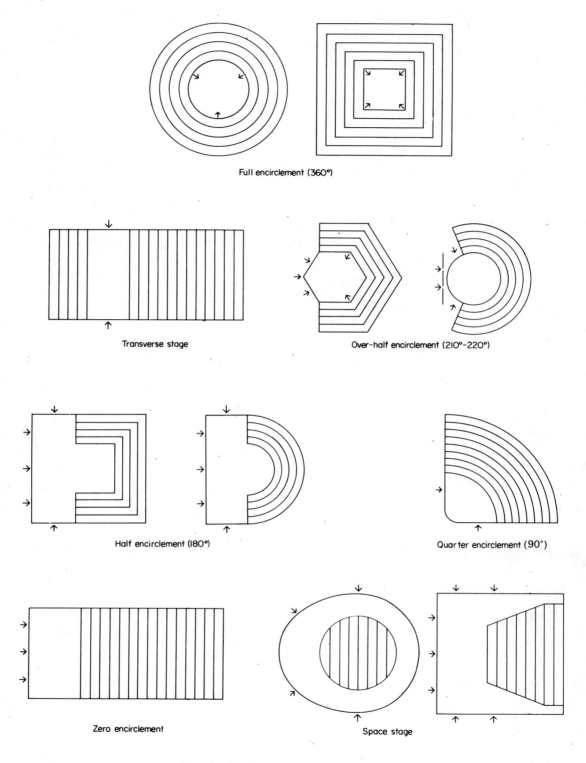

Full encirclement (360°)

Transverse stage

Over-half encirclement (210°-220°)

Half encirclement (180°)

Quarter encirclement (90°)

Zero encirclement

Space stage

Fig. 3.4. Degrees of encirclement of stage area by seating

fore at the heart of theatre planning and is one of the most important matters to be considered.

Within the long history of the stage, the separation of the audience from the action of the play by a proscenium is of comparatively recent origin, but it has dominated the design of most theatres standing in this country today and, indeed, most of our knowledge and experience is based on the proscenium form. Yet, in more recent times there has been a very strong movement towards the revival and development of closer relationships between actor and audience, by rejecting the proscenium and bringing the performance within the same space as the audience. If the performance is to remain at the focus of the audience's attention, some degree of encirclement of the stage area by the seating can be expected and the various forms which have developed over the ages can be defined by the extent of the encirclement achieved, as follows (Fig 3.4).

Full encirclement (360°)	Theatre-in-the-round; island stage; arena.
Transverse stage	
Over-half encirclement (210°–220°)	Greek/Hellenic theatre
Half encirclement (180°)	Roman theatre; thrust stage
Quarter encirclement (90°)	Fan stage
Zero encirclement	End stage
Space stage	

Greater encirclement has the obvious advantage of bringing more members of the audience within good acoustic and visual distance of the stage, but it also means that they will tend to be distracted in some instances by the audience on the other side of the acting area. Furthermore, it is not possible for an actor to convey facial expressions and gestures in two opposite directions at the same time—an angle of 135° is generally considered to be the limit (Fig 3.5)—and greater encirclement can therefore impose constraints on the type of performance undertaken.

The whole matter of auditorium/stage relationships is subject to continuing debate, but most new theatres have adopted an end-stage or quarter encirclement arrangement (or somewhere in-between). This limitation on the degree of encirclement not only permits normal directional acting, but also the production of a wide selection of plays, including many adapted from the proscenium stage.

It should be noted, however, that where a fly tower and/or stage wings are included, the effect of stage and auditorium being in the same architectural space is lessened and similarity with the proscenium theatre is increased. The architect should also be aware of the limitations placed on the amount and type of scenery in an open stage production, as well as the cost of fireproofing where a fire curtain is not used.

Even in the proscenium theatre, not all the acting space lies behind the fire curtain. The part of the stage in front of the setting line is referred to as the forestage and this is often extended towards the audience to form a large apron stage, providing some opportunity for a closer actor/audience relationship (Fig 3.6).

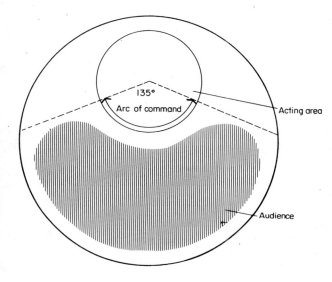

Fig. 3.5. Actors' arc of command

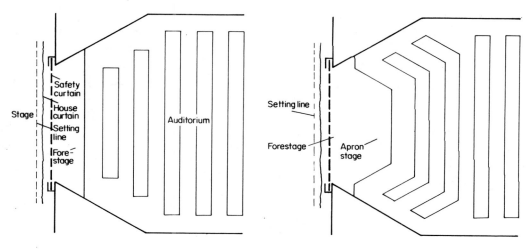

Fig. 3.6. Proscenium forestage and apron

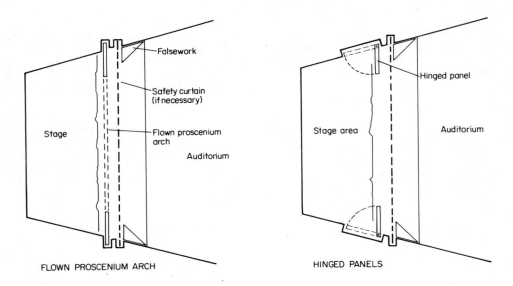

Fig. 3.7. Adaptation of end-stage to proscenium

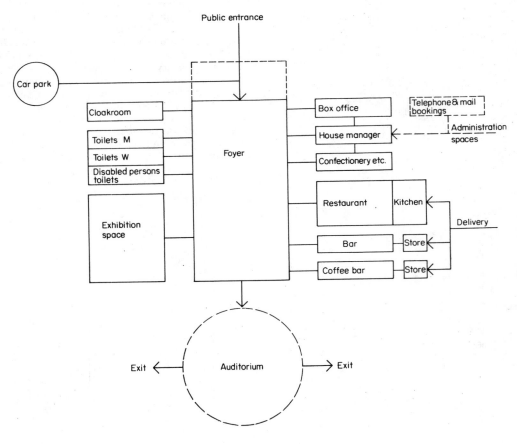

Fig. 3.8. Public spaces

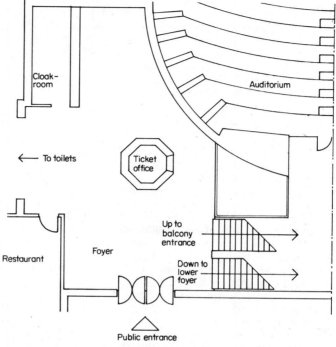

Cloak-room

← To toilets

Ticket office

Auditorium

Restaurant

Foyer

Up to balcony entrance →

Down to lower foyer →

Public entrance

EXAMPLE I: PLAYHOUSE, NOTTINGHAM

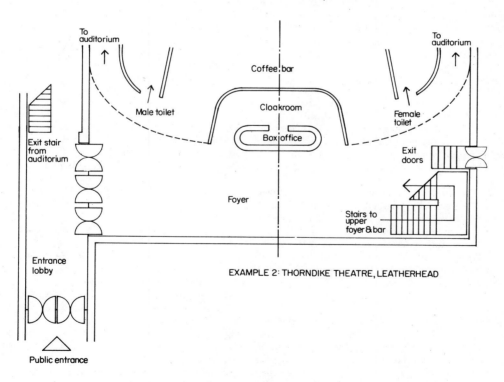

To auditorium

Coffee bar

To auditorium

Male toilet

Cloakroom

Female toilet

Exit stair from auditorium

Box office

Exit doors

Foyer

Stairs to upper foyer & bar

Entrance lobby

EXAMPLE 2: THORNDIKE THEATRE, LEATHERHEAD

Public entrance

Fig. 3.9.   Examples of foyer planning

LOCATION OF ORCHESTRA PIT

The provision of an orchestra pit for support music in a theatre has a direct effect upon the planning of the auditorium. For musical productions, the most convenient location for the orchestra is between the stage and audience, to enable both performers and orchestra to see the conductor.

Although other locations have been adopted and can work, especially with small groups of players providing incidental music or with the assistance of closed-circuit television, they lose the advantage of having a direct contact between stage and conductor.

ADAPTABILITY OF STAGE

Most theatres designed today are required to cater for many types of play and a range of other uses and some facilities for changing the form of the stage should be planned at the outset.

When the orchestra pit is not required for a production, its open area can be filled in and used either for additional auditorium space or as an extension to the stage. Similar consideration might be given to the construction of the stage floor by forming the acting area of adjustable units, to be arranged in a variety of different and effective ways.

Most end-stage or quarter-encirclement theatres can be designed for adaptation to a proscenium stage arrangement, but usually not without some loss of continuity of the auditorium side walls. One possible way of overcoming this problem is to fly the whole of the proscenium wall and another is to hinge parts of the auditorium walls to form the proscenium opening (see Fig 3.7), but particular attention must always be given to the fire regulations affecting the different forms of stage arrangement.

PUBLIC SPACES

Fig. 3.8 shows a typical arrangement of public spaces. Apart from the auditorium itself, the most important public space is the foyer, which should be planned to be easily accessible from the outside. An attractive, uncongested meeting place, a place of anticipation and excitement, it should help the audience to enjoy the sense of occasion that going to the theatre ought to be.

Entrances to the auditorium, especially from the foyer and bars, should be carefully planned to provide light and sound 'locks'; these are usually in the form of two sets of doors with dark absorbent material between.

The other accommodation in this group needs to be readily accessible from the foyer and planned to meet the sequence of needs before, during and after the performance. Two possible arrangements are illustrated in Fig 3.9.

On entering the foyer, people should be able to reach the box office easily, to deposit coats, visit the toilets and buy programmes and confectionery without being crushed or caught in too much cross-circulation. The bars and exhibition space should be planned with space for people to sit or stand without impinging on the main circulation routes. If the theatre bar is located within the same space as other public spaces, the bar itself must be capable of being closed down with shutters outside licensing hours.

Should the restaurant be required to serve the general public as well as theatregoers, its location will be determined by the extent to which the foyer, toilets, cloakrooms, exhibition space and other facilities will be open during the daytime and closed seasons. Management policy, or planned alternative options, should be agreed at the outset.

The house manager has to play an important public relations role and requires a comfortable office, accessible from the foyer and close to the box office. If he has a personal secretary or assistant, a separate office should be provided.

ARRANGEMENTS FOR THE DISABLED

In providing for the disabled, the following factors should be borne in mind:

(a) A person in a wheelchair should be able to reach any of the public areas, including the auditorium, without having to negotiate steps. Ramps should not exceed a slope of 1 in 12 and should have a flat area at the top. If a lift is provided, it should be large enough to take a wheelchair and attendant.

(b) It is very much better to provide special areas for wheelchairs and attendants in the auditorium, rather than expect the disabled to transfer to the normal seats.

(c) A separate escape route or routes for wheelchairs and attendants is desirable. Otherwise, it might be necessary for people in wheelchairs to wait with their attendants until the rest of the audience has left.

PERFORMANCE SPACES

The accommodation normally required for the performers and the performance organisation of a theatre is illustrated in Fig 3.10. The main relationships are self explanatory, but it should be pointed out that the lighting and sound control rooms are located at the rear of the auditorium above the heads of standing members of the audience. The dimmer room might also be best located away from the stage and, in all three cases, care must be taken to avoid sound generated by the equipment (or those using it) reaching the audience. Fig 3.11 illustrates a typical arrangement of control rooms and lighting galleries.

The stage manager's office should lead directly to the stage, close to the prompt corner. Other stage staff accommodation, the electrician's workshop/store and the performance properties store should also be planned as close to the stage as possible.

The dressing rooms, changing rooms and corridors can be a source of noise and, whilst there are considerable advantages in planning changing rooms close to the stage, it is more important to stop external sound (and light) entering the acting area. Dressing rooms may be planned at other floor levels, but no more than two floors above or below the stage. Fig 3.12 illustrates three possible locations for the dressing rooms; at the rear, at the side and below the auditorium respectively.

From their changing rooms, musicians and their conductor must be able to reach the orchestra assembly room or space, instrument room and then the orchestra pit without entering

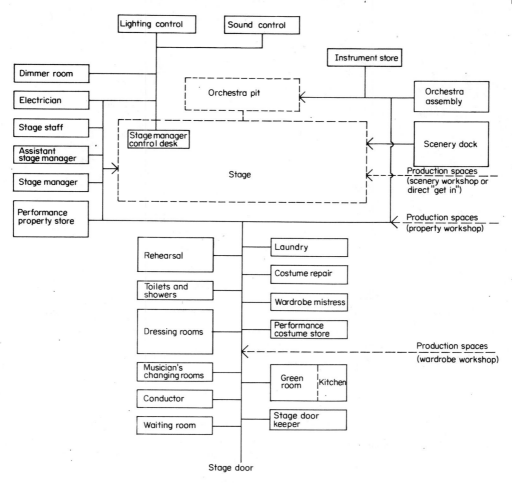

Fig. 3.10. *Performance spaces*

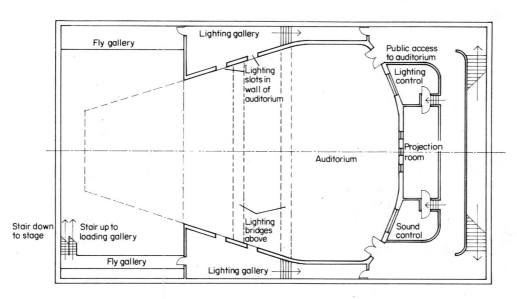

Fig. 3.11. *Typical arrangement of control rooms and lighting galleries*

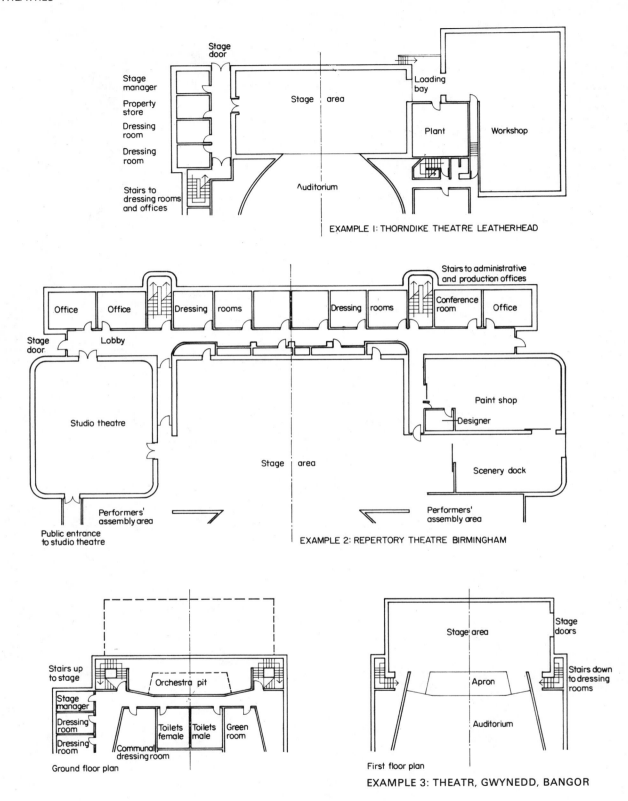

EXAMPLE I: THORNDIKE THEATRE LEATHERHEAD

EXAMPLE 2: REPERTORY THEATRE BIRMINGHAM

EXAMPLE 3: THEATR, GWYNEDD, BANGOR

Fig. 3.12. *Typical arrangments of dressing rooms and backstage accommodation*

the stage or auditorium. In small theatres, separate changing, assembly and instrument rooms are replaced by a single band room with lockers.

The scenery dock should be planned at stage level and accessible from the stage and loading door. It must be borne in mind that the largest piece of scenery will need to pass through the doors into the scenery dock.

A rehearsal room should ideally be the same size as the stage and accessible from the scenery dock, but this is often uneconomic if not also used for other purposes such as chorus dressing or ballet practice. It has an obvious potential for experimental theatre and will need to be very carefully planned in relation to public access and toilet facilities if the public are to be admitted.

Facilities for storing, washing, ironing and repairing costumes should be provided reasonably close to the dressing rooms, possibly in the form of a single wardrobe-room with separate washing room if the theatre does not have a large repertoire.

The green room or canteen should also be planned near the changing rooms to dispense frequent cups of tea or coffee, and possibly light snacks, during rehearsals.

Some control of the stage door is necessary to keep out unauthorised persons and, even if a full-time stage door keeper is not employed, an office with a telephone should be provided with a full view of the entrance and waiting space.

ADMINISTRATION SPACES

A possible arrangement of offices dealing with the management of the theatre is shown in Fig 3.13.

Note the links with front-of-house accommodation, box office, house manager, restaurant and bars, and with production offices (production manager, designers), if these are incorporated in the building.

The extent of the accommodation will, of course, depend on the scale and structure of the management organisation, but most theatres appoint a general manager and an artistic director who must work closely together. The general man-

ager is usually responsible for administration and finance, for building maintenance and the front of house activities whereas the artistic director is primarily concerned with the production and performance activities, although there are inevitably areas where the two roles overlap.

From time to time, the artistic director will need to hold meetings of section heads and, if a separate conference room cannot be justified, the director's room should be made large enough for this purpose.

Although auditions are normally held on stage or in the rehearsal room, the provision of a separate interview room will enable details and confidential matters to be discussed without interruption, if the number of private offices is limited.

PRODUCTION SPACES

The accommodation in this group of spaces (Fig 3.14) is concerned with the design and production of scenery, properties and wardrobe items. It is obviously an advantage if this work can be carried out in the theatre building, particularly with repertoire and repertory theatres, but site restrictions or site costs might make it economically necessary for the production to be prepared elsewhere and the sets transported to the theatre. If the production spaces are provided elsewhere, it will be necessary to make adequate provision in the performance spaces for the storage and repair of scenery, properties and costumes.

The spaces fall into four groups:

(a) Production offices
(b) Scenery section
(c) Property section
(d) Costume section

The production offices are concerned with design and organisation and the production manager normally has the job of coordinating the work of the other three sections and the stage staff.

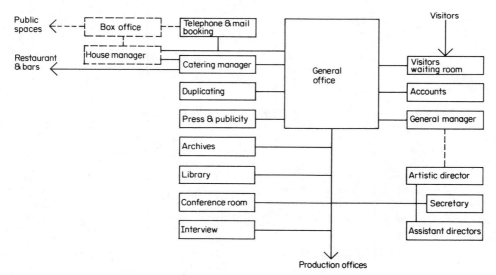

Fig. 3.13. Administration spaces

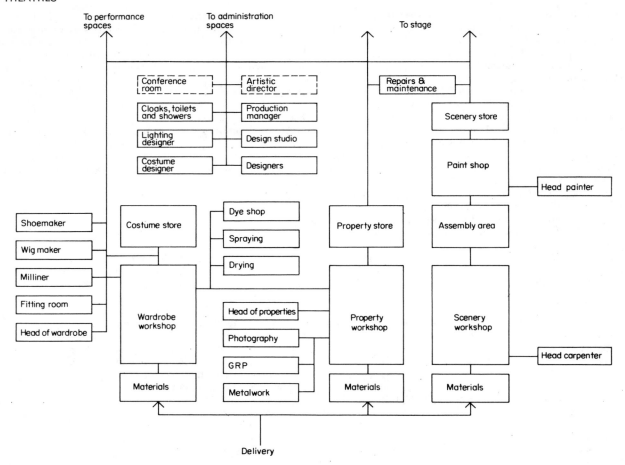

Fig. 3.14.   Production spaces

The workshop accommodation will vary in extent from one or two large spaces in which most, if not all, the scenery and properties are made to a highly specialised series of departments, each with its own section head. Much will depend on the scale of operations envisaged and the range of the company's repertoire.

SERVICE SPACES

Early consideration must be given to the location and adequate provision of service spaces within the building, with particular regard to:

Boiler/heat exchanger room, with associated pumps and controls.
Air handling plant, including refrigeration or cooling plant and humidifiers.
Air ducts, to and from fresh air and building spaces (especially auditorium).
Service ducts.
Cable and meter room and, if necessary, electricity sub-station.
Battery room.

It should be borne in mind that the air handling plant and air ducts are potential sources and conveyors of noise into the auditorium. They must, therefore, be separated from the auditorium by sufficient construction mass and duct length to enable the noise to be attenuated to acceptable levels.

SPACE REQUIREMENTS

AREA OF SITES

There is no direct correlation between the number of seats in a theatre and the area of site required, since the size of the theatre and the space required to give access to it will depend more on the amount and disposition of the other accommodation. It will therefore be necessary to establish the general size and shape of the building to be designed before the space requirements of the site can be properly determined.

For general guidance, however, it should be noted that a medium size theatre (500–800 seats), with ancillary accommodation, including workshops, on two or three levels, could occupy a site area of 40–60 m front to back and 30–40 m side to side. Additional site space will be required for service accesses and parking, as well as any forecourt treatment to the public entrance.

BUILDING SPACE REQUIREMENTS

The space requirements for individual activities in the theatre are set out under Accommodation, but the following factors affect the planning of the basic auditorium/stage relationship and should be borne in mind from the beginning:

Area of auditorium	0·6 m per person
Furthest seat from stage front	20 m
Volume of auditorium	3 m³ per person (greater above 300 seats)
Acting area	9 m × 9 m or 9 m diameter

If the stage is to have wings, they should be at least the same size as the acting area. With two wings, the full stage width should therefore be at least 27 m wide.

DATA

AUDITORIUM SEATING

No seat should be more than 20 m from the stage front if the performance is to be seen and heard clearly. The choice of seating arrangment is affected by the width of the seatway—the unobstructed vertical space between rows when the seats are tipped up—and the design of the seat itself. It will therefore be necessary to choose the type of seat before final dimensions are established but, at the initial planning stage, the minimum dimensions shown in Fig 3.15 and Tables 3.1(a), 3.1(b) and 3.2 will act as a useful guide.

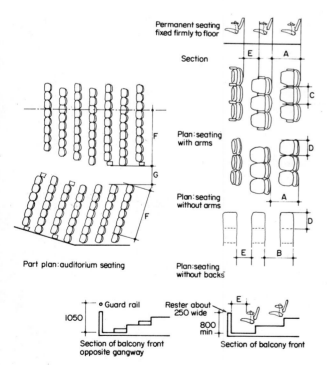

Fig. 3.15. Auditorium seating

Table 3.1(a) MINIMUM DIMENSIONS OF SEATING

A Back-to-back distance between rows of seats with backs: 760 mm (minimum).
B Back-to-back distance between rows of seats without backs: 610 mm (minimum).
C Width of seats with arms 510 mm (minimum).
D Width of seat without arms 460 mm (minimum).
E Unobstructed vertical space between rows (seatway) 305 mm. See Table 3.1(b).
F For normal maximum distance of seat from gangway see Table 3.1(b). But rows with more than twenty-two seats could be possible, provided that the audience was not imperilled.
G Minimum width of gangway 1070 mm.

Table 3.1(b) DISTANCE OF SEATS FROM GANGWAYS

Minimum seatway (measured between perpendiculars) E (mm)	Maximum distance of seat from gangway (510 mm seats) F (mm)	Maximum number of 510 mm wide seats per row	
		Gangway both sides	Gangway one side
305	3060	14	7
330	3570	16	8
355	4080	18	9
380	4590	20	10
405	5100	22	11

(Based on GLC Requirements)

In 'continental seating', the rows run continuously between side aisles and none of the better viewing positions are given over to gangways. Seatways have to be a little more generous, which in any case increases audience comfort, and the effect is to produce fewer rows of more seats than the traditional British arrangement. Until recently, continental seating was not permitted in this country but it has now been used in a number of new theatres. It is always advisable to discuss this matter with the appropriate authority at an early stage, as the use of continental seating might well require wider gangways and additional exits.

Where seats of standard width are set out within a non-rectangular auditorium, the ends of rows can be very untidy. To mitigate this, the manufacturers can often supply the seats in a number of widths.

SIGHT LINES

Good views of the acting area are essential and, for all practical purposes, this means that members of the audience should be able to see over the heads of the people in front of them. The rake of the auditorium floor required to give adequate sight lines can be worked out graphically as shown in Fig 3.16 and described below.

The lowest and nearest point which the whole audience should be able to see clearly is first established. For the single level auditorium, where a steep rake is acceptable, point P can be taken at the front edge of the stage (0.8–1.1 m above auditorium floor level). But where galleries are introduced or the headroom at the rear is otherwise restricted, a point between 0.6 m and 0.9 m above the front edge of the stage

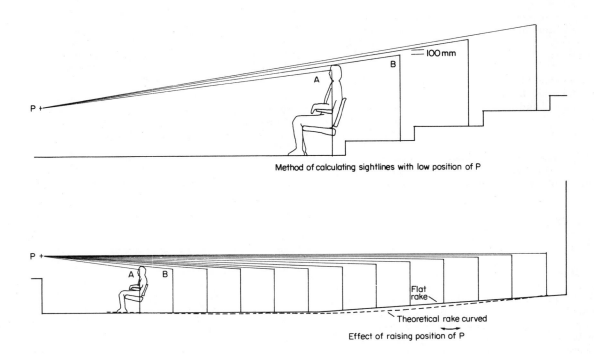

Method of calculating sightlines with low position of P

Flat rake

Theoretical rake curved

Effect of raising position of P

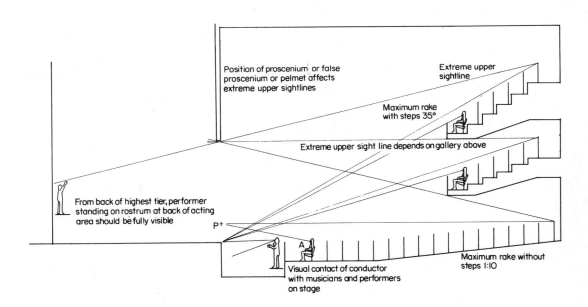

Position of proscenium or false proscenium or pelmet affects extreme upper sightlines

Extreme upper sightline

Maximum rake with steps 35°

Extreme upper sight line depends on gallery above

From back of highest tier, performer standing on rostrum at back of acting area should be fully visible

Visual contact of conductor with musicians and performers on stage

Maximum rake without steps 1:10

Fig. 3.16.   Vertical sight lines

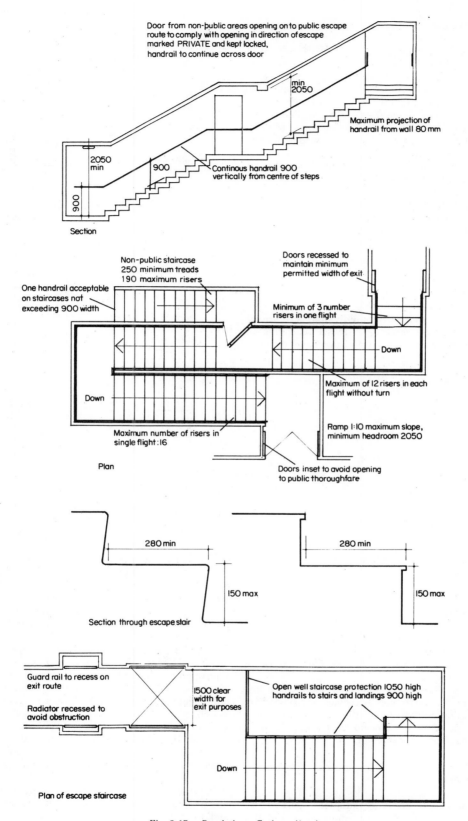

Door from non-public areas opening on to public escape route to comply with opening in direction of escape marked PRIVATE and kept locked, handrail to continue across door

min 2050

Maximum projection of handrail from wall 80 mm

2050 min

900

900

Continous handrail 900 vertically from centre of steps

Section

Non-public staircase 250 minimum treads 190 maximum risers

One handrail acceptable on staircases not exceeding 900 width

Doors recessed to maintain minimum permitted width of exit

Minimum of 3 number risers in one flight

Down

Maximum of 12 risers in each flight without turn

Down

Maximum number of risers in single flight : 16

Plan

Ramp 1:10 maximum slope, minimum headroom 2050

Doors inset to avoid opening to public thoroughfare

280 min

150 max

280 min

150 max

Section through escape stair

Guard rail to recess on exit route

Radiator recessed to avoid obstruction

1500 clear width for exit purposes

Open well staircase protection 1050 high handrails to stairs and landings 900 high

Down

Plan of escape staircase

Fig. 3.17.   Regulations affecting exit stairs

3–17

will flatten the rake but still give unobstructed views of performers above their knees.

The eye level (A) of a person in the front row is then plotted (allowing 1120 mm for the height between eye level and floor) and a vertical line drawn through the eye position of the second row. A sight line projected back from P over the head of the person in the first row will cross the vertical line at the eye level (B) of a person in the second row. The height allowed above eye level to clear the head is normally 100 mm. The same procedure is then applied to each row in turn until all eye levels are established.

The theoretical floor level, plotted 1120 mm below the eye levels, will be found to be slightly curved, but in most cases the rake can be straightened to give regular steps or slopes. The maximum gradient for aisles without steps is 1 in 10. Staggered seating can improve views of the stage, but the different viewing sections through the auditorium should nevertheless be re-checked finally for good overhead sight lines.

MEANS OF ESCAPE

The minimum number and width of individual exits are set out in Table 3.1, but more might be required depending on the layout of seating and gangways and the travel distance to an exit.

Table 3.2 NUMBER AND SIZE OF EXITS

Number of people accommodated on each tier or floor	Minimum number of exits*	Minimum width (mm)
200	2	1050†
300	2	1200
400	2	1350
500	2	1500
750	3	1500
1000	4	1500

* Plus one additional exit of not less than 1500 mm for each extra 250 persons or part thereof.
† Would not normally apply to exit corridors or staircases servicing an auditorium of a theatre.

The principal regulations affecting escape stairs are illustrated in Fig 3.17.

ORCHESTRA PIT

To avoid the orchestra being too obtrusive, it is usually accommodated in a pit, part of which is below the front of the stage (Fig 3.18a). (Figures 3.18b and 3.18c illustrate use of apron stage lift).

The floor of the pit should be 2–3 m below stage, preferably adjustable, but finally determined by the height required for instruments (e.g. double bass) below the stage construction, the acoustic design of the auditorium and any particular preferences of the orchestra or director.

STAGE PLANNING

The stage area has to be the most adaptable part of the theatre and, although the degree of adaptability and the

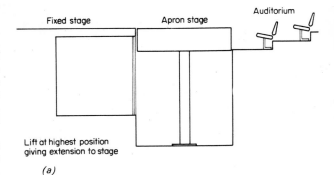

Fixed stage Apron stage Auditorium

Lift at highest position giving extension to stage

(a)

Movable seating

Stage riser

Lift at intermediate position giving extension to auditorium

(b)

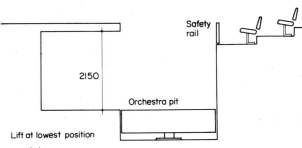

Safety rail

2150

Orchestra pit

Lift at lowest position

(c) *Fig. 3.18. Orchestra pit and apron stage lift*

extent of technical facilities required will depend on the particular auditorium/stage relationship adopted, most of the planning principles involved can be illustrated by a typical proscenium stage arrangement (Figs 3.19 and 3.20).

Fig 3.19 shows the main areas and their functions and Fig 3.20 shows a typical plan in more detail.

The size of the acting area—related, in the proscenium stage, to the width of the proscenium opening—should be determined at the outset. To provide some flexibility in the type of production to be accommodated, it is better to err on the large size, irrespective of the seating capacity of the auditorium, knowing that it is comparatively easy (although sometimes expensive in scenery) to reduce the effective acting area for the small productions. As a guide, an area of about 9 m wide by 7–9 m deep would be typical, some of it in front of the setting line. Outside the acting area, provision for setting and circulation space for performers, as shown on the plan, are both essential.

Provision for storing scenery adjacent to the stage area is also necessary in most cases, particularly in repertoire theatre and for productions with scene changes. Such scenery is

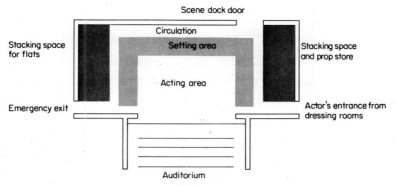

Fig. 3.19.   Main areas of stage

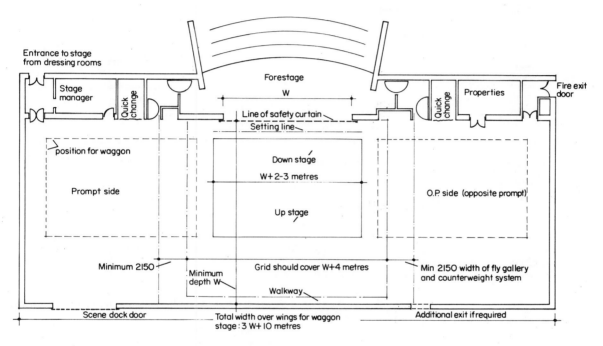

Fig. 3.20.   Typical plan of stage

accommodated mainly in three ways:

(a) Flown above the stage.
(b) Set out on wagons at the side or sides of the stage.
(c) Stored at the side or sides of the stage.

The most flexible arrangement is to provide both fly tower and stage wings.

Adequate space must also be provided for the prompt corner and stage manager's control desk without interrupting the performer's circulation space.

FLY TOWER

The height of the grid, a platform of steel slats over the stage, should be at least two-and-a-half times the working height of the proscenium opening to ensure that sets can be taken up out of sight. A further 2 m above the grid should be allowed for working space (Fig 3.21).

The minimum width of the grid should be 4 m wider than the proscenium opening and the internal width of the fly tower a further 2 m each side. The grid should run the full depth of the stage.

If wings are provided which extend beyond the fly tower, a double purchase counter-weight system must be used to reduce the height required for suspension cables (main counterweight system) and hemps (hand ropes).

PROSCENIUM

Although there is a movement away from the picture frame approach to theatre, the space requirements for masking

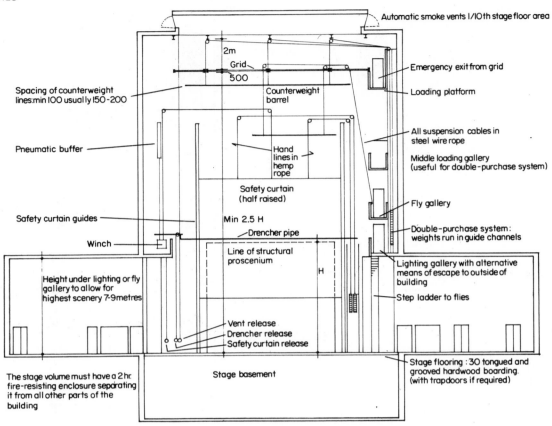

Automatic smoke vents 1/10th stage floor area

2m
Grid
500

Counterweight barrel

Spacing of counterweight lines:min 100 usually 150-200

Emergency exit from grid

Loading platform

All suspension cables in steel wire rope

Pneumatic buffer

Hand lines in hemp rope

Middle loading gallery (useful for double-purchase system)

Safety curtain (half raised)

Fly gallery

Double-purchase system: weights run in guide channels

Safety curtain guides

Min 2.5 H

Drencher pipe

Winch

Line of structural proscenium

H

Lighting gallery with alternative means of escape to outside of building

Step ladder to flies

Height under lighting or fly gallery to allow for highest scenery 7-9metres

Vent release
Drencher release
Safety curtain release

Stage flooring : 30 tongued and grooved hardwood boarding. (with trapdoors if required)

The stage volume must have a 2 hr. fire-resisting enclosure separating it from all other parts of the building

Stage basement

Fig. 3.21.   Typical section through stage and fly tower looking towards auditorium

house tabs and safety curtain might still be needed and these are illustrated in Fig 3.22. The normal proscenium height is about 6 m, depending on vertical sight lines, and the width varies from about 7 m to 14 m.

SAFETY CURTAIN

It is advisable to discuss the need for a safety-curtain with the local Fire Authority at the earliest possible moment. With an open stage, it would be impractical to provide one, but the authority will normally insist on the use of fire-resistant materials for scenery and other fire precautions.

Where a safety-curtain is used, it is usually made of steel framing with steel plates covered with asbestos cloth or steel framing with asbestos plates. If the height above the opening is restricted, a two or three piece rigid curtain may be acceptable. It must overlap the opening by 0.46 m at the top and sides and descend by gravity at a rate of 0.3 m per second. Above the safety-curtain, a drencher pipe must be installed on the stage side to discharge water onto the surface of the safety-curtain.

CYCLORAMA

If a cyclorama is to be provided, a convenient form is rolled on and off a cone at the side of the stage and is suspen-

ded on a track around the back and sides of the acting area. The location of the track should be carefully planned in relation to the setting area.

STAGE LIFTS, REVOLVES, TRAPS AND REMOVABLE SECTIONS

To give opportunities for variety in stage set and production, the stage area is sometimes divided into areas capable of being raised or lowered with stage lifts (Fig 3.23). Other stages are occasionally, but now rarely, provided with a revolve, which makes it possible for three or four changes of set to be made smoothly within a production without dropping the curtain. Other possibilities include the use of portable revolves and combined split revolves and lifts.

For any kind of stage adaptability, some form of basement is needed below the acting area, especially if traps are to be preformed or cut in the floor. The stage floor should be finished in timber (preferably hardwood strip) to enable traps to be formed if necessary, to give some slight springing underfoot and the possibility of screwing down sets. Some stages are completely demountable, with the facility to remove individual sections of the stage if required.

STAGE LIGHTING

The provision for stage lighting should make it possible for any part of the stage to be lit from as many different angles as

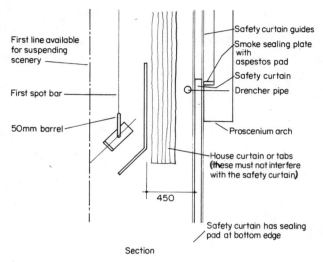

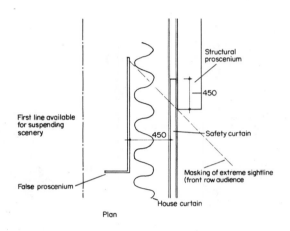

First line available for suspending scenery

First spot bar

50mm barrel

Safety curtain guides

Smoke sealing plate with aspestos pad

Safety curtain

Drencher pipe

Proscenium arch

House curtain or tabs (these must not interfere with the safety curtain)

450

Safety curtain has sealing pad at bottom edge

Section

Structural proscenium

450

First line available for suspending scenery

450

Safety curtain

False proscenium

Masking of extreme sightline (front row audience

House curtain

Plan

Fig. 3.22. Typical details of proscenium arch

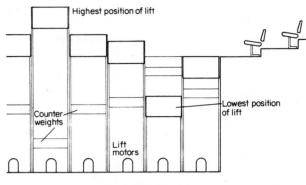

Highest position of lift

Counter weights

Lift motors

Lowest position of lift

Fig. 3.23. Stage lifts

possible. The main sources of light are overhead within the stage and auditorium, from the side slots and, less frequently, from footlights.

Overhead lighting is particularly important and should be arranged to strike the actor's face at about 45° above horizontal (35° minimum). But as spotlights are usually crossed onto an actor from sources away from the centre line, their position on a section through the building will need to be nearer 55° above horizontal (40° minimum). The location of lighting bars over the stage and lighting bridges over the auditorium can be worked out graphically by arranging the cone of light from each source on section to fall between 55° and 40°, so that the whole stage from front to back can be covered by one or other location, as illustrated in Fig 3.24.

CONTROL ROOMS

The stage manager will normally operate from the side of the stage, using his control desk to communicate with all parts of the theatre but particularly the lighting and sound control rooms at the rear of the auditorium.

The lighting control room should have a window large enough to give an unrestricted and undistorted view of the stage, even when members of the audience are standing. The room size will depend upon the actual equipment chosen

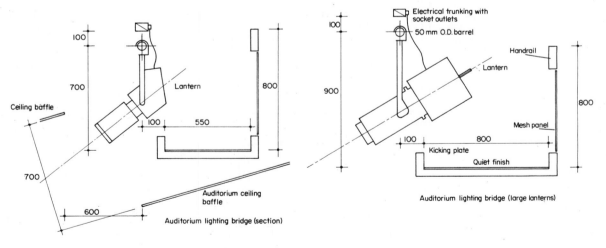

100

700

Ceiling baffle

700

100

Lantern

100   550

800

600

Auditorium ceiling baffle

Auditorium lighting bridge (section)

Electrical trunking with socket outlets

50 mm O.D. barrel

100

900

Handrail

Lantern

800

Mesh panel

100   800

Kicking plate

Quiet finish

Auditorium lighting bridge (large lanterns)

Fig. 3.24(a). Auditorium lighting bridges

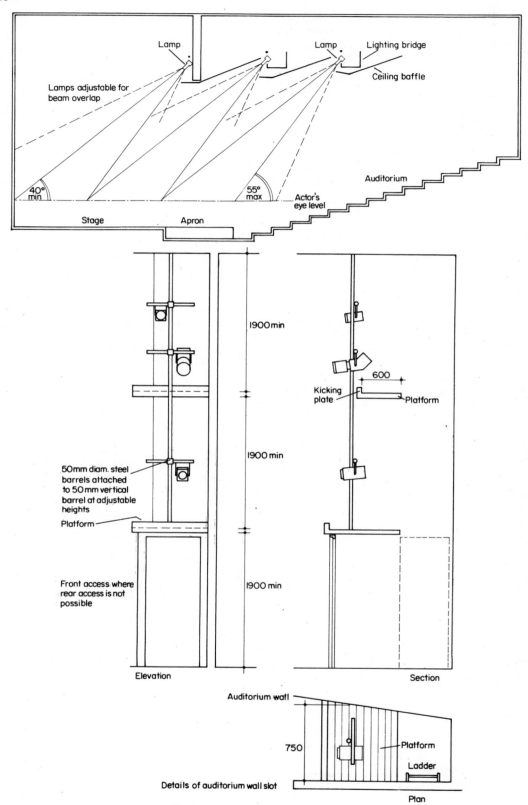

Lamp

Lamp

Lighting bridge

Ceiling baffle

Lamps adjustable for beam overlap

40° min

55° max

Actor's eye level

Auditorium

Stage

Apron

1900 min

1900 min

600

Kicking plate

Platform

50mm diam. steel barrels attached to 50 mm vertical barrel at adjustable heights

Platform

Front access where rear access is not possible

1900 min

Elevation

Section

Auditorium wall

750

Platform

Ladder

Details of auditorium wall slot

Plan

Fig. 3.24(b).   Stage lighting arrangement

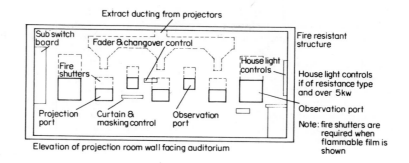

Extract ducting from projectors

Sub switch board

Fader & changover control

Fire shutters

House light controls

Fire resistant structure

House light controls if of resistance type and over 5kw

Observation port

Projection port

Curtain & masking control

Observation port

Note: fire shutters are required when flammable film is shown

Elevation of projection room wall facing auditorium

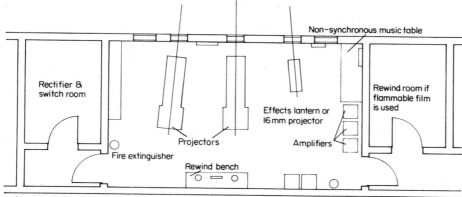

Non-synchronous music table

Rectifier & switch room

Effects lantern or 16mm projector

Rewind room if flammable film is used

Projectors

Amplifiers

Fire extinguisher

Rewind bench

Lobby may open on to public part of premises if ventilated and non-flammable film is used

Fig. 3.25. Typical layout of projection room

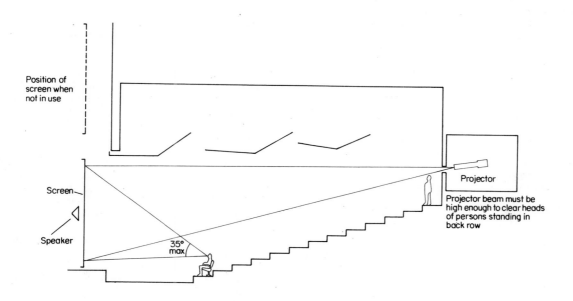

Position of screen when not in use

Projector

Screen

Projector beam must be high enough to clear heads of persons standing in back row

Speaker

35° max

Fig. 3.26. Film projection

and the detailed layout, but initially a space 3 m wide by 2.4 m deep should be sufficient for planning purposes to accommodate a lighting console and space for writing, storage and maintenance.

The sound control room has similar requirements and, if it needs to be separated from the lighting control room by a sound-proof wall, a connecting door or window can provide a useful means of direct communication between the two operations. It is also useful for the sound control room, in particular, to have direct aural communication with the auditorium by using a double or treble sliding sash for the window.

Access to both rooms should be outside the auditorium and preferably away from public circulation. It should also be possible for operators to get to the stage easily without crossing public areas, but this is not usually possible. In addition, space is required for dimmer racks, whose ventilation fans, if not insulated, can be a source of intrusive sound in the auditorium. A useful location for the dimmer rack room would be along the route between control rooms and stage, which could also provide access to lighting slots and lighting bridges.

FILM PROJECTION

Although the acoustic and sight line requirements of theatres and cinemas are different, film shows can take place quite satisfactorily in a theatre. The main additional requirements are a projection room and a screen.

The projection room will need to be located at the rear of the auditorium in a central position, often placed between the lighting and sound control rooms. A typical layout of a projection room is shown in Fig 3.25.

When not in use, the rigid screen can usually be flown towards the front of the acting area (Fig 3.26), where the flying of sets is likely to be least demanding. If there is no fly tower, the screen might be stored at the back of the stage, but sufficient space should be available without interfering with the circulation or setting areas.

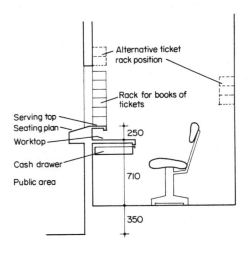

Fig. 3.27. Section through typical box office

DRESSING ROOMS

The layout of dressing rooms should provide adequate facilities for performers to put on their costumes, store their normal clothing and personal items, put on make-up and check their appearance before going on stage. There should also be provision for hand and face washing and reasonably convenient access to toilets and showers.

Particular regard should be given to the provision of artificial lighting for putting on make-up. It is normally in the form of bare tungsten bulbs each side of a mirror above a dressing table to simulate as near as possible the quality of lighting on stage.

See Figs 3.28 and 3.29 for layouts of dressing places and typical dressing rooms.

BOX OFFICE

The design of the box office should make it convenient and comfortable for the clerks to sell tickets to the public. About 5 m² is required for each clerk and Fig 3.27 shows the dimensions of a typical section.

Compartments for books of tickets are usually about 90 mm wide × 225 mm deep × 175 mm high.

WORKSHOP EQUIPMENT

The dimensions and spaces required for a woodworking machine, morticer, circular saw and bandsaw are shown in Fig 3.30.

ACOUSTICS

To achieve a satisfactory acoustic character in the auditorium space, it is necessary to control:

(a) The level of background noise,
(b) The reverberation within the space and,
(c) The elimination of echoes.

The sound of the actor's voice will decrease with distance, but it must never fall below the level of background noise which inevitably exists in an auditorium. Intrusive noise should therefore not exceed the background noise of a listening audience and particular attention should be given to the following:

1. External noise (from road traffic, aircraft or local industry for example), which should be controlled by the mass of the building, including the roof. Any external doors in the auditorium/stage envelope should provide sound 'locks', using two sets of doors and sound absorbent material between.
2. Internal noise (from bars and toilets for example) which should be controlled in a similar way.
3. Mechanical noise from the ventilation system. Plant vibration and noise should be absorbed by suitable mountings and structural mass and the ductwork should incorporate lengths of silencer.

Reverberation times depend on the volume of the space

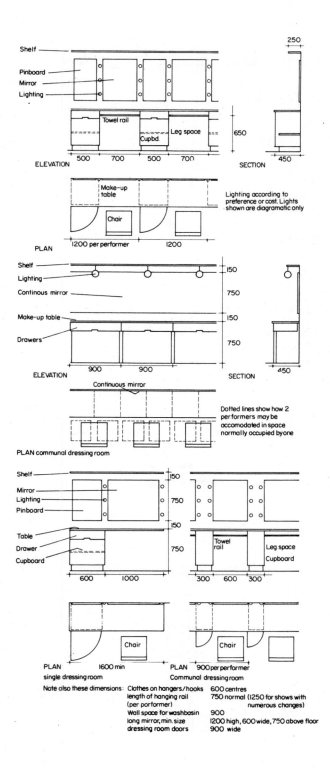

Fig. 3.28.   Dressing room spaces

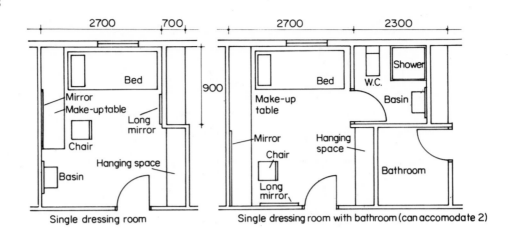

Single dressing room

Single dressing room with bathroom (can accomodate 2)

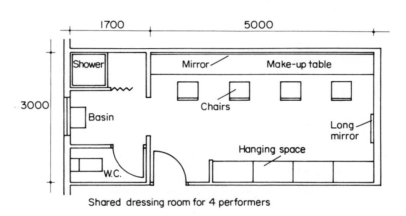

Shared dressing room for 4 performers

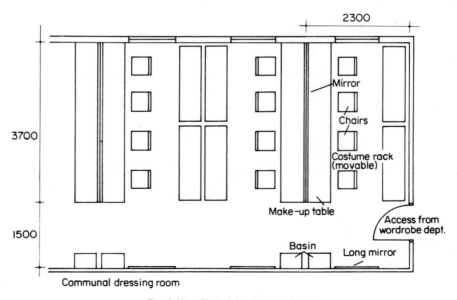

Communal dressing room

Fig. 3.29. Typical dressing room layouts

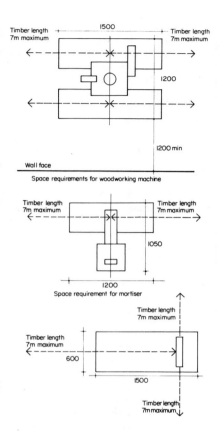

Space requirements for woodworking machine

Space requirement for mortiser

Space requirement for circular saw

Space requirement for band saw

Fig. 3.30. Workshop equipment

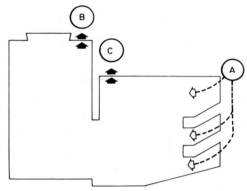

1.

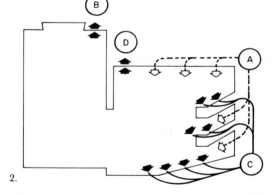

2.

1. Simple Plenum System with One Inlet Fan and Independent Stage and Auditorium Extract Fans.
   A. Inlet fan.
   B. Stage extract fan (capacity 40% of total).
   C. Auditorium extract fan (capacity 60% of total).
   Total capacity of extracts to equal 75% of input.
   Usual order of starting is B, A, C.
   (Where convenient the stage extract for B and the auditorium extract for C can be combined into one extract fan common to both.)

2. Downward System with Inlet Fan and Independent Stage and Auditorium Extract Fans.
   A. Inlet fan.
   B. Stage extract fan (capacity 40% of total).
   C. Auditorium extract fan (capacity 60% of total).

D. Auditorium emergency extract fan (capacity 60% of total). Total capacity of extracts to equal 75% of input.

Extract from the auditorium in normal circumstances is by ducts under the seating. The stage extract discharges directly to the open air. On lowering the safety curtain or operation of emergency controls the normal extract from the auditorium stops and the emergency auditorium extract fan starts.

Usual order of starting is B, A, C.

Note: a single fan may combine the duties of fans C and D; changeover dampers being arranged in the ductwork so that in normal circumstances, air is extracted from below the seats. In an emergency, this is shut off and extract duct above the proscenium arch is opened. Order of starting would then be B, A, (C, D).

Fig. 3.31. Displacement ventilation systems (based on GLC requirements)

and the amount of sound absorption with it. Generally, the audience and seats provide most of the absorption, but some additional dampening of sound is usually required on one or more wall surfaces. A volume of 3 m³ per person (up to 300 seats) should give optimum conditions for a reverberation time of 0.8–1.0 second suitable for speech, but larger numbers of seats require a greater volume per seat.

The most common conditions for the production of echoes are parallel reflecting surfaces, which produce 'flutter', and curved or faceted distant walls which concentrate delayed reflected sound. Both conditions should be avoided or one or more of the surfaces should be made sound-absorbent.

The control of noise, reverberation and echoes is less critical if the direct sound of the actor's voice is dominant. One way of reinforcing sound from the stage is to provide reflectors or 'clouds' above the front part of the auditorium to direct the sound to the back seats, where the direct sound is weakest; in some cases, the auditorium ceiling itself might be an appropriate reflecting surface. Acoustically, no seat should be further than 20 m from the front of the stage.

HEATING AND VENTILATION

Conventional heating and ventilation methods will normally be appropriate to the front of house and backstage areas, but the auditorium and stage present particular problems.

In the auditorium, air movement must ensure that there are no pockets of stale air and that a feeling of freshness is generated, but there must be no draughts. Some form of displacement ventilation system is required and Fig 3.31 illustrates two approaches based on GLC requirements. The inlet apertures should direct the air evenly over the audience and must be designed to avoid noise being generated; if the air velocity is too high, plenum boxes or silencers will be required. Low level extract grilles are normally located below the seats in the risers of row steps.

The temperature of auditorium air must be carefully controlled, bearing in mind the considerable heat generated by the audience itself during a performance. In the summer, it can rise well above ambient temperature and, if the difference is likely to be more than 6° C, cooling will be necessary. To avoid discomfort, cooled air should not be introduced into the auditorium at low level.

On stage, air movements can ruffle scenery and costumes, but heating is nevertheless required. Although no system is ideal, recessed radiators around the back of the stage probably give the best answer, but staff must avoid placing scenery and stage equipment in front of the radiators.

Automatic emergency extracts will be necessary over both stage and auditorium. In the event of fire, low level extracts must be automatically shut down to ensure that no smoke is drawn towards the audience.

ACCOMMODATION

The extent of the accommodation required in any particular theatre will depend not only on the type and size of theatre envisaged, but also on the kind of productions to be catered for, the theatre's management structure and the characteristics of the site. For example, the provision of production workshops might be prohibited by site restrictions or high cost and, consequently, scenery, properties and costumes will have to be made elsewhere. Alternatively, it might be management policy to exploit the location of the theatre to develop the restaurant and bar facilities for general public use during the daytime and closed seasons, as well as for the benefit of audiences.

The outline schedule of accommodation set out in Table 3.3 is therefore intended to provide a framework for the initial brief. In the smaller theatres, a number of the spaces listed will not be provided separately, but their functions will be combined and accommodated in fewer, smaller spaces. Conversely, larger theatres will require an expanded schedule, especially in the provision of individual rooms for administrative and production staff (e.g. assistant managers of various departments) and of rooms for specialist performers (e.g. music and ballet rehearsal rooms).

Notes on the following aspects of accommodation are given where particularly relevant:

(a) Space requirements.
(b) Services and internal environment.

Unless otherwise stated, spaces will be provided with normal background heating, natural ventilation and general artificial lighting (40–60 lux); also sufficient socket outlets for vacuum cleaning.

Table 3.3 SCHEDULE OF ACCOMMODATION

Accommodation	Space requirements	Services and internal environment
AUDITORIUM/STAGE		
Auditorium	0.6 m² per person; 3 m³ per person up to 300 (increasing volume per person above 300)	Dimming lighting; separate emergency lighting (between 0.01 and 0.025 lux); exit signs (BS 2560:1954) Loudspeakers (2 in main roof, 2 on prompt side, 2 on OP, 2 at back); deaf aids Microphone points (2 in main roof space; 1 on prompt side, 1 on OP, 1 at back); with socket outlets Upwards or (preferably) downwards ventilation system supplying minimum 28 m³ air per person per hour with even temperature and air movement (no draughts); in case of fire, automatic cut-off in low level extract coupled to emergency high level extract Special acoustic design; sound insulation giving maximum 25 dBA (20 dBA for larger theatres) Special seating arrangement and sight-line design

Accommodation	Space requirements	Services and internal environment
Orchestra pit	1 m² for each performer; 5 m² for piano; 5–6 m² for timpani; 2 m² for conductor	Emergency lighting and exit signs (as auditorium) Socket outlet for local lighting, microphones and instruments Loudspeakers (3 equally spaced) Microphone points (say 4) Ventilation—part of auditorium system Adjustable floor level using lifts; conductor's sight-lines
Stage	Acting area 9 m × 9 m or 9 m diam; for other spaces see Data: Stage Planning (page 3–4)	Special stage lighting (detailed design required); working lighting in fly tower, wings and basement; emergency lighting and exit signs (as auditorium) Independent socket outlets (3 each side of proscenium arch, 1 on working side of flies, 1 in grid); cable ducts in stage floor Loudspeakers (3 each side of stage, 1 each side of fly tower, 1 in grid) Microphone points (3 on prompt side, 3 on OP, 4 on working side of flies, 1 in grid, 1 in understage) Stage manager's control panel/cue board/intercom Fire fighting equipment; drencher; sprinklers Automatic high level extract and smoke vents in case of fire Heating system at stage level (radiators) Acoustics—part of auditorium design; sound insulation as auditorium
PUBLIC SPACES Entrance	Space for people to alight from car or coach preferably under cover	External lighting
Foyer	Adequate space for access to auditorium and ancillary accommodation (bars, toilets etc.) without undue cross-circulation; and for people to congregate before performances and during intervals	Separate emergency lighting (1 lux); exit signs Loudspeaker; microphone point Public telephones (2 nos. coin-operated) with kiosks or hoods Plenum ventilation
Circulation to auditorium and escape routes	1.370 m wide min	Separate emergency lighting (1 lux); exit signs
Cloakrooms	Allow 1 coat hook for each auditorium seat; 1 m counter length per 20 cloakroom users	Unattended cloakrooms to have ½ hour fire resistant enclosure; also security arrangments
Toilets	Separate normal provision for each sex (assume 75% male; 75% female; total 150%) also separate toilet for disabled persons	1 wc to 100 female public; 1 wc to 100 male public (1 wc to 250 over 400), 1 urinal to 25 male public; 1 whb (h & c) to each wc or urinal; 1 wc and 1 whb for disabled persons
Box office	5 m² per ticket-selling space (2 nos. min)	Telephone
House manager's office	12–20 m²	Telephone
Sales counter	(say) 5 m²	
Theatre bar	Space for people to sit or stand out of main circulation routes; bar length to serve up to half audience within interval of about 15 minutes Small store for crates and boxes (full and empty) and goods to be sold by floating sales staff	Washing up facilities

Accommodation	Space requirements	Services and internal environment
PUBLIC SPACES *(cont)*		
Coffee bar	Similar space requirements to theatre bar, but with small food preparation room and fuller provision of seating and tables	Washing up and tea/coffee making facilities, heating cabinets for pre-cooked food
Restaurant	Size depends on management policy. Allow 1 m² per restaurant seat	See also Section 5 'Public Houses and Licensed Premises'
Kitchen (to restaurant)	Allow 0.5 m² per restaurant seat, plus storage, staff rooms and toilets	Gas and electrical supplies for food preparation cooking and washing equipment Extract ventilation over cooking area
Exhibition space	Space for people to view exhibitions without blocking main circulation routes	Socket outlets at high and low levels for exhibition lighting
PERFORMANCE SPACES		
Dressing rooms: communal double single	For space dimensions, see Data (page **3**–15)	1 whb (h & c) to 4 performers; for single dressing room, 1 wc, 1 whb (h & c) and 1 shower Dressing position lighting (bare 40 W bulbs around mirror); general lighting to be tungsten Shaving sockets (1 between 2 dressing positions) Socket outlets for use by performers (hair driers, clothes vacuum cleaners etc.) Fire fighting equipment; sprinklers
Musicians' changing rooms	1.5 m² per person. (1 m², if separate orchestra assembly room is also provided)	
Conductor's room	18 m² (21 m² with piano)	Shower, wc and whb (h & c)
Toilets and showers	Separate provision for each sex	1 wc to 5 females; 1 wc to 8 males; 1 urinal to 5 males; 1 whb (h & c) to each WC or urinal; 1 shower to 4 or 5 performers
Green room	20 m² min	Sink (h & c); gas or electric cooking ring; socket outlet(s) for tea/coffee making Telephone (coin-operated) outside room, with hood. Quiet, restful atmosphere
Stage door keeper	Small office, say 7 m²	Telephone
Waiting room/space	Small area, say 10 m²	Telephone (coin-operated) with hood or kiosk
Rehearsal room	9 × 9 m (as acting area on stage) minimum; but usually larger, depending on flexibility of use	Socket outlets for temporary lighting If used for small public performances, then heating and ventilation, lighting and sound control, access and safety measures to be similar to auditorium and stage
Orchestra assembly room	1 m² per person	Sound and fire check separation from orchestra pit, auditorium and stage
Instrument store	For larger instruments. Allow 2 m² for upright piano, 5 m² for grand piano, 5 m² for timpani, 0.5 m² for each other instrument	Lift required for grand piano if not stored at stage level

Accommodation	Space requirements	Services and internal environment
The following space might be required to function without integral production spaces		
Wardrobe mistress	12 m²	Socket outlets for sewing machines and localised lighting
Costume repair and maintenance	12 m²	Socket outlets for sewing machines and localised lighting
Laundry	12 m² min	Washing machines and spin driers (3 or more large domestic type) Sink (h & c) Socket outlets for ironing boards or presses Drying conditions (e.g. heating pipes or radiators); extract fan
Performance costume store	Varies in size from racks and shelves in wardrobe mistress' room to large separate room for repertoire	
Scenery dock	Space for current production or repertoire only (not long term storage); 7 m high	Fire separation from stage; smoke vents
Performance property store	20 m² (approx), depending on size of productions envisaged and repertoire	
Repairs and maintenance	20 m² (approx)	Socket outlets for power tools
Stage manager's office	12–15 m²	Telephone
Stage staff room	22–25 m² (for deputy stage manager, ASM's and secretary)	Telephone
Electrician's workshop	12 m²	Socket outlets for power tools, etc
Backstage toilets and cloakrooms	Separate provision for each sex	1 wc to 10 females, 1 wc to 15 males, 1 urinal to 10 males, 1 whb (h & c) to each wc or urinal; 1 clothes locker per person
Lighting control room	For area, see Data: Control Rooms (page 3–21)	Control panel (console) with conduit runs to points in stage and auditorium Socket outlets for equipment Subdued and screened lighting during performance Sound separation from auditorium
Sound control room	As 'lighting control room'	As 'lighting control room', but sound insulated from all surrounding spaces
Projection room	For area, see typical layout in Data: Film Projection (page 3–23)	Electrical provision for projectors (15 A socket outlets for 16 mm; 45 A single or three-phase for 35 mm), amplifiers and rewind equipment Direct mechanical extract to open air (0.0174 m² effective clear area per projector) Water supply (direct or 700 litre storage tank with pump) for pulsed discharge lamps and 35 mm projectors with carbon arcs Fire fighting equipment, including asbestos blanket where inflammable film is used Temperature 18°C (10°C minimum) Subdued and screened lighting during performance Sound separation from auditorium
Dimmer room	Space for dimmer racks and ciculation	Electrical supply for racks and cooling fans Sound separation from auditorium

Accommodation	Space requirements	Services and internal environment
ADMINISTRATION SPACES		
General office	10 m² per person, including filing space	Telephone
General Manager's office	12–15 m²	Telephone
Catering Manager's office	12–15 m²	Telephone
Accounts office	10–12 m²	Telephone
Telephone and mail bookings room	10–12 m²	Telephone
Duplicating room	Space depends on extent of reprographic equipment	Socket outlets for equipment
Press and publicity room	10–12 m²	Telephone
Visitors room	10 m² (approx)	
Archives	Size depends on management policy and volume of material	
Library	As archives (above), but could be in the form of wall shelving in general or private office	
Conference room	20–30 m²	
Interview/audition room	25–35 m²	
Artistic director's office	20–30 m²	Telephone
Assistant director's office	10–12 m²	Telephone
Secretary's office	10 m²	Telephone
Toilets and cloakrooms	Separate provision for each sex. Coat hanging space within offices or locker rooms	1 wc to 10 females, 1 wc to 15 males, 1 urinal to 10 males, 1 whb (h & c) to each wc or urinal
PRODUCTION SPACES		
Production manager's office	15–20 m²	Telephone
Designers' room	15–20 m²	Telephone. Socket outlets for localised lighting (e.g. anglepoise lamps)
Design studio	30–40 m² (incl. model making and model storage)	Socket outlets for localised lighting and model making tools
Costume designer's room	12–17 m²	Telephone. Socket outlets for localised lighting
Lighting designer's room	12–17 m²	Telephone. Socket outlets for localised lighting (e.g. anglepoise lamps)
Toilets, cloakrooms and showers	Separate provision for each sex	Toilets and cloakrooms as for backstage; at least 1 shower for each sex
Scenery materials store	Space to take timber (in horizontal racks), rolls of materials and sheet materials stored on end vertically)	

Accommodation	Space requirements	Services and internal environment
Scenery workshop	Repertory 100 m²; repertoire 150–300 m²; height 7 m	Gas rings (2 nos.); large sink (h & c); electrical supply (single and 3 phase) Natural top light; general and localised artificial light
Head carpenter	12 m²	Telephone
Assembly area	9 × 9 m (acting area) minimum	
Paint shop	80 m² (minimum length: at least one paint frame 9 m; minimum width and height 7 m)	Gas rings (4 nos.); sinks (2 nos. h & c); electrical supply: natural light and tungsten lighting to simulate stage lighting
Head painter	12 m²	Telephone
Scenery store	Size depends on repertoire and management policy	
Repairs and maintenance	20 m² (approx)	Socket outlets for power tools
Property materials store	May be provided in the form of shelving (0.225 m deep) around workshop walls	
Property workshop	40 m² (minimum ceiling height 3 m)	Gas ring; large sink (h & c); electrical supply; natural light; adjustable table lights
Head of properties	12 m²	Telephone
Photographic dark room	6 m²	Sink; electrical supply
G.R.P. room } Metalwork room }	Separate room, minimum 3 × 3 m Separate room, minimum 3 × 3 m	Gas ring; large sink (h & c); electrical supply; natural light; adjustable table lights
Property store	Repertoire 50 m²; for future use 80 m²	
Wardrobe materials	May be provided in the form of shelving (up to 1.3 m. deep) along workshop walls	
Wardrobe workshop	Repair only, 20 m²; repertoire, 100 m²; large scale repertoire, 200 m²	Electrical supply; natural light and local artificial light
Head of wardrobe	10 m²	Telephone
Fitting room	10 m²	
Milliner	3.6 × 3 m for millinery work; 3.6 × 3 m for preparation of accessories	Gas ring, sink (h & c), electrical supply; natural light, adjustable table light
Wig maker } Shoe maker }	Size depends on repertoire and management policy; may be part of workshop, but with separate storage	Socket outlets for power tools
Dye shop	7.2 m × 3.6 m	Large sink (h & c); circulated warm dry air; gas and electrical supply; natural light
Drying	Space to accommodate drying rack 2.4 × 1.8 × 2 m high	Provide circulated warm dry air
Spraying	Spray booth 10 m² (approx)	Socket outlets for power tools and spraying equipment
Costume store	Size depends on repertoire and management policy	
Toilets, cloakrooms and showers	Accessible from scenery, property and wardrobe departments	Toilets and cloakrooms as for backstage; at least one shower for each sex

STATUTORY REQUIREMENTS, LEGISLATION AND AUTHORITIES

Along with other places of entertainment, theatres are subject to control under a number of national and local Acts of Parliament, regulations and rules.

ACTS OF PARLIAMENT

Theatres Act 1968. Requires licensing of premises for public performance of plays.

Cinematograph Acts 1909 and 1952. Requires licensing for cinematograph exhibitions, with certain exceptions (see also Cinematograph Regulations of 1955, 1958 and 1965).

Fire Precautions Act 1971. Fire certificates to be applied for and issued.

Public Health Acts 1936 and 1961. Includes provision to make regulations covering means of escape and building construction. (See also Building Regulations 1972 and London Building Acts 1930–1939).

Health and Safety at Work etc. Act, 1974, Part III provides 'power to make building regulations'.

Offices, Shops and Railway Premises Act 1963. Concerns administrative spaces.

Factories Act 1961. Concerns production spaces, (e.g. workshops).

Town and Country Planning Act 1971. Planning permission required for new theatres and for alterations to existing theatres which constitute "development" as defined by the Act.

London Building Acts 1930, 1935 and 1939. Concerned with building construction and fire precautions. Theatres are subject to special control by District Surveyor. Applies to Inner London Boroughs.

(Note: A list of Acts affecting places of entertainment and building works generally is given in the volume *Planning: Architects' Technical Reference Data*).

REGULATIONS AND BYELAWS

Building Regulations 1972 and amendments. Cover building work, including structural fire precautions and means of escape, in England (outside the Inner London Boroughs) and Wales. Detailed particulars and drawings to be submitted to the local authority for approval.

Building Standard (Scotland) Amendment Regulations 1965. Cover building work in Scotland.

London Building Construction Byelaws, 1972 (and amending Byelaws 1974). Cover building work in the Inner London Boroughs.

Technical Regulations for Places of Public Entertainment in Greater London, 1965. Issued by the Greater London Council, they are particularly wide in scope and cover siting, planning, construction and services.

Cinematograph (Safety) Regulations 1955, 1958 and 1965. Cover conditions for the use of premises for showing films, even where a licence is not required.

OTHER RULES AND CONDITIONS

Licensing authorities have power to make rules and regulations concerning the safety of buildings used for public entertainment. In particular, the Greater London Council issue 'rules of management for places of public entertainment', which are annexed to all licences granted.

AUTHORITIES

The following official and voluntary bodies are concerned, inter alia, with the planning of theatres:

Department of the Environment
Department of Education and Science
Scottish Office
Welsh Office
The Arts Council of Great Britain
Association of British Theatre Technicians
International Federation for Theatre Research
Society for Theatre Research
Society of British Lighting Designers
Society of Theatre Consultants
Standing Advisory Committee on Local Authorities and the Theatre
Theatres Advisory Council

EXAMPLES

Aberystwyth: Theatr-y-Werin   Completed 1972
(400 seats)
Architects: Alex Gordon & Partners
Architects Journal (24/7/74)

Bangor: Theatr Gwynedd   Completed 1975
(340 seats)
Architects: Percy Thomas Partnership

Billingham: Forum Theatre   Completed 1968
(593/643 seats)
Architects: Elder Lester & Partners

Birmingham: Cannon Hill Studio Theatre   Completed 1965
(200/300 seats)
Architects: Jackson & Edmonds

Birmingham: Repertory Theatre   Completed 1971
(901 seats)
Architects: S.T. Walker and Partners in association with the City Architect
Architects' Journal (22 and 29/12/71)

Bolton: Octagon Theatre   Completed 1967
(322/422 seats)
Architect: Geoffrey Brooks

Cardiff: Sherman Theatre   Completed 1973
(450/475 seats; also arena theatre of up to 200 seats)
Architects: Alex Gordon & Partners
Architects' Journal (24/7/74)

Chester: Gateway Theatre   Completed 1968
(500 seats)
Architects: Michael Lyell Associates

Chichester: Festival Theatre   Completed 1962
(1360 seats)
Architects: Powell & Moya with Christopher Stevens

Colchester: Mercury Theatre   Completed 1972
(400/500 seats)
Architects: Norman Downie Associates

Coventry: Belgrade Theatre   Completed 1958
(910 seats)
Architects: City of Coventry Architects' Dept.

Eastbourne: Congress Theatre   Completed 1963
(1678 seats)
Architects: B. & N. Westwood, Piet & Partners
Architect & Building News (31/7/63)

Exeter: Northcott Theatre   Completed 1968
(433 seats)
Architects: Sir William Holford & Partners

Farnham: Redgrave Theatre   Completed 1974
(356 seats)
Architect: Frank Rutter

Guildford: Yvonne Arnaud Theatre   Completed 1965
(568 seats)
Architects: Scott, Brownrigg & Turner
Architects' Journal (16/6/65)

Hornchurch: Queens Theatre   Completed 1975

Hull: Gulbenkian Centre   Completed 1969
(200 seats)
Architects: Peter Moro & Partners

Leatherhead: Thorndike Theatre   Completed 1969
(530 seats)
Architect: Roderick Ham
Architects' Journal (12/11/69)

Leicester: Phoenix Theatre   Completed 1963
(274 seats)
Architects: City of Leicester Architects' Dept. (Stephen
George)
Architects' Journal (18/12/63)

Leicester: Haymarket Theatre   Completed 1973
(710 seats)
Architects: Building Design Partnership in association with
City of Leicester Architects' Dept.

London: National Theatre   Due for completion 1976
(1165 seats; also smaller theatre of 895 seats)
Architects: Dennis Lasdun & Partners
(Design illustrated in *Architectural Design* (Feb 1968)

Manchester: University Theatre   Completed 1965
(300 seats)
Architects: Building Design Partnership

Newcastle-upon-Tyne: University Theatre Completed 1970
(449 seats; also studio theatre of 100/200 seats)
Architect: William Whitfield
Architects' Journal (5/5/71)

Nottingham: Playhouse   Completed 1963
(756 seats)
Architects: Peter Moro & Partners
Architects' Journal (1/1/64)

Peterborough: Key Theatre   Completed 1973
(399 seats)
Architects: Mathew Robotham Associates

St. Albans: Abbey Theatre   Completed 1968
(240 seats)
Architects: Michael Meacher & Partners

St. Andrews: Byre Theatre   Completed 1970

Sheffield: Crucible Theatre   Completed 1971
(1000 seats; also studio theatre of 250 seats)
Architects: Renton Howard Wood Associates
Architects' Journal (22 and 29/12/71)

Southampton: Nuffield Theatre   Completed 1964
(420/500 seats)
Architects: Sir Basil Spence & Partners
Architect & Building News (1/4/64)

Stirling: MacRobert Centre   Completed 1971
(475/497 seats)
Architects: Robert Mathew Johnson, Marshall & Partners

Swindon: Wyvern Theatre and Arts Centre Completed 1971
(652 seats)
Architects: Casson Condor & Partners
Architects' Journal (22/12/71 and 29/12/71)

Worcester: Swan Theatre   Completed 1965
(353 seats)
Architect: Henry Gorst

Wythenshawe, Manchester: Forum Theatre   Completed
1971

Cork, Eire: Opera House   Completed 1965
(996 seats)
Architects: Michael Scott & Partners

Dublin, Eire: Abbey Theatre   Completed 1966
(628 seats)
Architects: Michael Scott & Partners

BIBLIOGRAPHY

Aloi, R, *Archittetture per lo Spettacolo*, Hoepli Milan (1958)

Aloi, R, *Teatri e Auditori Theatres and Auditoriums*, Hoepli Milan (1972)

Joseph, Stephen (ed) *Adaptable Theatres*, Association of British Theatre Technicians, London (1962)

Bellman, Willard F., *Lighting the Stage,* Chandler Publishing Company, San Francisco (1967)

Bentham, Frederick, *Theatre of Stage Lighting,* Pitman, London (1969)

Bentham, Frederick, *New Theatres in Britain,* Rank Strand Electric Ltd, London (1970)

Burris-Meyer, H and Cole E. C., *"Theatres and Auditoriums"* (2nd ed), Reinhold, New York; Chapman & Hall, London (1964)

Burris-Meyer & Mallory, *Sound Reproduction in the Theatre,* Theatre Arts Books, New York (1965)

Corry, Percy, *Community Theatres,* Pitman, London (1974)

Elsom, John, *Theatre outside London,* Macmillan, London (1971)

Gasgoigne, Bamber, *World Theatre,* Ebury Press, London (1968)

Graubner, Gerhard, *Theater-Aufgabe und Planung,* Callway, Munich (1968)

Greater London Council, *Places of Public Entertainment technical regulations,* Publication 378 GLC, London (1971)

Greater London Council, *Play safe—A guide to standards in halls used for occasional stage presentations,* GLC, London (1968)

Ham, Roderick (ed), *Theatre Planning,* Association of British Theatre Technicians, Architectural Press, London (1972)

Hartnoll, Phyllis (ed), *Oxford Companion to the theatre* (3rd ed), Oxford University Press, London (1967)

Joseph, Stephen (ed), *Actor and Architect,* Manchester University Press, Manchester (1964)

Joseph, Stephen, *Theatre in the Round,* Barrie & Rockliff, London (1967)

Joseph Stephen, *New Theatre forms,* Pitman, London (1968)

Parkin, P. H. & Humphries H. R., *Acoustics, noise & buildings,* (2nd ed) Faber & Faber, London (1963)

Pilbrow, Richard, *Stage Lighting,* Studio Vista, London (1970)

Schubert, Hannelore, *The Modern Theatre,* Pall Mall Press, London (1971)

Southern, Richard, *The Open Stage,* Faber & Faber, London (1953)

Southern, Richard, *Proscenium and sight lines,* Faber & Faber, London

Sweeting, Elizabeth, *Theatre Administration,* Pitman, London (1969)

"Tabs" Publications, *Stage planning 1971,* Rank Strand Electric Ltd, London

The Arts Council of Great Britain, *The Theatre today in England and Wales,* The Arts Council of Great Britain, London (1970)

Warre, Michael, *Designing and making scenery,* Studio Vista, London (1967)

Hughes, Peter, *A.A.Dipl. FRIBA is a partner of Percy Thomas Partnership. He has been concerned with the design of auditoria, multi-purpose halls and a theatre during the last few years, mainly for University Colleges in Wales.*

Lovibond, Malcolm, *B.Arch., Dip. TP, FRIBA, MRTPI set up his own practice in 1973. From 1959 to 1973, he was with Percy Thomas Partnership and was Associate-in-charge of the theatre for the University College of North Wales, Bangor. He is a member of the Association of British Theatre Technicians and part-time tutor at the University of Manchester School of Architecture.*

4 CINEMAS

ANTHONY WYLSON, F.R.I.B.A., A.A. Dip (Hons)

INTRODUCTION

Cinematograph film is a thin, flexible, transparent base material coated with a photo-sensitive layer of emulsion capable of recording an image. This image can be projected onto a screen. A sound track is incorporated on the film to provide the synchronised sound effects.

The projection equipment is normally located in a projection room and the relationship between projection equipment and screen varies according to space available and type of equipment used. The conditions relating to sound production, acoustics, heating, ventilation and lighting require specialist advice when considered in detail.

The arrangement of seating, gangways, exits and lighting in public cinemas are controlled by statutory regulations and local authority licensing. This section endeavours to cover basic material affecting space planning. It cannot cover the full extent of design and techniques in detail. Cinema techniques have developed considerably over the years and continue to do so. Statutory requirements have changed with necessity. Thus the original inflammability of film required strict precautions which was covered in early Cinematograph legislation and clearly evident in early projection room planning.

In addition to Government Safety Regulations, Local Authorities exercise powers to maintain security for the public. For this analysis, reference is made to the Home Office Regulations and the Technical Regulations imposed by the Greater London Council. Obviously, it would be necessary for the designer to obtain detailed information for the project.

The commercial cinema fulfils two roles. To the exhibitor the purpose of the cinema is to provide an acceptable investment. To the patron the purpose is to provide an environment in which the film show can be enjoyed in comfort and safety to the extent that he is willing to invest in the price of a seat.

ENCLOSED CINEMAS

As much architectural work for cinemas nowadays consists of altering existing cinemas, the background history is important. It is also important to see a particular audio-visual technique in context.

The history of the 'moving film' dates back to the end of the last century, although buildings constructed specially for film presentations were not in evidence until around 1910. Prior to this, the exhibition of films given in a variety of places which basically had to meet only one requirement—to contain a seated audience. Enterprising exhibitors hired concert and lecture halls. In the country districts, shows were performed in fairground marquees competing largely with the circus and other side attractions. The programmes of the Edwardian music halls and variety theatres included films during the intervals. This gained popularity and more time was allotted to them. Ultimately the films took over and comprised the full programme.

Thus the first cinemas, to some degree, were imitations of the music hall, both in design and decor including proscenium opening, stage and orchestra pit. As cinemas gradually increased in size and number in the 1930s, the decor of the music hall in turn gave way to more flamboyant and exotic motifs. This was an attempt to complement atmospherically, the genre of romantic and adventure films which were then in vogue. At the same time, one group of architects produced more restrained and often streamlined designs, and soon became known as the 'hard-top' school. In any case, the introduction of the sound film in the late 1920's had little effect on auditorium design. If the acoustics of an auditorium proved unsatisfactory on completion, modifications would be made to improve the situation. This consisted mainly of positioning sound absorbent materials in the appropriate places until acceptable results were achieved. W. C. Sabine, who pioneered the science of acoustics half a century earlier, was almost totally ignored, and it was not until the beginnings of the widescreen processes introduced in the early 1950's, that cinema design did undergo a radical transformation.

As a result of the Second World War, there was a period of about eleven years in which no new cinema buildings could be built. By the early 1950's, when the restrictions were removed and economic conditions allowed the construction of new buildings, the pattern of life in the western world had also changed. Educational standards had greatly improved; most people were enjoying a much higher standard of living; and there was more time available for recreation and leisure. Radio and television, were replacing the cinema as the principal media for mass entertainment. The potential decline in audiences encouraged the film industry to find new methods of attracting the audiences back to the cinema.

In 1952, Cinerama was introduced. Technically an impressive development, this had as its objective the creation of a powerful visual and aural impact upon the audience, on a scale hitherto unknown. To achieve this objective, three projectors were synchronised to provide a large and complete image on a semicircular screen. The sound was reproduced stereophonically through five speaker systems behind the screen as well as several surround speakers positioned in the auditorium. The system, on the whole, demanded considerable modifications to existing auditoria which generally proved inadequate to house the enormous screen. Productions costs were high and only a few Cinerama films were eventually made. Showings were restricted to the big cities whose populations would justify the presentation of the same film for a lengthy period.

Although the production and exhibition side of the film industry has been disrupted by the war, the same could not be said for the technical developments in cinematography. Improvements had been achieved in the quality of photographic emulsions as well as colour systems. Lenses for cameras and projectors had been improved allowing larger apertures and shorter focal lengths. This permitted the transmission of more light which allowed larger screen sizes without any appreciable reduction in picture quality.

In 1953, 20th Century Fox introduced the Cinemascope system, which made use of an auxiliary anamorphic lens attachment in front of the normal projection lens (see subsection on Film Systems). This effectively permitted screen widths to be doubled. It had become clear that if larger screens were to be installed in existing cinemas, the restrictions on the height of a screen would prove more critical than that on the width. In a cinema having both stalls and balcony, the height of the screen was obviously regulated by the sight lines of the audience sitting in the rearmost row of seats in the stalls to clear the soffit of the balcony.

Also, increasing the height of the screen would provide unsatisfactory viewing angles to those sitting in the front rows, and hence more rows of seats would have to be removed. Thus the Cinemascope screen proportion that increased the width without necessarily affecting the height, could be more easily adapted to existing cinema buildings. Furthermore, Cinemascope was to pave the way for even larger pictures. With improved technology, cinema owners began projecting even ordinary films at greater magnification, and to obviate the necessity for extra screen height, smaller apertures at the projection gates were used. These techniques with aspect ratios (the ratio of height of screen to its width) between 1:1·65 and 1:1·85 are broadly termed 'wide-screen, and are

particularly relevant to current auditoria design with an optimum ratio of 1:1·75.

The quest for greater impact and audio-visual communication is expressed in experimental techniques such as, Imax and Circarama. These techniques synchronised projectors to project films on three, six, nine, twelve and as many as fifteen screens. The layout of the screens range from the complete cylindrical enclosure of Circlorama in which the picture extends all around the audience, to a complex configuration of shapes and flying screens removed and replaced as and when required. The latter are techniques adopted in various recent expositions and require particular technical appraisal to establish planning requirements.

DRIVE-IN CINEMAS

Drive-in cinemas have been constructed in countries with equitable climates and large towns of car-owners. These replaced the enclosed auditorium with a terraced car-park orientated towards a very large screen. Each car space is supplied with individual loudspeaker equipment and in some cases, individual heating units are also supplied. Patrons remain in their cars.

SITING

GENERAL CONSIDERATIONS

The siting of a commercial cinema must reflect the objective of attracting the attention of the public or being easily accessible to a well populated area. It must be able to take advantage of generators of activity such as communication centres, shopping centres and centres with evening amenities. A cinema can benefit by the capacity of its neighbours to create a lively atmosphere in the evening, in preference to a daytime prestigious location. The impression to the public of the immediate surroundings to the cinema is important to engender an atmosphere of warmth, well being, and occasion.

The commercial cinema consists basically of four sections (Fig 4.2):

1. Auditorium with seating facing a screen on which a picture is projected from a projection room.
2. Adjoining public spaces to provide for access, circulation, essential services, and ancillary functions depending upon the complexity of the project.
3. Management spaces necessary for the administration and maintenance of the cinema.
4. Engineering services.

The largest of these functions is the auditorium and projection room. The auditorium requires reasonable proportions and acceptable means of access and exit.

The relationship between access and the auditorium (Fig 4.1) is particularly important when the cinema forms part of a complex in which other independent uses are included. The value of an urban property may render the use simply for one cinema auditorium uneconomic—in fact the limited time use of the cinema demands that the site is used profitably during normal working hours. This could lead to associating the cinema with shop use at ground floor and easily accessible to the street, offices, hotel or flats on the upper floor, and

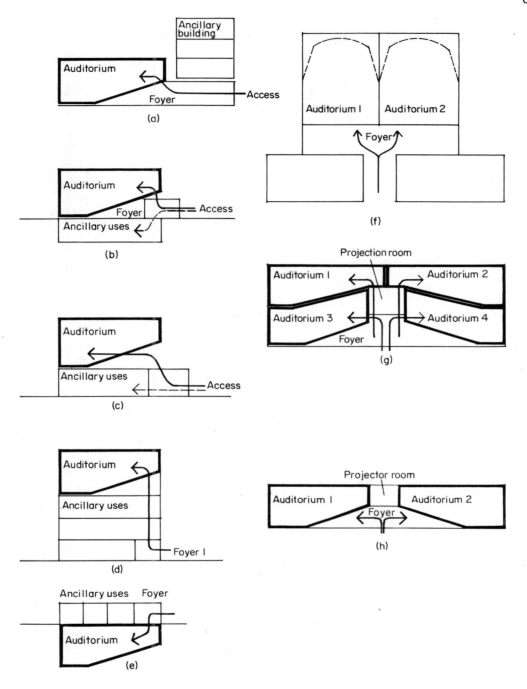

Fig. 4.1   Access to auditoriums

(a) *Cinema at ground floor. Deep foyer allows for ancillary uses over front section of the building.*

(b) *Cinema at ground floor. Ancillary uses in basement under auditorium. Consider compatability of structural solution, noise problem and access.*

(c) *Cinema at first floor level. Ancillary uses at ground floor. Consider ease of access to first floor.*

(d) *Cinema on upper floor. Ancillary uses below. Consider access and exits in relation to number of people concerned.*

(e) *Cinema at basement level. Consider compatability of structural solution and location of exits.*

(f) *Two cinemas sharing entrance and foyer.*

(g) *Four cinemas sharing foyer and projection room.*

(h) *Two cinemas sharing foyer and projection room.*

ballroom or restaurant above or below the cinema.

Although reasonable situations can be provided for gaining access to a cinema at basement level, ground level and first floor level, above first floor creates difficulties. It is unlikely that large numbers of people would accept lift access and lift exit from a cinema on an upper floor. Neither lifts or escalator qualify as means of escape.

The present trend to have several auditoria in one project necessitates the careful planning of access (see sub-section on Foyers). The foyer must provide space for guiding patrons to the correct auditorium.

Obviously, the surrounding conditions are important. Noise factors of nearby traffic or industrial processes could be disturbing although much can be done to overcome such siting disadvantages. (i.e. Odeon, Marble Arch and Odeon, Elephant and Castle; both in London).

The siting must also be relevant to the intended style of the cinema, whether it is to be a Super Cinema with separate performances or a standard popular cinema with a continuous programme. In the first case the size necessary for the wide/deep screen auditorium, luxurious seating, ancillary bar, lounge accommodation and spacious foyer will differ considerably from the economic screen, maximum seating arrangements, and small foyer space of the standard popular cinema.

DRIVE-IN CINEMAS

It is assumed that basic market research including an analysis of car ownership has been carried out. A 1500 car capacity drive-in requires approximately 8 ha of land easily accessible from a main road. Details of access would require the approval of the highway authority. In one particular situation the capacity of a drive-in giving one performance a day has been calculated as being 5% of the total sum of private vehicles registered within the area. Areas susceptible to mist or fog should be avoided, and electricity, water and drainage must be available. Satisfactory entrances and exits should be determined early in the proposals. It is advantageous to have trees at the screen end to provide a dark background to the screen, to cut out glare and to maintain privacy.

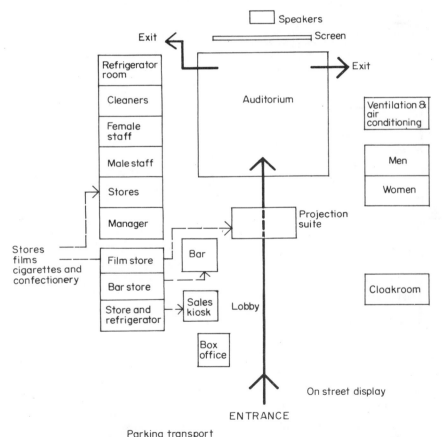

Fig. 4.2 Circulation diagram

PLANNING

The basic planning of the normal commercial cinema consists of four elements: auditorium and projection suite; entrance foyer and box office; administration offices; engineering services (see Fig 4.2). These are detailed in the following paragraphs.

AUDITORIUM AND PROJECTION SUITE

This is the largest space and satisfactory proportions for good seating layout is fundamental to the best use of the site area (Fig. 4.3).

The auditorium provides a secure area for seating and screen, allowing adequate space in the form of gangways, seatways and cross-overs for circulation. Local authority conditions regulate seat spacing, the length of rows and width of gangways and both widths and numbers of exits. There are also regulations governing securing seats. Provision for wheelchairs is permitted at the discretion of the Local Authority and the Cinema Management and particular provision would be required regarding access, accommodation in the auditorium and toilet facilities.

General circulation within the auditorium must be related to the best areas for viewing the screen, control and the degree of disturbance to a seated audience that would be acceptable.

Entrance at the centre of the rear gangway provides least disturbance as the usherette and patron circulate behind and at the sides of the direction in which the audience is facing. However, the back of the auditorium is the highest level and, in the case of a ground floor or first floor auditorium, could prove difficult to achieve as the point of access. A central access provides an alternative but obviously creates a disturbance in view of half the audience if access is permitted during the performance. Side entrances require increase of staff. Access either side of the screen causes the most distraction unless screened. Lavatory accommodation for the public should be available from the auditorium. Accommodation should also be provided in a refrigeration room for the administration of auditorium sales (Fig. 4.3).

The projection room should be on the axis of the centre of the screen and various methods of projection are discussed later. The projection suite includes ancillary accommodation.

THE ENTRANCE FOYER (See Figs 4.13 and 4.14)

This accommodation should include ancillary rooms for the public. The entrance foyer forms a baffle to reduce the transmission of noise and dirt from the street, to reduce heat loss in winter and heat gain in summer, and to provide a space for grading the lighting levels from street to auditorium. It provides a means of directing the public and also accommodates the box office and kiosk. It also provides access to cloakroom, bar and other facilities, and in the case of the hard-ticket super cinema, it would form a lounge or waiting area.

The paybox provides secure accommodation for cashier and ticket machine and should be clearly visible to the public. The kiosk provides for the sale of confectionery, cigarettes, and refreshments. Cloakroom and bar are more associated with hard-ticket Super Cinema layout, in which the foyer is used as a waiting area prior to the performance.

ADMINISTRATION AND ANCILLARY ACCOMMODATION

Depending upon the size of the cinema and associated activities, the staff accommodation will consist of manager's office, assistant manager, clerical staff, female staff room and toilets, male staff room and toilets, administration stock room, cleaners room, and refuse store.

Stockrooms and refuse room should be accessible from the street and the manager's office should be accessible from the foyer. The staff section could have separate access from the street, but this should not impair the general security of the cinema.

ENGINEERING SERVICES AND PLANT ROOMS

The plant rooms comprise boiler room, oil storage, plenum, electrical intake, switch room, water storage, and battery room store. Floor and ceiling voids should provide adequate service ducts as the auditorium and projection room complex are heavily controlled by services to provide the appropriate environment. Public areas and stores will also require extensive ducted ventilation that must be accommodated.

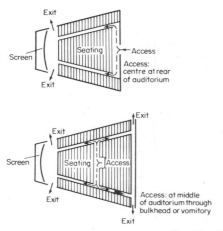

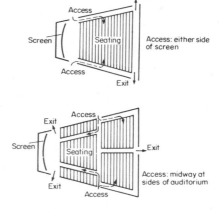

Fig. 4.3 Circulation within auditorium
(See also Statutory Requirements, page 4–30)

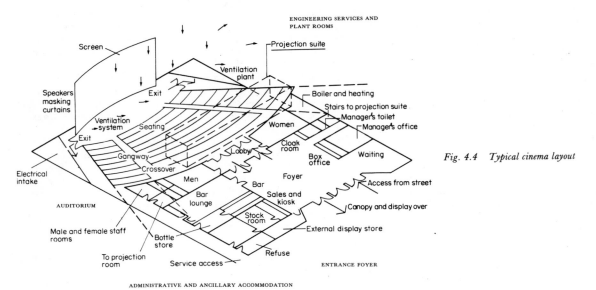

DECORATIVE, PRIMARY SAFETY
AND CLEANERS LIGHTING

ENGINEERING SERVICES AND
PLANT ROOMS

Fig. 4.4   Typical cinema layout

ADMINISTRATIVE AND ANCILLARY ACCOMMODATION

*Figs. 4.5(a) to (f) show the Dimensional Criteria for
the Auditorium.
(For optimum dimensions relating to acoustics, see page 4–29)*

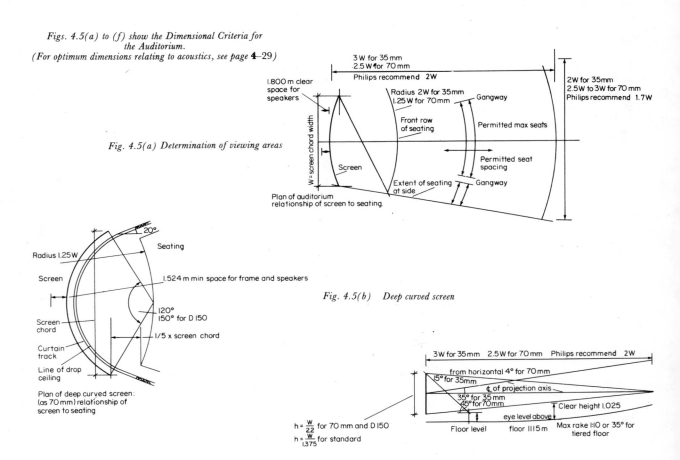

Fig. 4.5(a) Determination of viewing areas

Fig. 4.5(b)   Deep curved screen

$$h = \frac{W}{22} \text{ for 70 mm and D 150}$$
$$h = \frac{W}{1.375} \text{ for standard}$$

Fig. 4.5(c)   Section of stadium type auditorium

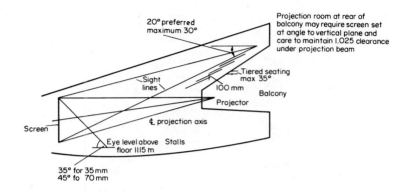

Fig. 4.5(d) Section for stall and balcony

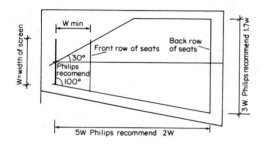

Fig. 4.5(e) Plan for flat screen (matt white non-directional)

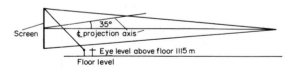

Fig. 4.5 (f) Section for flat screen (matt white non-directional)

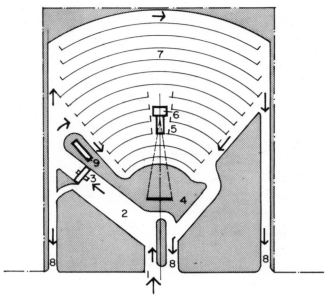

Fig. 4.6   Single drive-in cinema theatre
(Architects: William Riseman Associates, Boston, Mass)

1. Main entrance	5. Snacks and toilets
2. Holdout	6. Projection room
3. Toll booth	7. Exits
4. Screen	8. Office

DRIVE-IN CINEMAS (See Figs 4.6, 4.7 and 4.8)

These are most suited to countries with equitable climates, with traffic conditions that provide the necessary demand, and road conditions that can cope with inflow and outflow of traffic ranging from 250 to over 2000 cars. In general, the smaller cinemas cater for about 400 cars whilst about 1200 is representative of the larger. Similar to recent trends in cinema buildings, dual drive-in cinemas are not uncommon. These usually have auditoria placed either back-to-back or side-by-side, but sharing a common projection booth (Fig. 4.7).

Although patrons generally remain in their cars to watch the films some drive-ins provide cafeterias and snack bars, and even playgrounds for children. The essentials of a drive-in cinema are an adequate site for terraced car positions with easy access to a suitable road (see Fig 4.8), a very large screen, a projection booth, ticketing facilities. The site must permit a traffic circulation system to allow easy and independent entry and departure. The choice of location and other problems associated with layout, construction and land drainage must also be considered carefully.

Layout. The plan of a drive-in, similar to an enclosed cinema auditorium, is generally fan shaped i.e. a segment having an inclusive angle of approximately 80°. The orientation of the plan should avoid the setting sun shining onto the screen or into the spectators looking at the screen. Screens should face East or North. The site should be protected from extraneous noise such as road traffic, aircraft, or industry.

Landscaping. This should be provided on either side and the rear of the screen tower to give the necessary protection from both wind and light. Surrounding trees and shrubs can also reduce extraneous noise.

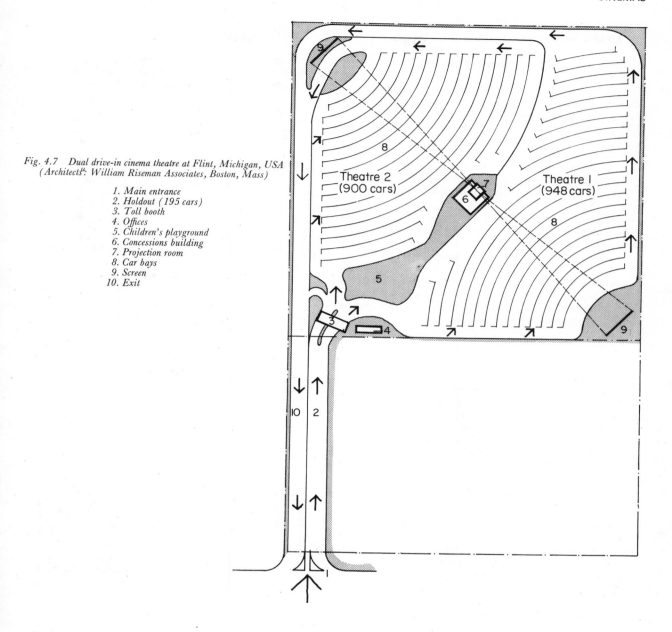

*Fig. 4.7   Dual drive-in cinema theatre at Flint, Michigan, USA
(Architects: William Riseman Associates, Boston, Mass)*

1. Main entrance
2. Holdout (195 cars)
3. Toll booth
4. Offices
5. Children's playground
6. Concessions building
7. Projection room
8. Car bays
9. Screen
10. Exit

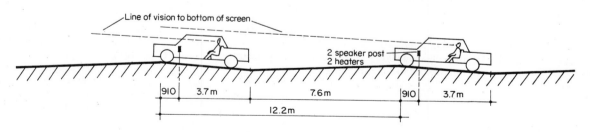

Fig. 4.8   Typical section through ramp

SPACE REQUIREMENTS

ENTRANCE FOYER AND BOX OFFICE

The foyer is the first space entered by the public. Therefore, after the impression conveyed by the external appearance and advertising, the foyer provides an opportunity to express the character and atmosphere of the cinema and the management.

In the Super Cinema, cinema going represents an occasion which may be pre-booked. The foyer provides a waiting space and could provide access to a bar, refreshments area, cloakrooms or exhibition area. In the Standard Cinema, the public arrive shortly before the film commences, or during the programme, buy a ticket or queue and proceed as directly as possible to the auditorium. The foyer is in effect an entrance lobby between street and auditorium.

Generally the temperature of the foyer should be 12°C in cold weather or 1° below outside temperature over 15°C if the building is cooled. Adequate ventilation should be provided. The lighting intensity should be graded from appearing bright from the street, to a lower level of illumination nearer the entrance to the auditorium.

BOX OFFICE

The layout of the box office in relation to the entrance foyer, kiosk, queuing space and exit routes, depends upon the cinema type (Figs. 4.9 to 4.11). The main objective is to avoid the cross circulation of entry to and exit from the auditorium if this can occur at the same time, and to avoid queuing or the slow operation of advance booking to obstruct movement through the foyer. In all cases it is necessary to provide a film classification programme board and a layout indicating the seating prices in the auditorium.

Super cinemas. The box office will have provision for advance booking for hard-ticket sales. The location of the box office must be easily accessible from the street. The island type of box office is less appropriate for advance booking. A box office for the 'Super Cinema' should have two windows, one of which has an 'advance booking' layout for reference.

Standard cinemas. Provision for advance booking and spontaneous booking should be considered, i.e. at least two windows. For cinemas of over 1000 seats, a separate advance booking window should be considered in addition to two windows for spontaneous booking.

Self-service cinemas. The provision of automatic sale of tickets related to availability is yet to be developed on a commercial basis. Entry to the auditorium would be controlled by a mechanically operated gate. Any price division within the auditorium would also require separation. The system would need a change machine and supervisor. The mechanically operated gate would not count as an exit.

Wall position. More suitable for advance booking and can be accessible to the manager's office. Incoming traffic can be separated from outgoing (See Figs. 4.9 and 4.10).

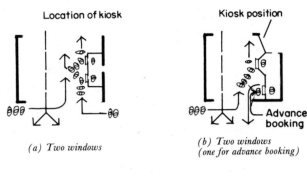

(a) *Two windows*

(b) *Two windows (one for advance booking)*

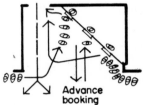

(c) *Two windows and one for advance booking*

Fig. 4.9   Box office in side-wall

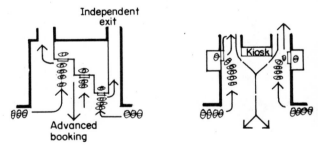

Fig. 4.10   Box offices structurally separated

Island position. This provides a prominent position in relation to the foyer, and can be linked with a kiosk. In the case of a wide pavement, where queuing can be limited to one side of the entrance, the incoming and outgoing traffic can be reasonably separated (see also Figs. 4.10 and 4.11).

Equipment. The basic equipment consists of an automatic ticket machine, a cashdrawer and the statutory priced seating layout plan and film classification board (see Figs. 4.12, 4.13 and 4.14).

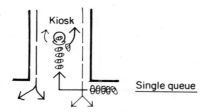

Single queue

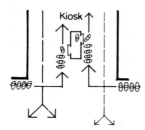

Double queue
(restricted exit circulation)

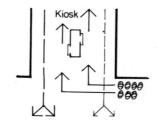

Double queue (less restricted circulation
but requiring wide pavement or waiting
space)

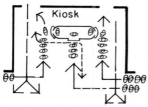

3 windows (one for advance booking
or 3rd price range)

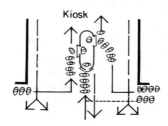

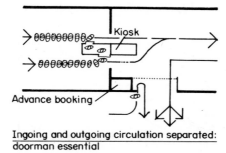

Advance booking

Ingoing and outgoing circulation separated:
doorman essential

Fig. 4.11   Island box office circulation

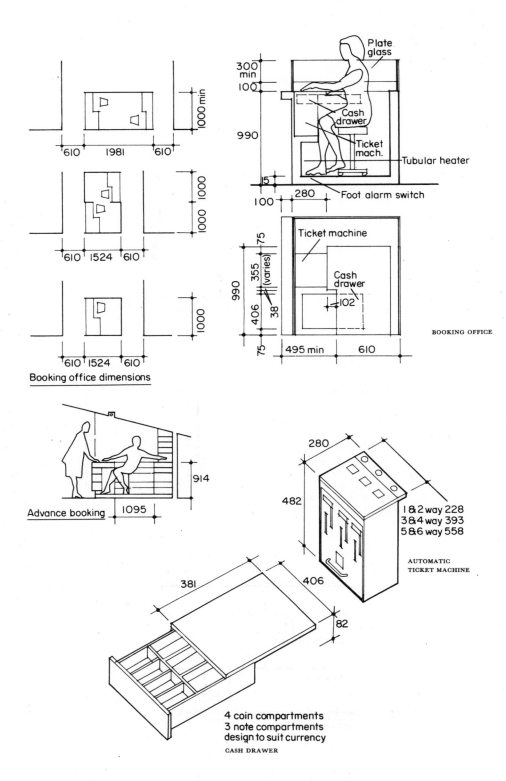

Booking office dimensions

Advance booking

BOOKING OFFICE

AUTOMATIC
TICKET MACHINE

1 & 2 way 228
3 & 4 way 393
5 & 6 way 558

4 coin compartments
3 note compartments
design to suit currency

CASH DRAWER

Fig. 4.12   Dimensional criteria for box office

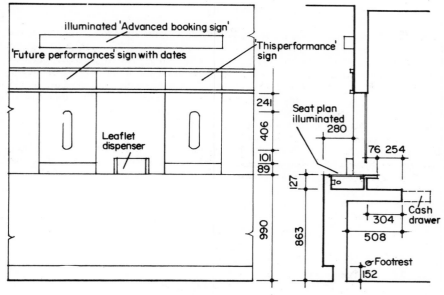

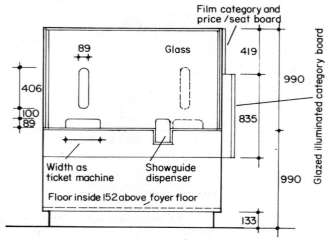

Fig. 4.13   Example of advance booking window arrangement

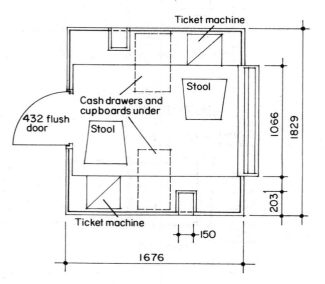

Fig. 4.14   Island box office. Example of two cashier unit

SALES KIOSK (See Fig 4.15)

This consists of fixed sales counter to sell ice-cream, confectionery, soft drinks, hot dogs and cigarettes (see Fig 4.15).

It may incorporate the main and/or secondary pay box. The kiosk should be located between paybox and auditorium entrances and positioned to give maximum sales impact without restriction to normal traffic flow.

A suggested minimum length for auditoria up to 750 seats is 5.5 m with an additional 300 mm for every further 250 seats. The minimum working space of 900 mm is recommended and the floor raised 150 mm. A hand basin is required with cold water if protected food is served and both hot and cold water if unprotected food or drinks are served. Ventilation will be required for certain foods.

Roll up or removable security grilles to protect merchandise should be available for simple installations when the kiosk is unattended.

STOCK ROOM

It is necessary to provide a secure store to accommodate the stock of confectionery and cigarettes. The stock room should be located as near to the sales kiosk as possible, and also provide easy access for deliveries from the street. It should be possible to maintain a cool temperature and the space should allow for circulation and stocktaking. The quantity of shelving should be proportional to the size of the cinema with approximately 12 m run of shelving for up to 1250 seats and 15 m run for over 1250 seats.

Natural ventilation should be provided if possible, otherwise mechanical ventilation providing 21.23 m³/hr per 4.65 m² of floor area.

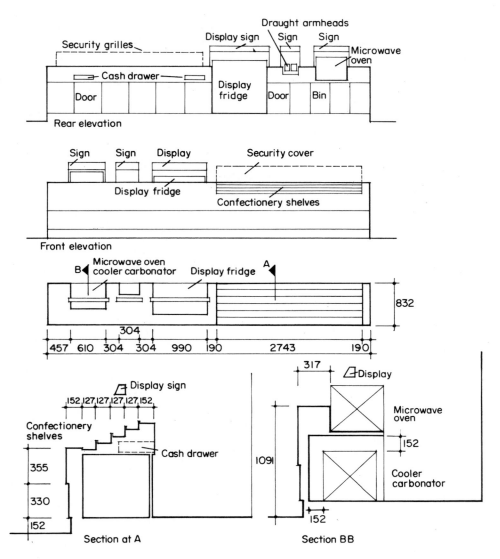

Fig. 4.15   Example of sales kiosk

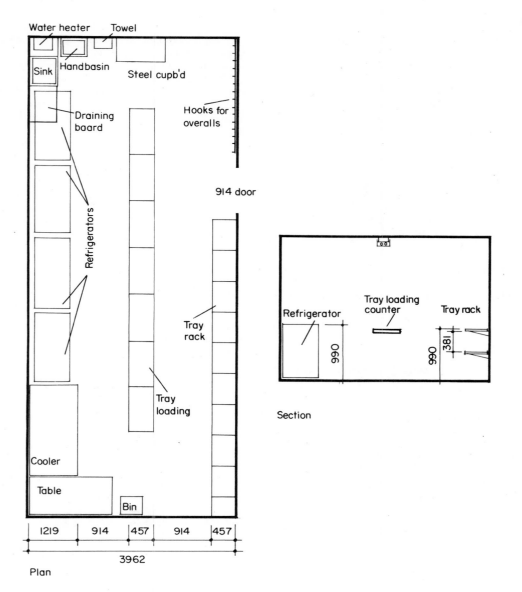

Fig. 4.16   Example of refrigerator room

REFRIGERATOR ROOM (See Fig 4.16)

Items for sale from trays in the auditorium must be securely stored and space should be provided for loading and returning trays and receiving cash from auditoria sales staff. Refrigerated storage is required for ice-cream and soft drinks. Other items should be stored separately in appropriate containers.

The refrigerators are approximately 1.370 m × 0.750 m × 1 m and the coolers are 1.829 m × 0.914 m × 0.610 m. The space includes coat hooks, handbasin and mirror.

The refrigerator room (Fig. 4.16) should be as near the auditorium as possible with reasonable access for street deliveries. The number of refrigerators and coolers could be:

Seats	Refrigerator	Coolers
0–250	1	1
251–500	2	1
501–750	3	1
751–1250	4	2
1251–2500	5	3

The room should be adequately ventilated providing eight air changes per hour. Hot and cold water supply should be provided for equipment, handbasin and sink. The door and door furniture must be arranged in a way that is suitable for a sales tray attendant.

REFUSE ROOM

The refuse room has to accommodate waste prior to collection. This should be located for easy access from the street preferably as an extended screened area. For internal refuse rooms ventilation should be 21.33 m³/hr per 465 m² of floor area, and the wall and floor surface should be washable.

CLEANERS' ROOM

A cleaners' room will require a sink, draining board, hot and cold water, hooks for overalls and space for cleaning materials and equipment. A 500-seat cinema would require three vacuum cleaners. The room should be separately ventilated and should comply with fire standards.

LICENSED BAR (See Fig 4.17)

The details of bar design (see Fig 4.17) are covered in detail in section 5. However, in cinemas, licensed bars are becoming more popular in all types of cinema.

The bar should be located with access to the main foyer, and the layout should permit the speedy service of drinks during short intermissions. The sales area should be protected with a lockable grille or screen when not in use. The layout of this area will require the approval of the appropriate liquor licensing Authority.

Stock room. Immediately adjoining the licensed bar there should be a stock room or area, with adequate security to stock spirits, beer and ancillaries together with empty bottles. Ventilation should be natural or mechanical providing 21.23 m³/hr per 4.65 m² of floor area. Space should be provided for coolers and pumps for conveying beer to the counter fitments.

Bar wash-up. Wash up facilities should also be immediately adjoining or in the licensed bar, for attending to glassware. The area requires services for sink, and glass washing machine and hand basin.

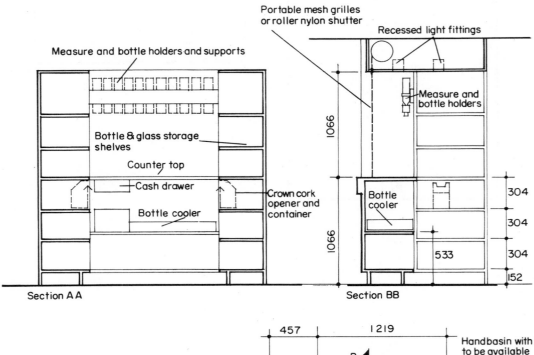

Fig. 4.17   Example of licensed bar

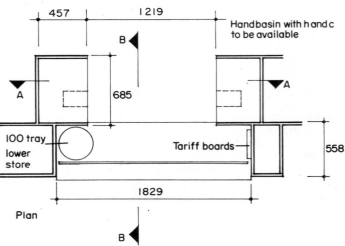

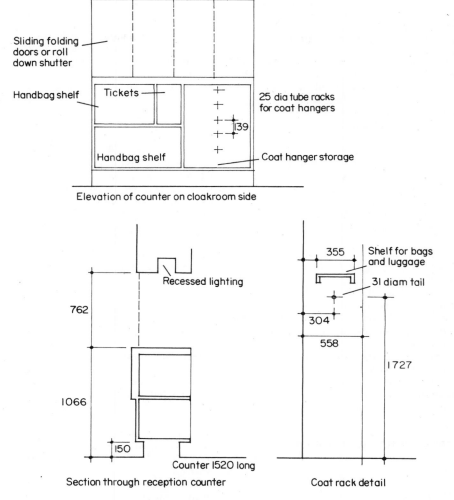

Fig. 4.18 Example of cloakroom reception counter and coat rack

CLOAKROOM (See Fig 4.18)

This should accommodate hats, coats, umbrellas and luggage securely, and should be accessible from the foyer. The coat rack should be suspended to maintain a clear floor space. The front of the reception counter should have sliding folding doors or a roller grille so that the area can be closed off when not in use (see Fig 4.18).

LAVATORIES

All public toilets should be related directly to the main circulation routes, preferably to auditorium entrance points. There can be loss of control of access to the auditorium if lavatories are located via exit routes. For standard cinemas with a continuous programme and a range of seat prices, it is important to relate lavatories to the auditorium rather than the foyer.

In Super Cinemas, where separate hard ticket performances are normal, lavatories can serve both auditorium and foyer without creating a security risk. In cinemas seating more than 750 it is better to provide separate lavatories to serve the front and back of the auditorium.

The following points should be noted:

1. The primary Ladies toilet should have a powder room or area.
2. Lavatories close to the auditorium must be well sound insulated.
3. Door closers, rubber door stops, quiet operating cisterns and fitting and sound absorbent surfaces should be considered to reduce noise.
4. Clean design, durable materials for easy cleaning, light and cheerful finishes and concealed fittings, can do much to reduce vandalism.
5. Ventilation should be not less than eight air changes per hour if mechanical extraction. Natural ventilation should be provided by opening not less than 1/20 of the total floor area. Additional provision should be made if smoking is not permitted in the auditorium, a practice common in Europe. As a fire precaution, the GLC require a fire-proof shutter to close off cloakroom accommodation if there is no full-time attendant.

SIGNS

A co-ordinating element of design and should give a clear, correct and logical sequence to selling, information, and traffic flow. The height of the letters for exit signs should accord with either BS 2560 (for internally illuminated signs) which includes directional arrows, or BS 4218 (for self-powered signs). The height of the letters is 112.5 mm when the viewing distance does not exceed 21.3 m and 225 mm in excess of this distance. BS 4218 provides only for 225 mm letters.

FIRE HOSES AND EXTINGUISHERS

Allowance should be made for adequate recesses for fire hoses and extinguishers. This equipment should be visible without being an intrusion on the design.

EXTERNAL DISPLAY

External display will include illuminated sign, a company symbol and readograph giving film titles at a scale relative to the siting of the cinema. In relation to pavement traffic and the entrance foyer, there will be display panels, programme boards and poster units.

Most cinema companies have a distinct identity conveyed in their advertising format, but it is essential that the display is designed as an integral part of the external appearance of the building. There should be a stock room available for all display equipment, and maintenance equipment.

SCREEN AND ANCILLARY EQUIPMENT

SCREEN TYPE

For 8 mm and 16 mm films a flat high gain screen aluminised silver, perlux or glass beaded) with an aspect ratio of 1:1.375. When larger screens are used for 35 mm and 70 mm certain factors must be taken into account. As the distance from the lens to the outer edge of the screen will be greater than the distance to the centre of the screen, to obtain uniform focus it is necessary to curve a larger screen to keep the screen surface reasonably equidistant from the centre of the lens. This curve is formed only in one plane for practical reasons. It also is necessary to curve the screen to provide a more uniform distribution of increased luminance that can be provided by new screen materials.

Screens are normally placed on the centre line of the auditorium, and except for deeply curved screens may be tilted from the vertical plane. The amount of tilt must be related to the location of the projector, type of auditorium and system of projection, see Fig 4.20.

MASKING

Adjustable masking is provided to contain the picture projected on to the screen, and to obtain the maximum apparent brightness. Masking is provided by black wool serge carried on rails to permit adjustment vertically and horizontally.

SPEAKERS

In commercial cinemas, a clear space of approximately 1.3 m should be allowed for the speakers to be situated between the screen and the structural wall.

DEMOUNTABLE AND REMOVABLE SCREENS

Where auditoria are planned for both cinema and stage performances other factors must be taken into account. A flat screen can be housed in a roller box at floor or ceiling level. In this case, the width of the proscenium opening would limit the screen width. However, screens are better retained stretched on a frame and lifted vertically or moved to the back of the stage.

Curved screens accommodated behind the proscenium are more difficult to move away and should be lifted vertically or rolled to the side or back of the stage.

SUPPORTING STRUCTURE

Screens are mostly constructed from fire resistant material stretched into position by cord lacing to hooks on a special frame. This frame can be of steel or aluminium lattice construction, either free standing or supported on the rear wall or ceiling and floor.

Screen frames are 450 mm to 900 mm larger overall than the maximum picture size to allow for fitting eyelets, localised rucking and lacing. Provision should be made in planning the auditorium for the transport of and replacement of a screen.

The screen is contained in a timber box approx. 300 mm longer than the height of the screen and up to 900 mm square. This is necessary as screens cannot be folded.

CURTAINS

Curtains can be provided to protect the screen and to provide a visual effect at intervals. Screen curtains are suspended on rails which can be secured to the screen frame. Curtains are usually drawn to each side of the screen and allowance must be made for curtains to overlap at the centre when closed and to hang at each side when open.

If there is not enough space at the sides for storing curtains, they can be raised vertically. A storage space 600 mm deep is required for curtains with up to a 7.9 m drop. A pelmet or valence can be used to hide the curtain track.

If decorative lighting is used to illuminate the curtains, spotlights can be accommodated in a recess at ceiling level. If there is a balcony in the auditorium, such lighting could be arranged along the front of the balcony. Alternatively, where there is adequate space between the screen and the front row of seats decorative lighting can be recessed into the floor.

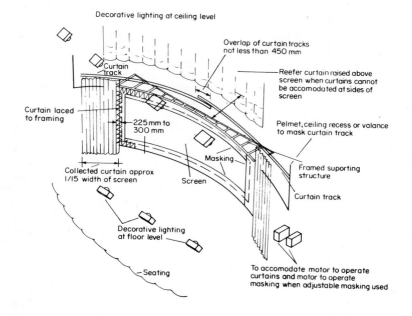

Decorative lighting at ceiling level

Overlap of curtain tracks not less than 450 mm

Reefer curtain raised above screen when curtains cannot be accomodated at sides of screen

Curtain track

Curtain laced to framing

225 mm to 300 mm

Pelmet, ceiling recess or valance to mask curtain track

Masking

Framed suporting structure

Screen

Curtain track

Collected curtain approx 1/15 width of screen

Decorative lighting at floor level

To accomodate motor to operate curtains and motor to operate masking when adjustable masking used

Seating

Fig. 4.19   Curved screen layout with curtains

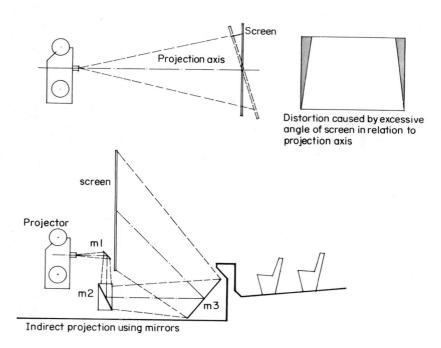

Screen

Projection axis

Distortion caused by excessive angle of screen in relation to projection axis

screen

Projector

m1

m2

m3

Indirect projection using mirrors

Fig. 4.20   Siting of screens

PROJECTION SUITES

A projection suite forms the operational core of a cinema. It contains not only the projection and sound equipment but includes other apparatus for operating the curtains and variable masking, house lights, interval music and public address systems. During the past decade, the manual operation technique of many cinemas has been replaced by automatic control. In recent years automation has been introduced. Current trends in modern equipment tend towards lighter construction and obsolescence, compared with the earlier equipment which were much more solidly built. Flexibility within the projection room should be provided for the inevitable changes in equipment and layout.

A projection suite may consist of the following: projection rooms, rewinding room, dimmer and switch room, workshop and store, remote control room and rest room and toilet for the projection staff. In multiple cinema complexes, whenever practicable, a single projection suite can be centrally located to serve all the auditoria. Such examples usually utilise both direct and indirect projection systems.

PROJECTION BOOTH OF DRIVE-IN CINEMA (See Fig 4.24)

Projection rooms (Fig 4.21) are statutorily required for the projection of 35 mm and 70 mm films in premises licensed for cinematograph exhibitions. 16 mm projectors are not generally used in commercial cinemas, but when they are, and if the light source is not an enclosed incandescent lamp, they have also to be located in projection rooms.

With manual operation, a projectionist's duties comprises controlling the exhibition of films (which includes ensuring that the image is accurately focused, regulating the sound reproduction and adjusting the variable masking when different aspect ratios are used), playing non-synchronous music during the intervals and controlling the curtains and house lights. Additionally, he has to rewind and relace films as well as taking charge of all the technical equipment, including undertaking any minor repairs which may become necessary from time to time.

The majority of the tasks which the projectionist has to perform such as opening the curtains and dimming the house lights, operating the screen masking, changing over from one projector to the next, selecting the interval music, etc are largely of a repetitive nature, and therefore lend themselves ideally to the process of automation. With the larger spool capacities presently available and the existence of a xenon arc lamp which practically requires no attention, automation will undoubtedly grow increasingly popular, and indeed has been already adopted by the major exhibitors. One result of this current trend is that it is now possible for some film programmes to be run entirely on one projector (instead of the two previously needed). Indirectly this may account for the present tendency to use a centrally located projection suite in the case of multi-cinema complexes and conversions.

SIZE

The Cinematograph (Safety) Regulations 1955 stipulates that 'projection rooms shall be large enough to enable the operators to work freely at the film projectors and any other equipment therein'. Nowadays, the size of the room obviously varies with the number of auditoria it has to serve, and hence the amount of equipment which will be used.

In a projection room serving one auditorium, using minimal equipment, a convenient size is 3.9×4.0 m. When an effects lantern and spotlight are added as part of the equipment, the minimum size should be increased to 3.9×5.5 m. Projection room sizes of modern commercial cinemas serving a single auditorium are usually 4.6×7.3 m. The floor to ceiling height should not be less than 2.5 m.

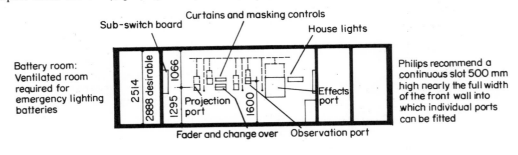

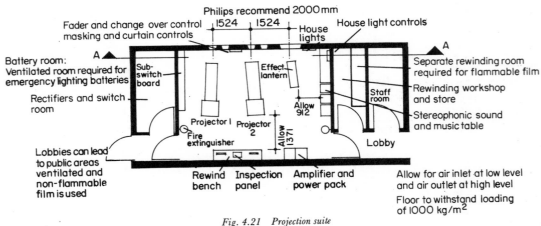

Fig. 4.21   Projection suite

EQUIPMENT

In commercial cinemas, the basic equipment for manually operated projection rooms consists of at least two projectors, sound amplifier racks, curtain and masking control, lighting dimmer control, switchboard, rectifiers, rewind bench, effects lantern, spotlights and non-synchronous music desk. Within the projection suite, some of these items may be in separate rooms.

For automatically controlled projection rooms or cinemations, there will be in addition to the above items, a console which programmes the film performance.

The equipment available that permits a complete programme to be fed through one projector without interruption requires space adjacent to the projector.

The ST200 new rewind system provides a full programme of up to four hours without changeover or rewinding. The system can be used with any projector currently in service. The non-rewind unit, if fitted with three film discs of up to 132 cm dia, allows for a new programme to be made up whilst projecting. The maximum height of the equipment is 2.25 m. The equipment is complete with motorised winder for making up and breaking down the programmes and a separate control unit (see Fig. 4.22). Complete automation can be achieved with the addition of the ST450 matrix programmer.

Westrex 5035 Film Carrier Assembly designed for a complete film programme giving a film capacity of 2 × 13,500 ft. Normally situated at the rear of the projector assembly or alongside if space is limited (on the non-operating side). The assembly consists of a motor cabinet mounted on a turntable, with control panel and for reels (see Fig 4.23).

LAYOUT OF EQUIPMENT

All the equipment and controls in the projection room should be located in such a way that they provide for easy accessibility with the least physical effort. A typical layout is shown bility with the least physical effort (see Fig. 4.21).

Projectors are normally spaced 1.5 m apart, and installed equidistant from the centre line of the auditorium. To enable projectionists to work easily at the projectors, a minimum clear space of 760 mm must be left at the sides and back. The projectors must also be accessible from the front, so the bases of the projectors should be positioned 500 mm from the front wall.

It should be noted that the effects lantern, which may also serve as a spotlight, is usually located on the right of the projectors, next to the non-synchronous music table and lighting dimmer controls. These items are used simultaneously in conjunction with an observation port. Duplicate controls for curtains, variable masking, and sound fader are usually mounted on the front wall on the right of each projector.

PORTS

The normal minimum provision is one projection port for each projector, one observation port for each projector, and a port and observation panel or large port for the effects lantern. Both projection and lantern ports are glazed with optical quality glass, while observation ports are fitted with plate glass. To simplify cleaning, they are usually mounted on lift out metal frames.

Metal shutters to cover the projection room side of all the ports are no longer required when only safety film is used. Shutters must be provided, however, when inflammable film is used. These shutters are made from heavy gauge sheet (3 mm steel plate) in guides. Statutorily, the shutters must be capable of being released from both within the projection room as well as from outside.

AMPLIFIER RACKS

The location of amplifier racks is not so critical, but the controls and changeover switches must be fitted on each side of the projection ports except when remote control is used (see 'Remote control room' below). The racks are usually placed against the side or back walls of the projection room.

Some types require access to wiring for maintenance purposes so an allowance of 500 mm for moving them forward has to be provided. In the projection room layout given above, the three amplifiers are for stereophonic sound reproduction; monophonic sound requires only one amplifier and a power pack.

PROJECTOR POWER SUPPLY

For 35 mm projectors using carbon arc lamps up to 75 A, a single phase supply is adequate; but above this three phase supply is required. Three phase supply is also necessary for 70 mm projectors. For xenon arcs which operate at not more than 80 A, a single-phase supply is required, although 3-phase supply to the rectifiers is sometimes required.

WATER SUPPLY

All 35 mm and 70 mm projectors having carbon arc lamps working above 75 A have to be water cooled. A 12 mm diam. supply pipe and 18 mm or 25 mm drainage pipe is sufficient for this purpose.

Some local authorities will not permit direct connection with the mains supply, and in these circumstances, a closed circuit system utilising a circulating pump will have to be employed. A tank having a capacity of up to 150 gal (472 litres) is necessary, with the pump working at 30 lb/sq. in. (2 kg/cm^2). Additionally, it is also usual to provide a stand-by pump, and in both cases water is circulated at the rate of between 4 to 9 litres/min.

LIGHTING, HEATING AND VENTILATION

Lighting has to be carefully arranged so that no unnecessary light is spilled onto the screen via the projection ports. Bracket fittings mounted on the front wall to the right of each projector or narrow beam spotlights on adjustable arms suspended from the ceiling are usually recommended.

When safety film is used and stored overnight, a minimum temperature of 7°C is required; tubular electric heaters worked by thermostat switches are normally used. The recommended working temperature of projection rooms is 18°C.

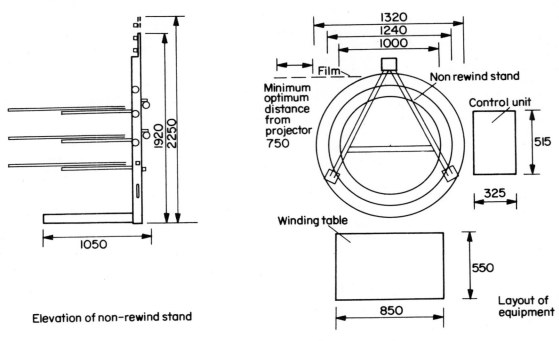

Fig. 4.22   ST200 non-rewind installation

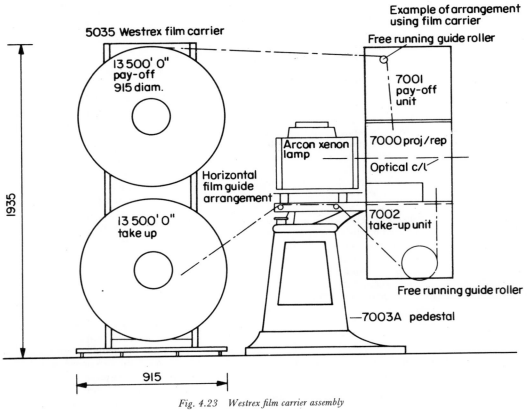

Fig. 4.23   Westrex film carrier assembly

A natural or mechanical ventilation system separate from the one used to serve the rest of the cinema must be provided for the projection suite. For carbon arc lamps, the ventilation required must be of adequate volume and low velocity to prevent uneven burning and thus undesirable changes in light intensity during projection. The ventilation system must include both inlet and outlet registers. The size of registers and any ductwork necessary can be based on a minimum of 0.18 m² effective (clear) area per projector installed.

When carbon arcs or xenon arc lamps are used for projectors and effects lanterns, additional outlet ventilation is required. This may connect directly with the open air by ductwork, using an extract fan where necessary. The ductwork must be fitted with access panels to enable it to be cleaned along its length. Xenon arcs produce ozone which is a toxic gas. The concentration in any area where people work should not exceed 0.01/1 000 000 of atmosphere. Whilst ventilation is required for the lamp house, a rapid flow of cold air should be avoided. Up to 2.2 kW capacity ozone-free xenon lamps are available which do not require ventilation ducting.

FIRE FIGHTING EQUIPMENT

When safety film is used the Home Office recommendation for the provision of fire fighting equipment in projection rooms is two 2 gal. (9 litre) soda-acid or water-gas expelled extinguishers. For the use of inflammable film, an asbestos blanket must be provided.

PROJECTION BOOTH OF DRIVE-IN CINEMA

In a typical single drive-in cinema, the projection booth (Fig 4.24) is normally located at a distance of between 3 to 4 screen widths away from the screen. The booth is usually supported on slender columns to allow cars to be positioned behind without obstructing the view of the screen.

Because of the considerably larger screen area, sometimes exceeding 930 m², very powerful arc lamps are employed, but despite this, the screen luminance provided is generally less that of an indoor cinema. In a dual drive-in, a common concession building can serve both audiences in terms of projection facilities and other amenities (Fig 4.24).

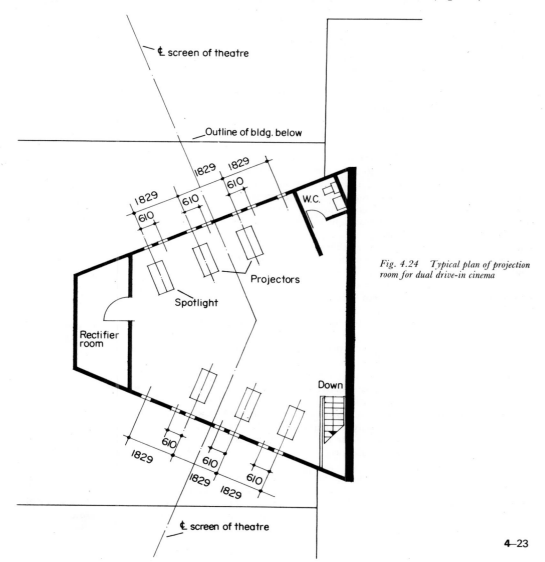

Fig. 4.24 Typical plan of projection room for dual drive-in cinema

DATA

In order to appreciate basic projection equipment, it is necessary to outline existing film gauges, light sources and sound reproduction.

FILM GAUGES

Although in the 80 years of cinematography many film gauges have been developed, only four have become generally accepted. These are 8 mm, 16 mm, 35 mm and 70 mm.

8 mm film. This is the smallest of the narrow gauge films, and is used mainly for commercial and amateur uses. There are three types.

(a) Standard 8 with double perforations which is silent.
(b) Standard 8 with single perforations which may incorporate a sound track.
(c) Super 8 with double perforations which may include a sound track.

Most 8 mm projectors are dual gauge or dual format machines. This permits the above three types of 8 mm film to be shown generally. The projectors are small, portable and only require normal electricity supply. The light source usually consists of low-wattage filament lamps. The projectors are capable of producing a satisfactory screen picture of up to 690 × 910 mm. Small self contained projectors incorporating a rear projection screen are also available for small audiences. The planning implications of this gauge and equipment are relatively simple.

16 mm film. This is the most commonly used of the narrow film gauges. It is extensively used for commercial, educational, scientific, industrial and television work, although rarely in the commercial cinema. Either a magnetic or optical sound track can be incorporated. Projectors are available using different classes of light source—an incandescent lamp (or halogen-tungsten lamp) or alternatively carbon arc, xenon arc, or pulsed discharge lamp. A projector using an incandescent lamp is usually compact and portable. The other projectors tend to be built to the same technical standards as 35 mm projectors.

The largest size of incandescent lamp permits a screen size up to 1.98 × 2.74 m and about 20% larger for halogen-tungsten. In premises licensed for cinematograph exhibitions, 16 mm projectors utilising incandescent lamps may be set up in the auditorium only provided that certain conditions are fulfilled. These include the condition that the projector is surrounded by a clear space at least 910 mm wide, defined by a barrier or other effective means to prevent the entry of unauthorised persons.

When 16 mm films are shown on a large screen, projectors using the more powerful light sources are used, and it would be installed in a projection room. The requirements for this would be similar to those for 35 mm projectors.

35 mm film. This is the standard gauge for all forms of professional cinematographic work, and is the gauge most widely used for the commercial cinema. On premises licensed for cinematograph exhibitions all 35 mm projectors must be located within a projection room and space should be allowed for sound and ancillary equipment. Some projectors are fitted with incandescent lamps and are portable. These are used in such situations as lecture theatres, and can utilise screens of up to 4.12 × 5.64 m.

The standard equipment for commercial cinemas consists of 35 mm projectors with carbon arc, xenon arc, or (formerly) pulsed discharge light sources. Spool capacities have been limited to 2000′, which required a changeover from one projector to another every twenty minutes. This affects the size and layout of projection rooms. Nowadays, projectors with handling spool capacities of 2000′ and 6000′ are available. The shift towards automation in projection rooms encourages the tendency towards a one projector arrangement to handle a complete film programme. In the circumstances, a carbon arc light formerly preferred is being replaced by the xenon arc which can operate continuously.

Some forms of 35 mm projectors are available in the 'dual-gauge' format, which allows both 35 mm and 70 mm film to be shown.

70 mm film. To date, 70 mm is the largest gauge of film used in the commercial cinema. The release prints have two rows of perforations with very wide margins to allow for six track stereophonic sound along both edges of the film. 70 mm film presentations, such as Todd AO, are shown on extremely large and deeply curved screens. Dimension 150 (D150) is another 70 mm system which can be shown on an even larger screen. Special projectors were originally required but it is possible to obtain projectors that show both 35 mm and 70 mm films. The high production costs are making 70 mm currently uneconomic.

LIGHT SOURCES

The most common sources of illumination used in connection with cinematograph projectors are: incandescent lamps, halogen-tungsten carbon arc, xenon arc and formerly pulsed discharge lamps. Each type has its own advantages and disadvantages as well as separate requirements for ventilation.

Incandescent lamps. The advantage of an incandescent filament lamp is its simplicity. It is used in conjunction with all 8 mm projectors, most 16 mm projectors and some 35 mm projectors. It provides the least efficient source of light and the low light output enables screen widths of only up to 2.7 m for 16 mm and 5.64 m for 35 mm films to be obtained. It is less suitable for colour projection.

Carbon arc lamps. The carbon arc lamp is the most common source of illumination for film projection. A wide selection of carbons are available and screen sizes of up to 45.7 m wide can be satisfactorily illuminated. Different sizes or combinations of carbons can be used in one lamp to provide the same screen luminance when projecting either 70 mm or 35 mm films. This form of lighting requires ventilation ducts to the open air to dispel the products of combustion, and the high power carbon arc systems need water cooling. One pair of carbons is burned within 20 or 60 minutes according to the electric power in circuit.

Xenon arc lamp. With the shift towards automation in most cinemas nowadays, many projectors now utilise the xenon arc lamp which operate continuously when switched on. In the xenon lamp, the arc is struck between tungsten electrodes in an atmosphere of xenon gas at a pressure of several atmospheres. These arcs are made in only five sizes ranging from 450 W to 5000 W, and cannot be interchanged in any one lamp housing. The larger sizes provide a screen centre luminance of 8 ft.-1 to 10 ft.-1 (85.6 col/m^2 to 107 col/m^2) on a screen 15.24 m wide. The xenon arc, requires no attention (other than replacement), and is thus easily automatically controlled. Like the carbon arc lamp, some attention must be given to ventilation and it is usually desirable to connect the lamphouses with the open air by means of an extract duct (ozone free xenon lamps are available up to 2.2 kW) because of the ozone produced when the arcs ionise the surrounding atmosphere.

Pulsed discharge lamp. In a pulsed discharge lamp, two electrodes are enclosed in a vacuum containing a small amount of mercury vapour. Electricity is supplied intermittently to the electrodes, and the arcing is timed to coincide with the periods when the film is not moving. These lamps are used only in specially designed projectors. Pulsed discharge lamps have been available in two sizes—800 W and 1000 W, with the latter capable of illuminating screens up to 9.14 m wide. Double lamp projectors have also been made, which gives 60–70 per cent more light and can illuminate adequately screens up to 12.19 m wide.

Pulsed discharge lamps can be adapted to automatic control, and do not require special ventilation or skilled attention. Usually when a lamp fails it is instantly and automatically replaced. They require a continuous water supply and drainage at a rate of 1–1½ gal/min (4–7 litres/min), which is similiar to that required by other high powered light sources.

SOUND REPRODUCTION

The aural component of a cinematograph presentation is contained in the release print on one or both edges of the film either in the form of an optical (photographic) or magnetic sound track. Most projectors, except the simplest equipment in the narrow gauge range, have integrated sound systems built into them. The optical sound track is the most widely used method of sound reproduction in the commercial cinema. However, increasing interest in high-fidelity sound systems has highlighted the limited resolution which can be obtained by photographic means.

In optical sound reproduction, photographic sound records appear as variations in density or width in the sensitive emulsion layer along the length of the film next to the picture area. These variations are made to modulate the illumination falling upon a photocell, and the resultant variations in electrical energy are amplified to drive the loudspeakers. In magnetic recording, the variations in magnetisation contained in the track produce variations in current (as the magnetic record passes across a narrow gap in the pole piece structure of the soundhead). These signals are (similarly) amplified to drive the loudspeakers.

When standard 35 mm films are projected, a single sound track (whether optical or magnetic) is usually used. 35 mm film enables up to four magnetic tracks to be produced, and these are channelled to three loudspeaker systems behind the screen as well as several surround speakers located in the ceiling or walls of the auditorium.

Some of the large film formats, however, such as Cinerama and Todd-AO employ stereophonic sound. Although in the past multi-track sound has been produced optically, nowadays currently they are all done by magnetic recording because of the sound quality obtainable. On 70 mm film, six track stereophonic reproduction can be obtained; these are fed to five loudspeaker systems behind the screen and surround speakers in the auditorium.

Some sound systems come as separate reproducers which are synchronised with the projectors; these are known as magnetic 'dual systems' and are capable of having a greater number of stereophonic sound tracks than the optimum available with either 35 mm or 70 mm film. An example of the magnetic 'dual system' is the original cinema presentation, which in addition to the three synchronised projectors, had 8 stereophonic sound tracks on a 35 mm strip played by 8 separate reproducers.

PROJECTION SYSTEMS

The three methods presently used for projection are direct, indirect and back projection. In order to achieve an acceptable standard of presentation, the technicalities of projecting the picture on to the screen have strict planning implications.

Direct projection is the most common method in use. Indirect projection (using mirrors) and back projection are employed usually when either direct projection proves impracticable (such as may be the case in a cinema conversion) or where the location of the projection room will not permit direct projection (as in a multiple cinema complex, using a centrally located projection room).

Standard method. In direct projection, an enclosed light source emits light rays through the film image located at the projector gate, and is focused by a lens on to a screen. The quality of the image thus projected, apart from its intrinsic properties, depends upon accurate focusing, intensity and colour of the light source, characteristics of the screen surface and contrast with any other illumination present.

Indirect (mirror) projection. Much of the output of cinema building in Britain today involves the conversion of the larger cinemas into several smaller ones. Although generally direct projection methods are to be preferred, in some of these conversions, structural restrictions, such as a low ceiling height, may prevent the use of the direct method.

Equally, economic considerations may favour the indirect method. When there are two or three auditoria within a cinema complex it is obviously logical to try to achieve as little duplication as possible. Recent developments in projection technology have made equipment more compact, and with the introduction of the one projector system made possible by the availability of much larger film spools, it is now not uncommon to find cinemas having common projection rooms serving multiple auditoria. However, certain compromises have been reached. These normally entail the inclusion of metal shutters to projection room ports even though they are not required when only safety film is used. Essentially, the practice of using a common projection room has contributed towards the more general usage of the indirect projection method, and a typical example is shown in Fig. 4.20.

Rear projection. Like indirect projection, back projection is used in cases of expediency when direct projection proves impracticable. It is by far the least common method adopted in the commercial cinema, but when used it is associated with flat screens for standard aspect ratios, and not for widescreen. Direct back projection involves a lateral reversal of the screen picture, except when specially adapted projectors and sound heads are employed. Consequently, whenever it is used, it is considered advisable and economic to introduce mirrors (Fig. 4.20).

THE SCREEN

Location and size. The size, angle and plan profile of the screen are relevant to the projection system and the seating layout. The ratio of height to width (h:w) of the projected image on the screen is called the aspect ratio. The standard aspect ratio is 1:1.375 and is based on the Academy frame on cinematograph film which was adopted as a standard in the early days of the cinema. The image on the screen therefore represents a proportional enlargement of the film frame, and this 3:4 format is usually shown on flat screens. Curved screens are often used nowadays in the larger commercial cinemas and they are associated with the greater magnification of the widescreen film systems. In every auditorium of conventional shape, the axis of the projector light beam should be coincident with the centre line of the auditorium and normal to the screen surface. Where two projectors are used, they should be positioned equidistant from the centre line of the auditorium and as near to it as working space will allow. Where there are three projectors, the optical axis of the central projector should be on the centre line, and the other two as near as practical to it, one on each side.

In the vertical plane, ideally the optical axis of the projectors should be horizontal and coincident with the centre of the screen. In practice, this situation may not be always easy to attain, so the projector axis might be placed at an angle to the horizontal. This angle is known as the projector rake or angle of rake. If the screen is vertical the projected image is distorted as shown in Fig 4.20.

Similar deformations are produced when the projector axis is tilted upwards or set off-centre from the screen. Within specific limits these distortions are unimportant, and is usually corrected by shaping the aperture plates, and by the presence of the black screen masking along the picture edges. In general, the limits of deviation for flat screen projection can be stipulated thus:

α downward = maximum 12°
α upward = maximum 5°

where α is the angle of rake.

It is of course possible to limit these distortions by tilting the screen backwards from the vertical so that it again becomes at right angles to the projector axis. When this is done care has to be taken to ensure that the spectators in the front row do not see the picture at too acute an angle. The screen should therefore not be tilted to an angle of more than $\frac{1}{3}$α.

Although flat screen projection using the standard aspect ratio is still commonly used in the smaller commercial cinemas and elsewhere, with greatly improved film technology, the larger commercial cinemas have mainly resorted to applying greater magnification factors in film projection, and thus utilising much bigger screens. This has brought about the widescreen projection systems. These and other types of projection systems which are used are as follows.

WIDESCREEN

The principal objective of the widescreen process is to achieve a greater sense of involvement in the film. Normally human vision encompasses a greater field of view laterally than vertically. Increased magnification made possible by new lenses was directed towards giving greater picture width than height. The term 'widescreen' describes a variety of forms of film presentations which have aspect ratios greater than the standard 3:4 format. Widescreen processes may further be technically subdivided into two main groups—systems using anamorphic lenses and systems using normal projection lenses. In the first system, the image on the film is optically compressed (squeezed) in the horizontal sense by means of a cylindrical anamorphic lens during photography, and is later expanded to the right proportions during projection by means of a similar lens which gives greater magnification laterally than vertically. The second system uses normal projection lenses, but the projector aperture is masked to give the required aspect ratio. Since the image on the film is not optically compressed, as in the first system, copies of this type are usually referred to as flat prints.

Since 1950, aspect ratios of between 1:1.65 and 1:1.85 have been used for many widescreen processes, even though BS 2784:1956 'Aspect ratios for 35 mm motion picture films' has stipulated 1:1.75 as an optimum for such presentations. Whatever proportion is used for a specific auditorium largely depends upon structural arrangements and the kind of film to be shown (e.g. with or without subtitles).

CINEMASCOPE

When Cinemascope was first introduced it had an aspect ratio of 1:2.55 with sound reproduced stereophonically from four magnetic sound-tracks. The prints with stereophonic sound, however, were not entirely accepted by exhibitors, and so an optical sound track was introduced. Eventually an aspect ratio of 1:2.35 was adopted with release prints having only a single optical sound-track.

70 MM SYSTEMS

Todd AO System. The Todd-AO system, uses 65 mm film in the camera and 70 mm prints for projection. It incorporates six track stereophonic sound, and has a frame area equal to four times the 35 mm frame. The aspect ratio employed is 1:2.2.

In existing cinemas which are being adapted, the screen height for 70 mm film should not be less than 20% greater than screens for widescreen or Cinemascope.

D150 System. Dimension 150 (D 150) uses the same aspect ratio as Todd-AO, but is capable of increasing the screen surface laterally by another 10% due to its deeper curvature.

IMAX

Imax is a recent invention which represents an even more spectacular use of 70 mm film. It is not only a sophisticated projection system but equally a unique film format. Developed by Multiscreen Corporation of Canada and first displayed at Expo 70 in Osaka, it is now permanently installed in the Cinesphere at Ontario Place, Toronto's new lakeside cultural and entertainment complex. Using an aspect ratio of 1:1.43, roughly equivalent to the standard 3:4 format, Imax is presented on a huge 24.4 × 18.3 m hemispherical screen. To obtain this extremely large image the projector utilises 70 mm film transported horizontally by a 'rolling loop' and has a 25 kW xenon short arc light source which provides a screen centre luminance of 25 ft.-l.

In every respect technically, Imax is a radically different projection system and film format to conventional forms. Taking advantage of the advanced projection system, the film format was designed to give as flexible a presentation as could possibly be achieved within the layout, and thus each Imax frame is capable of incorporating either nine 35 mm images or three vertical 70 mm images or the full Imax image (photographed with a prototype camera), or any combinations of these, for a new type of multi-image presentation.

CINERAMA

In the original Cinerama presentation introduced in 1952, three separate but synchronised 35 mm projectors were used to project a panoramic picture on to a deeply curved screen which covered an arc of 140°. The eight track stereophonic sound, contained in a separate 35 mm strip synchronised with the projectors, was reproduced over five loudspeakers behind the screen and a further eight surround speakers positioned both at the sides and rear of the auditorium.

The very special nature of this presentation required accuracy in matching the three slightly overlapping images which constituted the panorama, and as a result, Cinerama has now been replaced by a one-projector system which uses 70 mm film to give the required screen area. In consequence, the arc of the screen has been reduced to 125°.

CIRCLORAMA

There are several systems which have attempted to provide a 360° picture which totally surrounds the audience. In 1955, Walt Disney introduced his Circarama system which initially used eleven 16 mm projectors, but later modified to incorporate only nine 35 mm projectors.

The Russians brought out a similar system known as Kinopanorama which had eleven pairs of projectors for presenting a double height picture. Another called Circlorama employing eleven projectors had a brief run in a London Cinema, but was eventually phased out.

AUDITORIUM ACOUSTICS

The acoustic quality of the cinema auditorium is as important as the viewing conditions. The acoustic analysis should be based upon obtaining the clear reception by the audience of the spoken word. The degree to which members of the audience can hear intelligibly will be effected by reverberation in the auditorium and the nature of sound decay. Furthermore, the nature and positioning of speakers involves technicalities beyond the scope of this appraisal and thus the designer would be advised to seek expert advice. However, the effect on basic planning can be stated as follows:

The optimum reverberation time for a cinema, at medium frequency, is indicated in Figs. 4.26 and 4.27 and is related to the volume of the hall and amount of absorption as

$$T = 0.16 \frac{V}{A}.$$

where T = reverberation time;
V = volume of room;
A = total absorption of internal surfaces compared with an open window.

When the reverberation time is shorter, the hall sounds dead. When the reverberation time is long each sound masks the following sound causing loss of clarity. However, as the film

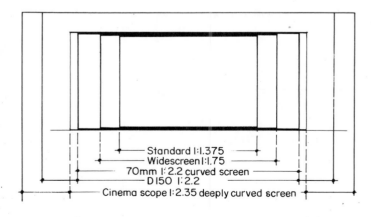

Fig. 4.25 Aspect ratio of projection systems

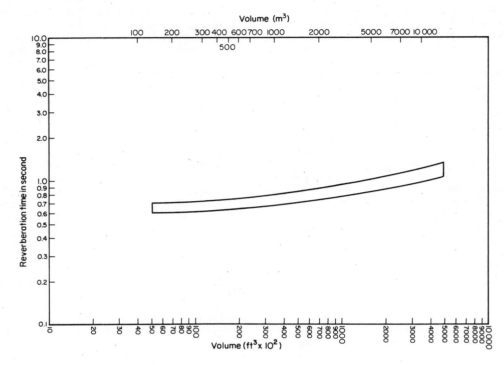

Fig. 4.26   Preferred mid-frequency reverberation times of cinemas
(Sound Research Laboratories Ltd.)

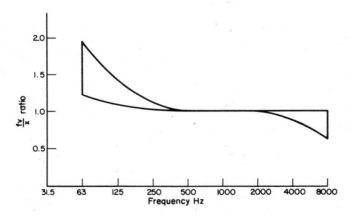

Fig. 4.27   Permissible variation of cinema reverberation times from mid-frequency values
(Sound Research Laboratories Ltd.)

recording has reverberation qualities in it, it is desirable to keep the auditorium reverberation time to practical minimum.

The quality of reverberation is effected by the shape and dimensions of the hall, also the nature and location of absorbent and sound reflective surfaces within the hall. The sound can be reinforced by making the sound pattern directional. In a simple layout, sound should be directed towards the rear of the hall by giving the ceiling and walls the necessary angles to act as reflectors. However, strong reflections or a concentration of reflections caused by a concave surface could produce an echo. Disturbing reflections can be remedied by applying sound absorbing material to the surface concerned.

Each hall has a great number of natural frequencies at which it comes into resonance. For good sound reproduction, the natural frequencies must be distributed over the whole frequency range. This can be achieved by an irregular shape to the hall, or by breaking wall surface without obstructing the pattern of useful sound reflections. Thus diverging side walls are important to the quality of sound reception in a cinema auditorium. Any reflected sound that travels more than 14 m than the direct sound, and is not reduced by at least 15 dB will seriously affect intelligibility; sound reaching the ears 30 ms or more after the direct sound can appear as an echo if it is not adequately reduced.

In planning the amount of absorption it is important to select and position the relevant absorbing material; *either* porous material, which as a rule increases in effect with the frequency, *or* panels, such as plasterboard applied at some distance from the wall, that absorb sound energy through vibration (the system can be made more efficient by damping with a soft material) *or* resonators. The latter provides a void in which sound energy can be absorbed. It is also important to remember that the audience forms a significant part of the total absorption of the hall and the seats should be upholstered to form a substitute for seats not occupied.

Generally, for good sound transmission to the rear of the hall, the ceiling should be acoustically hard whereas the rear walls of the auditorium should be faced with a material with a very high absorption coefficient.

Thus in practise, extreme differences between length and width of auditorium should be avoided. The total length of the auditorium should not exceed 35 m and the total length under a balcony should not exceed $2\frac{1}{2}$ times the floor to ceiling height under the balcony. A volume of 3 to 5 m^3 per person for small halls is a reasonable basis on which to work.

Parallel walls and concave wall faces should be avoided and sound should be directed towards the rear of the auditorium.

Particular attention should be given to sound insulation between auditoria. [56 db] Within each unit footstep noise should be deadened by a resilient floor finish, and the reverberation time should be made independent of the number of people actually in the auditorium by using heavily upholstered seats.

AUDITORIUM LIGHTING

The illumination within the auditorium must not only provide sufficient light for the audience to find their seats during the intervals and decorative lighting to animate the area of curtains when drawn across the screen, but also safety lighting with illuminated signs and cleaners lighting. Decorative lighting will be designed to enhance the auditorium space with special effects, dimmer controlled and in some cases linked to the interval music to provide a mobile lighting effect of changing patterns and colours. Decorative lighting is also used to create a sympathetic spatial effect within the large auditorium space. Managerial lighting (primary maintained lighting) is the lighting in both the auditorium and other parts of the building usually used when the public is present. Where there is inadequate daylight, the building must be illuminated by Managerial lighting and Safety lighting.

Safety lighting, required by law, must make provision for an illumination level at all times that the public is present in the building. Safety lighting must be supplied by a source of electricity independent of the mains, usually by batteries. A lighting level of about 2 lux (2 ft c) would be sufficient.

Cleaners lighting (panic lighting) should provide a high level of illumination for cleaning, and as panic lighting it should be available to be switched on in an emergency.

HEATING AND VENTILATION

The auditorium requires an air temperature of 65°F (18.3°C) and air should be moved at the rate of 1,000 cu ft/hour (28 m^3/hr) per person of which three-quarters should be fresh air from outside where complete air conditioning is not required. For comprehensive air conditioning, the humidity should be 55% in summer and 65% in winter.

STATUTORY REQUIREMENTS

The two statutes relating to cinematograph exhibitions presented in the UK are the Cinematograph Acts of 1909 and 1952. The type of film used during the early days of the cinema was of inflammable cellulose nitrate base, and thus the Act of 1909 was introduced to ensure public safety at cinematograph exhibitions where such films were used. With the introduction of safety film the 1952 Act was passed. This was followed by the Cinematograph (Safety) Regulations 1955, 1958 and 1965. These are arranged in five parts:

Part 1 deals with general requirements in connection with cinematograph exhibitions, and is thus the most relevant section as far as commercial cinemas are concerned.
Part 2 gives additional requirements for exhibitions utilising inflammable films; this mainly concerns archival cinemas or premises used by film societies in which nitrate based films might still be frequently shown.
Parts 3 and 4 apply respectively to premises used occasionally for cinematograph exhibitions and premises used in connection with television presentations.
Part 5 provides miscellaneous information such as definitions and repeals. Licensing authorities are also empowered to issue regulations.

In the Greater London Area, Technical Regulations for places of Public Entertainment are applied in addition to the Home Office Cinematograph (Safety) Regulations, 1955, 1958 and 1965. These regulations are discussed below only in so far as they affect the planning aspects of cinema. It is for the designer to obtain all the necessary information on requirements relevant to the location of the particular project.

EXITS

Regulation 2.(1). The premises shall be provided with an adequate number of exits, so placed and maintained as to afford the public ready and ample means of safe egress.

The minimum number of exits prescribed by statutory regulation for premises built, or substantially altered, after 1 January 1956 are given in Table 4.1.

Table 4.1 NUMBER OF EXITS

No. of Persons	No. of exits
1–60	1
61–600	2
601–1000	3
1001–1400	4
1401–1700	5
1701–2000	6
2001–2250	7
2251–2500	8
2501–2700	9

Although the maximum travel distance from seat to exit and exit widths are not governed statutorily, they are of great importance in the consideration of the safe evacuation of audiences from the auditorium in the event of a fire. Hence there are recommendations affecting these.

Experience has shown that although the structural fire resistance of a cinema building is an important consideration in fire safety, the surface finishes are of great importance. In consequence, the maximum travel distance from seat to exit is related to BS 476: Part 7: 1971 'Fire Tests of Building Materials and Structures: Surface Spread of Flame Test for Materials' which categorises surfaces according to Classes 1–4, with Class 1 having lowest flame spread ranging to Class 4 having rapid flame spread. It is recommended that no cinema wall and ceiling surfaces should fall within Class 4.

In premises permanently used for cinematograph exhibitions, not more than 25% of the wall and ceiling surfaces within the auditorium should fall within Class 3, and not more than 50% in premises occasionally used. The remaining surfaces should be of Class 1 and 2. Exit corridors of less than 12 m in length must have wall and ceiling surfaces not more than 50% of Class 2, and exceeding 12 m in length, only Class 1 surfaces should be used. Neither Class 3 or 4 should be used in exit corridors. If the surface finishes comply with the above, then the maximum travel distance from a seat to the nearest exit door can be stipulated as shown in Table 4.2.

Table 4.2 MAXIMUM DISTANCE TO NEAREST EXIT

Structure	Cinema occupancy only	Multiple or dual occupancy
Wholly fire resistant	30 m	26 m
$\frac{1}{2}$ hr fire resistance	20 m	20 m
Less than $\frac{1}{2}$ hr fire resistance	15 m	12 m

The width of exits can be determined in one or two ways. Some licensing and other authorities provide minimum exit widths in terms of feet and inches, which in general, experience has shown to be adequate. In more recent codes of practice and recommendations, however, a 'unit width of exit' is specified. This is defined as the width required by one person freely to pass through a doorway or down a flight of stairs. Unfortunately, no agreement has been arrived at as to what this 'unit' ought to be, so variations of between 482 mm and 558 mm exist. In the 'Fire Grading of Buildings', the recommendation for the rate of flow in theatres based on a unit width of 535 mm is for 45 persons per minute. In new buildings, however, exit doorways should not be less than 2 units ie 1.066 m, and in existing buildings they should not be less than 965 mm in width.

Table 4.3 UNIT WIDTHS

No of Unit Widths	2	3	4	5	6
Minimum width in new buildings	1·006 m	1·524 m	2·235 m	2·438 m	2·895 m
Minimum width in existing buildings	0·965 m	1·422 m	1·854m	2·286 m	2·667 m

EXITS, STAIRCASES, ETC

The Greater London Council (GLC) standards are as follows:

1. At least two separate means of egress shall be provided from every floor or tier for the accommodation of the public, with independent access to the street.

2. If any floor or tier is divided into two or more parts, exits shall be provided from each part.

3. Any tea room, lounge, restaurant or foyer or part used for public assembly to be provided with exits.

Table 4.4 WIDTHS OF EXITS

Max. No. of persons	Two exits not less than
200	1·066 m
300	1·219 m
400	1·371 m
500	1·524 m
For every additional 250 persons over 500	an aditional exit to be provided not less than 1·524 m

Width of gangways in relation to number of seats

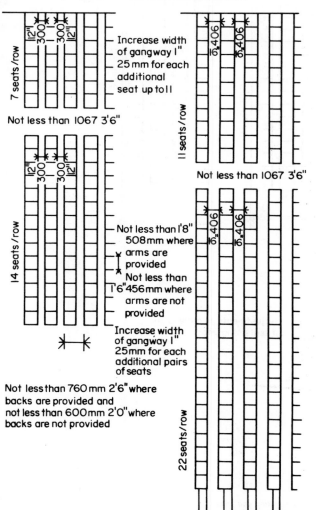

In licensed premises regularly used for closely-seated audiences all seating (except for chairs in boxes or other approved enclosures) shall be firmly fixed to the floor.

End seats of all rows shall be so aligned as to maintain a uniform width of gangway throughout its length.

Longer rows than 22 seats may be permitted subject to such further precautions as the Council may require.

Any stepped side gangway shall be provided with a handrail . . .

Fig. 4.28   GLC regulations for seating and gangways

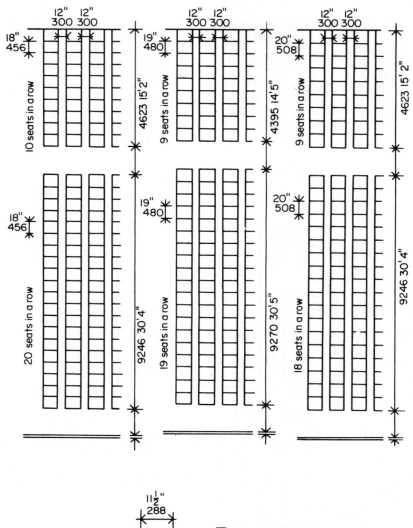

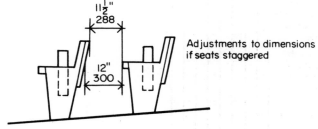

Fig. 4.29 GLC regulations for seating and gangways

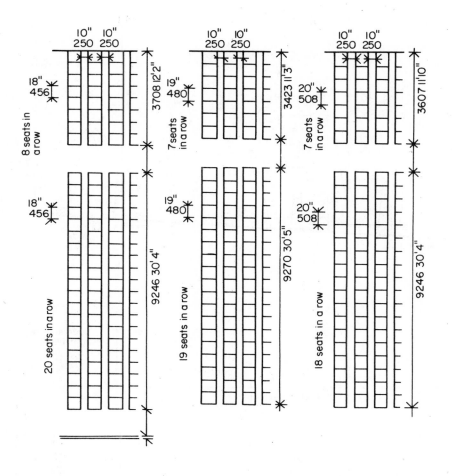

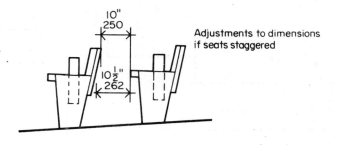

Adjustments to dimensions
if seats staggered

Fig. 4.30 Home office recommendations for places of public entertainment. Seats and gangways: wide spacing

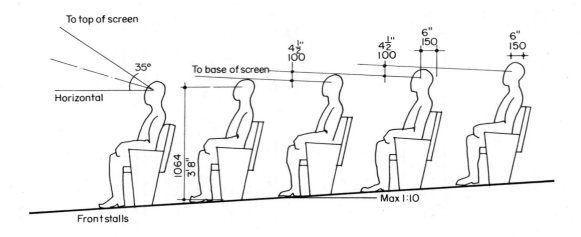

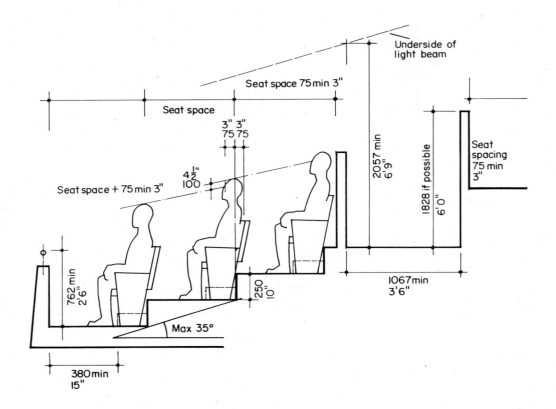

Fig. 4.31   Usual arrangement for seats and gangways

NUMBER AND CLEAR WIDTHS OF EXIT WAYS

SEATING

Any staircase, lobby, corridor or passage where forming part of the means of exit to be no less than the width of the exit or the aggregate widths of exits from which it leads (Fig 4.32).

The clear height of staircases, lobbies, corridors etc. to be not less than 2.057 m clear of any projections from walls or ceilings.

The floor of any passage or corridor shall not be inclined more than 1 in 10 to the horizontal, and should be level for a distance not less than its width from the top or bottom step of any stairway.

Any staircase to be without winders, and to have flights of not more than 16 or less than 3 steps. The staircase should not have more than two successive flights without a turn, or more than one flight without a turn if there are more than 12 steps in a flight. The depth of landings should not be less than the width of the flight.

Auditorium seats can be arranged staggered or in line. The minimum back-to-back spacing is 760 mm, although the current comfort standard is 900 mm. In the more expensive balcony and rear stalls seating, this back-to-back spacing could be increased to 990 mm or more. The minimum seatway between the back of one seat and the front of the seat immediately behind is 300 mm in the 'Technical Regulations for Places of Public Entertainment in Greater London 1965' the maximum number of seats in each row is stipulated thus:

(i) Seven seats where there is only gangway; this may be increased to eleven seats, if the seatway is increased by 25 mm for each additional seat over seven.

(ii) Fourteen seats where there are gangways at either end; similarly this may be increased to 22, if the seatway is increased by 25 mm for each additional seat over fourteen.

The continental and Scottish standards permit seating to extend the full width of the auditorium except for gangways at either side. The width of the seatway is increased accordingly.

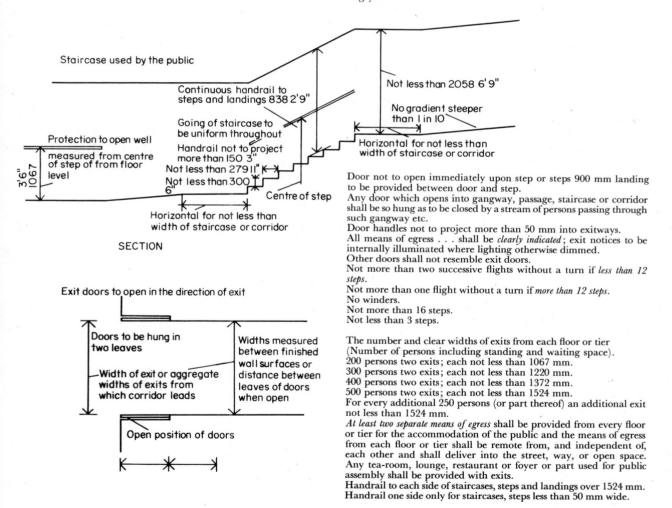

Door not to open immediately upon step or steps 900 mm landing to be provided between door and step.
Any door which opens into gangway, passage, staircase or corridor shall be so hung as to be closed by a stream of persons passing through such gangway etc.
Door handles not to project more than 50 mm into exitways.
All means of egress . . . shall be *clearly indicated*; exit notices to be internally illuminated where lighting otherwise dimmed.
Other doors shall not resemble exit doors.
Not more than two successive flights without a turn if *less than 12 steps*.
Not more than one flight without a turn if *more than 12 steps*.
No winders.
Not more than 16 steps.
Not less than 3 steps.

The number and clear widths of exits from each floor or tier (Number of persons including standing and waiting space).
200 persons two exits; each not less than 1067 mm.
300 persons two exits; each not less than 1220 mm.
400 persons two exits; each not less than 1372 mm.
500 persons two exits; each not less than 1524 mm.
For every additional 250 persons (or part thereof) an additional exit not less than 1524 mm.
At least two separate means of egress shall be provided from every floor or tier for the accommodation of the public and the means of egress from each floor or tier shall be remote from, and independent of, each other and shall deliver into the street, way, or open space. Any tea-room, lounge, restaurant or foyer or part used for public assembly shall be provided with exits.
Handrail to each side of staircases, steps and landings over 1524 mm.
Handrail one side only for staircases, steps less than 50 mm wide.

Fig. 4.32 Exitways

SITE AND GENERAL ARRANGEMENT

The GLC Regulations give particular attention to the frontage of the building, or access to open space to ensure rapid dispersal of persons from the premises in the event of fire and to permit satisfactory access for fire brigade appliances. The Regulations refer to width of streets, and control over private ways or private open space. They also refer to standards of separation from adjoining buildings.

The general arrangement of the premises must permit safe and orderly evacuation in the event of fire. This particular section states that the level of any part of any floor for the accommodation of the public shall not be more than 12·192 m above or 6·096 m below the principal street or ground level unless the building has frontages to two or more streets or satisfactory additional exits are provided with ventilated lobbies and a high standard of fire resistance.

The regulations also limit the slope of any floor to 1 : 10 or tiers not to rise more than 35° to the horizontal.

FIRE SEPARATION

Fire separation is laid down by Part III of the GLC Regulations. This section relates to the construction of the premises to minimise the risk of fire involving the structure. The structure of premises accommodating less than 500 people is to be one hour fire resistant and 2 hours for premises accommodating more than 500 people. External enclosures are to be constructed of non-combustible materials. The fixing of wall or ceiling linings are to be approved by the Council, and to have a Class 1 surface spread of flame. Decorative surface finishing including any fabric are to be non-combustible.

The regulations also relate to the construction of pay boxes, sales kiosks, showcases or bars and other fittings in ancillary rooms.

The regulations stipulate precise standards for the enclosure of means of egress, lifts and shafts, and both the ventilation requirements for ancillary rooms and the standard of construction of the necessary ducting.

OTHER RELEVANT ACTS

Shops and Offices and Railway Premises Act, 1963.
Health and Safety at Work etc, Act, 1974.
Building (Scotland) Act, 1959.
The Building Standards (Scotland) (Consolidation) Regulation, 1971.

Table 4.5 SANITARY ACCOMMODATION AS GLC REGULATIONS

W.C.'s	Fitments required for each category	Male Public (Persons)	Female Public (Persons)	Male staff (Persons)	Female Staff (Persons)
W.C.'s	1	1–200	1–100	1–15	1–12
	2	201–500	101–250	16–35	13–25
	3	501–1000	251–500	36–65	26–40
	4	1001–1500	501–900	66–100	41–57
	5	1501–2000	901–1300	—	58–77
	6	2001–2500	1301–1700	—	77–100
URINALS	Nil	—	—	0–6	—
	Urinals required for each category				
	1	1–50	—	7–20	—
	2	51–100	—	21–45	—
	3	101–150	—	46–70	—
	4	151–200	—		
		etc. at 50 persons increment	—	71–100	—
LAVATORY BASINS		One for each W.C. or range of urinals			

Note. It is assumed that half the audience are men and half are women.

EXAMPLES

SCALA, BIRMINGHAM

Architects: James A. Roberts and Associates.

The redevelopment of Smallbrook, Birmingham on the site of a previous cinema, incorporated an auditorium at basement level with entrance foyer at ground level (see Fig 4.33). An entrance canopy extends over the pavement providing long sides clearly visible from the pavement for advertising. A vertical sign rises above the canopy gaining the advantage of a corner site. The ticket office extends the full width of a deep foyer, with a staircase leading down to the auditorium at one side.

The lower vestibule provides access to the rear of the auditorium and is also served by a sales kiosk and cloakroom.

The auditorium is a four gangway stadium type with seating for 604 persons. There are three exit ways. The floor of the auditorium rises in front of the screen, and the void under the screen accommodates a ventilation chamber. Air is blown into the auditorium through grilles in front of the screen. Extract ventilation is at the rear of the auditorium.

The screen was designed for 70 mm projection, with variable horizontal and vertical masking allowing a range of picture sizes.

The original projection room layout allowed for Todd AO. The sound system consisted of six channel pre-amplifiers and main amplifiers for 70 mm projection connected to five sets of speaker units behind the screen with 24 ambient speakers recessed in the ceiling.

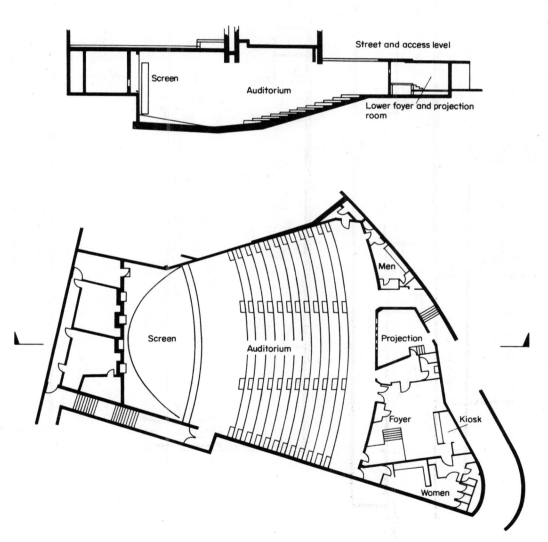

Fig. 4.33   Layout of the Scala Cinema, Birmingham

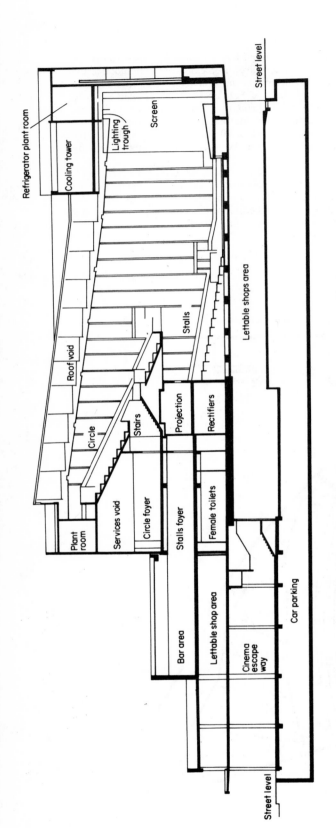

Refrigerator plant room

Cooling tower

Lighting trough

Screen

Street level

Roof void

Plant room

Services void

Circle

Circle foyer

Stairs

Projection

Rectifiers

Stalls foyer

Female toilets

Stalls

Lettable shops area

Bar area

Lettable shop area

Cinema escape way

Car parking

Street level

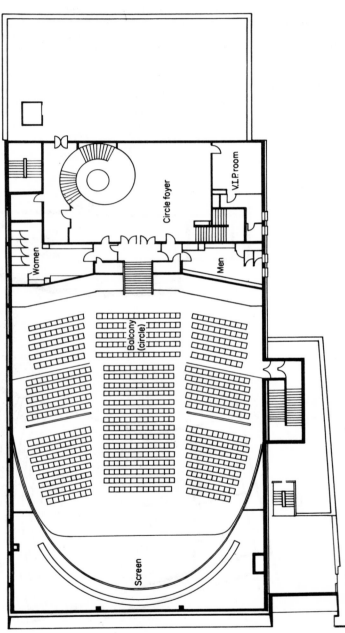

Women

Circle foyer

V.I.P. room

Men

Balcony (circle)

Screen

Fig. 4.34   Plan views of Odeon Cinema, Marble Arch, London

THE ODEON, MARBLE ARCH, LONDON W1
(See Figs 4.34 and 4.35)

Architects: T. P. Bennett and Son.

The site on the corner of Marble Arch (see Fig 4.34) was originally occupied by a cinema. The redevelopment released the commercial potential of the site by placing a new cinema at first floor level, with shops at pavement level. The access to first floor has been made less arduous by the use of escalators. These extend from an entrance foyer at pavement level, to a spacious lounge foyer at first floor. The noise of street traffic and underground trains presented a severe problem which has been overcome by structurally isolating the entire cinema auditorium from the main building, thus eliminating structure borne noise.

The auditorium seats 1360 with 790 in the Stalls and 570 in the Balcony. The large screen, constructed for D150 projection, cinerama and Todd AO measures 23.165 m on the chord. The first floor foyer is generous and provides a sales counter. Access to the Stalls is from the rear of the auditorium and at either side of a centrally positioned projection room. A circle foyer gives access to the circle at 2nd floor level.

The cinema is fully air conditioned with the cooling plant situated in a tower over the screen end of the auditorium.

The total development includes offices and commercial uses. The prominent position of the site is used to advantage with the external walls of the auditorium used for illuminated night display.

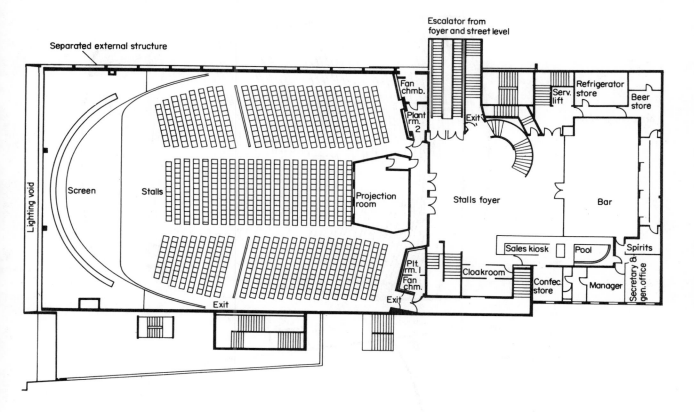

Fig. 4.35   Sectional view of Odeon Cinema, Marble Arch, London

ODEON, ELEPHANT AND CASTLE

Architects: Erno Goldfinger and Associates

The Odeon, Elephant and Castle (see Fig 4.36), is a rare example in which an independent cinema has been built as part of a redevelopment scheme. The site was previously occupied by a large cinema, and lies in close proximity to a railway line. The new cinema is part of the Elephant and Castle redevelopment plan including a shopping centre, extensive office development, and a major traffic reorganisation.

The entrance foyer is visually open to the wide pavement.

The relatively small foyer provides space for ticket offices and sales kiosk. The lavatory accommodation is positioned between auditorium and entrance foyer, providing sound insulation from street traffic. The auditorium seating 1040 is a stadium type plan with a roof construction which is profiled to the sight and projection lines. Access into the auditorium is centrally placed with a cross-over. The screen is designed as a structure independent of the auditorium walls, and was originally provided without masking.

The exterior form and the internal planning are direct in their interpretation of requirements.

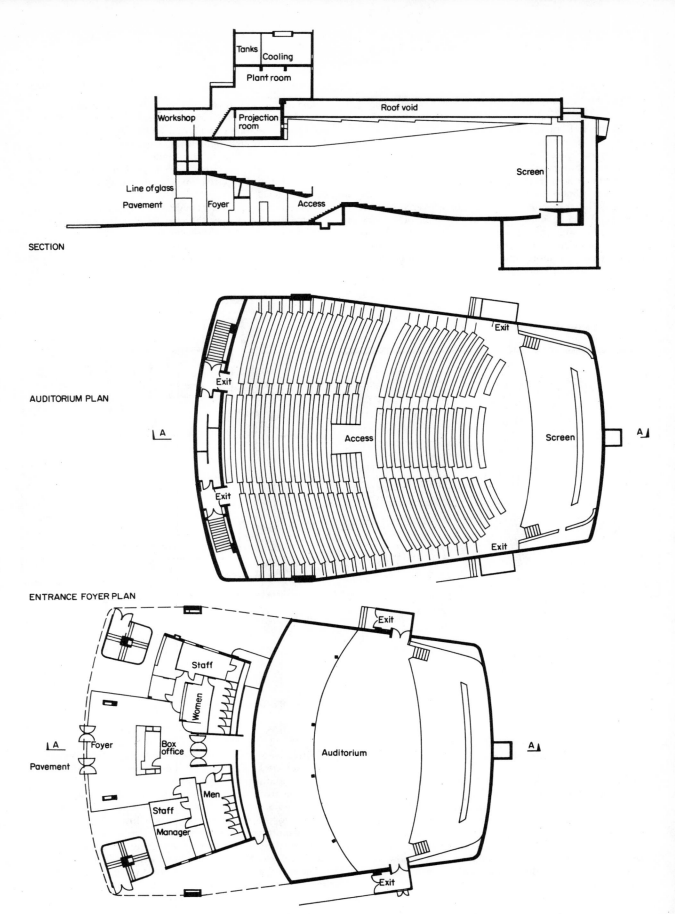

SECTION

AUDITORIUM PLAN

ENTRANCE FOYER PLAN

4–40   *Fig. 4.36   Section and plans of Odeon Cinema, Elephant & Castle, London*

CINEMA CONVERSION FOR THE CLASSIC, BANBURY
(See Fig 4.37)

Architects: Dowton and Hurst.
The original cinema consisted of a typical layout with circle and stalls and a projection room at the rear of the circle. The conversion into two cinemas consists of separating the circle as one auditorium and the stalls as another.

The alteration consists of extending the balcony floor and constructing a double skin wall between the two auditoria. The projection room is repositioned to ground floor level at the rear of Cinema 1 with a telescope mirror arrangement to project onto the screen of Cinema 2. The original cinema accommodated 751 seats, the new arrangement provides 470 seats in Cinema 1 and 241 seats in Cinema 2.

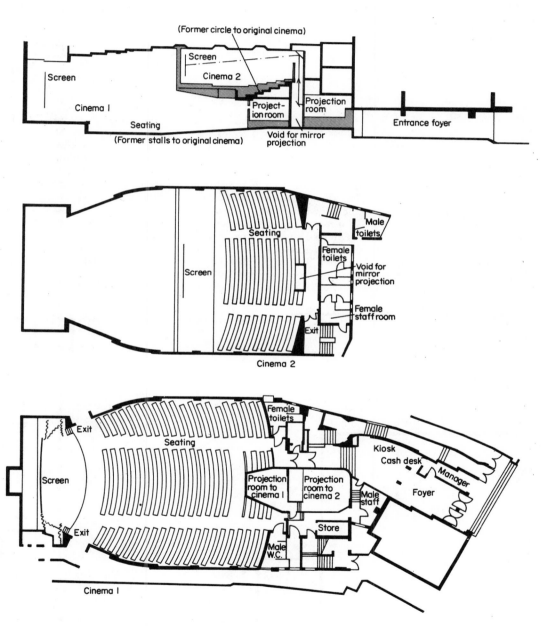

Fig. 4.37   Conversion to two cinemas. Rank Cinema, Banbury, Oxon

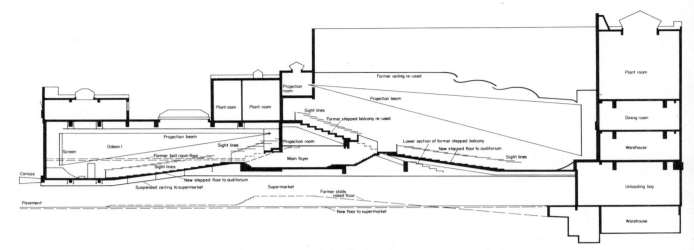

Fig. 4.38 Longitudinal section. Astoria Cinema, Southend

ASTORIA CINEMA, SOUTHEND (See Figs 4.38 and 4.39)

Architects: Rank Organisation Architects.

Many existing cinemas built for pre-war audiences have been found to be too large and inflexible. Some cinema companies have carried out a programme of twinning or dividing the existing auditorium into two or more separate cinemas. The Astoria at Southend has been divided into two cinemas and the ground floor has been separated and let to a Supermarket. The former back stage area has been converted to offices, staff rooms and stores for the supermarket, and the upper floors provide two auditoria, a foyer, bar, cloakrooms, lavatories, a manager's office and staff rooms.

The original balcony was extended to form one cinema seating 1235. The second auditorium seats 455 occupying the former dance floor. The larger auditorium has a sales kiosk at the side opening into the auditorium which provides a focus of interest during intervals.

Both cinemas have fully transistorised sound systems and cinemation, and include a hearing aid system for deaf patrons. The main foyer at first floor level is spacious and provides access to the ticket office, generous sales counter, bar, lavatories and the two auditoria. Guiding patrons from box office to auditorium is achieved by means of coloured illuminated panels suspended at ceiling level.

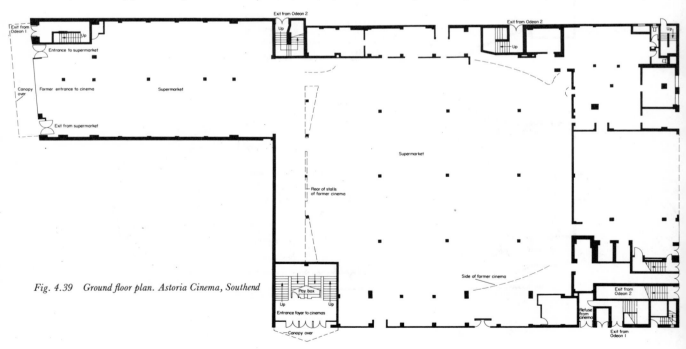

Fig. 4.39 Ground floor plan. Astoria Cinema, Southend

4–42

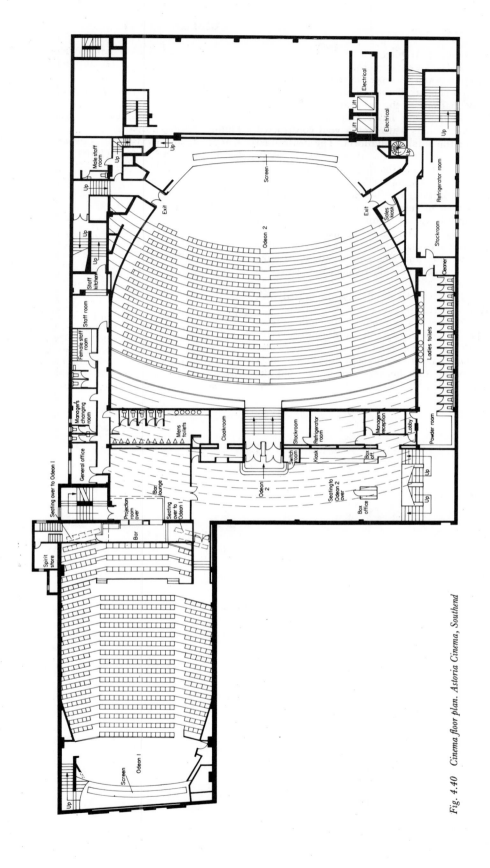

Fig. 4.40 Cinema floor plan. Astoria Cinema, Southend

4–43

STAR CINEMA AT SUTTON

BIBLIOGRAPHY

Aloi, R. *Architetture per lo spettacolo,* Hoepli, Milan (1958).
Sharp, D. *The Picture Palace and other buildings for the movies,* Hugh Evelyn, London (1969).
Knopp, L. *The Cinematograph Regulations, 1955,* The Cinema Press Ltd.
Bode, P., *Kinos,* Verlag Callway, Munchen (1957).
Philips. *Planning a Cinema.*
Knopp, L and Wylson, A. *Cinema Technical Study. Design Guide,* Architects' Journal (1967).

Architects: Star Company Architects.

Star Cinemas have developed numerous schemes using a centralised projection room to serve several auditoria. At Sutton, the complex consists of three auditoria; two small units immediately in front of the projection room, and a large auditorium on the same level. This means that the projection to the larger unit is through a void constructed over the ceilings of the smaller auditoria. The centralised projection room aims to serve the three cinemas. With suitable equipment and co-ordinating programming the total staff content can be used most efficiently.

With small auditoria design, it is important to consider the scale of the screen in relation to the auditoria space. Furthermore, control of seating, points of access, position of staff are all important in relation to the size of the space concerned. In this particular case, the internal lighting which consists of moving and changing coloured patterns projected onto the screen and wall, reduces the awareness of the auditorium size.

The external display for the building is integrated with the external fabric and cladding.

With this form of layout, it is important to guide patrons from the box office or box offices to the auditorium entrance door concerned. This can be done by a colour indicator system, motifs, floor carpet or direction signs; but it is essential to have some link between box office and the auditorium it serves.

Anthony Wylson *FRIBA, AA Dip (Hons), a partner in the firm Anthony Wylson and Munro Waterston, has had a long standing interest in cinema design. He has been responsible as a Consultant on new cinemas incorporated within development projects, modernising existing cinemas and converting existing buildings into cinemas. He was joint author of the Architects Journal's Cinema Design Guide and has contributed articles on cinema design to the architectural and technical press.*

5 PUBLIC HOUSES AND LICENSED PREMISES

C. J. MAIN, B. Arch., ARIBA
Assistant Director of Architecture, London Borough of Camden
(formerly Chief Architect, Whitbread London Ltd.)

INTRODUCTION

The public house is a specifically British institution, with a tradition of association with the national beverage dating back to the Roman occupation. Its generic name proclaims its origins as a dwelling where beer was brewed for sale, and the pole sign which is still its principal advertisement originated in the 'ale stake' the fifteenth century brewer put out to summon the 'ale conner' to approve his latest brew. Many curious and historic public house names testify that the ale-house selling beer, the tavern selling liquor and food, and the inn offering residential accommodation as well, have been for generations woven into the fabric of British history; and today the 'pub' is usually the first communal facility to open in a new town or redevelopment.

Dating back to the first Licensing Act of 1495 there is an almost equally long tradition of the regulation of public houses by national laws administred by Local Authorities. Appendix J of the Erroll Commission Report of 1972 lists nine main headings under which Local Authorities are empowered by a total of eighteen Acts to regulate the planning and construction of, and the operation and staff working conditions in, public houses. Acting in parallel with the Local Authorities and advised by their police, fire and public health officers, are the Licensing Justices, whose jurisdiction was first defined in 1828 and to whom all applications for new licences, and for alterations and extensions to existing licensed premises, must be submitted. The Erroll Commission Report describes the powers of the Licensing Justices as 'theoretically unlimited': in granting a licence the Justices are empowered to impose any conditions they think proper in the public interest, although the right of appeal against their decision was introduced in 1949.

The powers of Licensing Justices were the instrument used by the Government during the 1914–18 war to mount a concerted nationwide attack on liquor consumption and the licensed trade owes much of its structure today to the consequences of the measures and attitudes reflected in the Defence of the Realm Act of 1914. Since the turn of the century, beer consumption has fallen from 32.5 to 26 gallons per head of population per annum, and convictions for drunkenness from 65 per 1000 to 15.

The gravity of beer was diluted during the 1914 war to release agricultural land for more necessary purposes, and strong beer selling at 2d. per pint in 1914 had by 1919 been replaced by weaker beer selling at 7d per pint, the difference being mostly represented by increased Excise Duty. The wartime restriction of permitted hours of sale to eight was consolidated in the Licensing Act of 1921. Amongst subsequent legislation, the introduction of breath testing in the Road Traffic Act of 1967 has had a significant effect on the volume and pattern of public house trading.

The resultant reduction in both market and profit margins accelerated the rationalisation of the industry. Of 4000 property-owning brewers registered in 1914, only 300 survive today and a high proportion of these are subsidiaries of major conglomerates. The number of full on-licenses has fallen from 102000 in 1900 to 65000 today, representing 1 per 700 population. The license to sell beer only is obsolete and the independent Free House rare.

In superseding traditionally brewed draught beer, the condition of which required of the landlord expert cellarmanship, with top pressure beers which the brewers can rely on being served in consistent condition, today's brewing industry requires scientific and financial investment beyond the reach of the small company. Such technical innovations directly affect the planning of public house work. The Architect must plan to facilitate the delivery of beer in bulk, tanked storage in temperature controlled conditions, and electrically operarated metered dispense equipment.

The emphasis on the social function of the public house also gained impetus from the 1914–18 climate. A joint sub-committee of the Brewers Society and the National Trade Defence Association in 1918 recommended that 'improvements which involve enlargement and greater social amenities are more in the interests of temperance than a rigid adherence to existing restrictions on licensed premises'. Extended provision for the service of food and non-alcoholic beverages, and for recreation, entertainment and performances were amongst the recommendations put forward.

In 1944, the relevant recommendations of the Morris Committee on the rebuilding of war damaged licensed premises were to encourage the amalgamation of licences in redeveloped areas to provide larger units with more varied facilities, the increased provision of outdoor amenities such as gardens and bowling greens, added emphasis on the provision of seating at the expense of 'at the bar' drinking and the service of food, snacks and alcoholic beverages. Pioneered by the Carlisle houses of the recently dissolved State Management scheme initiated in 1916, the 1920's and 30's and the immediate post-war years saw the building of large 'improved public houses' with very varied facilities of the type illustrated in Basil Oliver's 'The Renaissance of the English Public House'. Whilst today development on such a scale can rarely be justified, this view of the public house as an informal community centre still subsists with the brewers and their public alike, and the successful 'pub' combines an atmosphere of intimacy with facilities for efficient service and direct supervision.

The Erroll Commission's Report of 1972 proposed a considerable relaxation of public houses' permitted trading hours and the exemption of restaurants and places of public entertainment, to accommodate a more mobile and leisured population and the growth of staggered working. In its definition of alcohol as a 'social solvent', its identification of a growing demand for a greater diversity of leisure provisions and facilities for the family in public houses, and in its recommendation of various limitations on the absolute discretion of Licensing Justices the report implies a far reaching liberalisation of British licensing law. Should its provisions ever reach the statute book, increased competition for leisure and the marginal propensity to consume will bring great changes to the future of the public house.

The launching by brewers of Discothèques, speciality catering operations, games facilities, and children's soft drinks bars in houses are amongst recent developments which demonstrate their sensitivity to the changing climate. It is impracticable to include in this survey all such present developments and impossible to foresee those which lie in the future. Any Architect working in this field is well advised to pay particular attention to the formulation of an exact and detailed brief with his client.

Some public houses have separate restaurants in addition to facilities for bar snacks. Restaurants have not been covered in detail in this section but readers wishing further information on this subject are referred to Section 2 'Hotels' in the volume *Planning; Buildings for Habitation, Commerce and Industry*.

SITING

The selection of a public house site is never governed by architectural considerations. The primary requirement is always the combination of clear visibility to passing traffic with a reservoir of residential, tourist or business population within easy walking distance of the site, and of the right number and social mix to provide a trading level adequate to justify the predicted investment. However, the architect must be prepared to advise that the proposed site satisfies the following criteria before his client reaches the point of commitment.

1. *The acceptablitiy in principle of its use for a public house to the statutory Planning Authority and the Licensing Justices.* Both are obliged to consider objections from any quarter, and particularly in predominantly residential areas the public house although popular as an amenity, is unwelcome as a neighbour. Opposition to the granting of a fresh licence is also occasionally presented to the Licensing Justices by licensees already established in the area. The commonly held belief that in rebuilding existing licensed premises it is necessary to provide for continuous trading to preserve the license in erroneous. All justices will hold a licence in suspension between the granting of provisional and final licensees. They will require to inspect the premises before granting the final licence to satisfy themselves that the executed work coincides with the drawings submitted to support the provisional application.

2. *The adequacy of the site to meet the Statutory Planning Authority's car parking standards.* These vary widely between Authorities, as can be seen from Table 5.1, which tabulates the results of a 1974 canvass of 50 administering authorities in the Home Counties and E. Midlands areas. Several of the answers received were qualified to take account of already available off-street parking facilities, and in the 'historic centre' of one city, the Authority's policy is to forbid private parking. From the operator's viewpoint the provision of parking facilities is less vital in the case of a public house serving bar snacks only than if a full meals service is on offer. The further up the market the operation, the more important parking becomes; and the site layouts of high class restaurants and evening function accommodation should ideally make it possible for drivers to set down the passengers under cover before parking.

3. *The adequacy of the site for deliveries. Beer, wines and spirits and food all exemplify the distributive trades' tendency to make larger deliveries less frequently.* A schedule of critical dimensions of typical brewer's delivery vehicles which are normally the largest to be catered for is given in the Data section below. All newly built public houses should provide hard standings for off loading within the curtilages of their sites, and sufficient manoeuvring space to obviate the necessity to back vehicles out onto a public thoroughfare.

4. *Visibility.* The success of public houses, and to a lesser extent, restaurants, depends on their ability to attract 'impulse sales'. Their siting, signing and design must therefore invite the public to use them, and the Architect must advise his client if the proposed site poses insuperable problems in the production of a design capable of generating its own publicity.

To ensure that these criteria are met, an outline Planning Consent and a provisional licence are minimum requirements before the client commits himself to the acquisition of the site. Informal consultation is insufficient since officials of Planning Authorities cannot bind their Committees prior to the consideration of applications and many Licensing Benches have very positive attitudes on the pattern of trade they are prepared to approve. For some sites criterion 4 will also require a detailed Planning Consent, in which case the prudent Architect will advise his client in advance of his fee commitment in the event of the application failing.

Table 5.1 TYPICAL STATUTORY AUTHORITIES PARKING REQUIREMENTS: NON-OPERATIONAL

No. of Authorities	Public Houses: Car Parking Space Ratio	No. of Authorities	Restaurants: Car Parking Space Ratio
11	1 : 4.6 m²	10	1 : 4 seats
8	1: 2.8 m² up to 28 m² 1: for each additional 6.5 m²	9	1 : 9.3 m²
4	10: not exceeding 28 m² 1: for each additional 4·6 m²	6	1 : 14 m²
2	25 spaces minimum	7	1 : 4.6 m²
2	1 : 2.2 m²	4	1 : 5 seats
1	1 : 3.7 m²	3	1 : 5 seats (or where public car parking is available it can be relaxed to 1 : 10 seats).
1	10: 28 m² (20 spaces min)	2	1 : 3.1 m²
2	1 : 2.8 m²	1	1 : 10 m²
1	1: 20 persons capacity (central town) 1: 10 persons capacity (other parts)	1	1 : 10 seats
1	1 : 4 seats	1	1 : 5.8 m²
1	1 : 2.3 m² (15 spaces min)	5	No standards
1	1 : 18.6 m²		
1	1 : 3 persons		
1	1 : 15 persons		
5	No standards		

Notes: 8 out of 50 replies failed to mention Public Houses   One out of 50 replies failed to mention Restaurants

Table 5.2 TYPICAL STATUTORY AUTHORITIES PARKING REQUIREMENTS: OPERATIONAL

Requirements	Number of Authorities	
	P.H's	Rest's
Adequate loading, off-loading and turning facilities within curtilage	5	2
One space/garage per managerial flat One space/garage per six inside staff One space per 15 outside staff	6	6
Sufficient manoeuvring and parking space shall be provided within the site boundary for the maximum number of operational vehicles normally visiting the site at any one time.	4	0
For dining/bar floorspace not exceeding 92.9 m²/65 m² For dining/bar floorspace, not exceeding 232.2 m²/125 m².	3	8
Space for at least five cars to set down and pick up persons and for one commercial vehicle.	5	5
For dining/bar floorspace not exceeding 100 m²/75 m². For dining/bar floorspace not exceeding 250 m²/125 m².	1	1
No operational parking standards	26	28

PLANNING

The need to attract people to use the house has already been stressed in the section on 'siting'. Once inside the premises, they must be made to feel comfortable by planning intimate corners for private conversation, particularly important in the single bar house often dictated by economic circumstances today. Each bar of a multi-bar house must have ready access to toilets for both sexes, which should not involve traversing another bar. The single bar house therefore tends to produce a more favourable ratio between sales area and non-income ancilliaries.

All seating areas in a bar must be visible from the servery. It is preferable for toilet entrances also to be visible from the servery where possible: If toilets are planned directly off an unsupervised entrance lobby, particularly in an urban location, the client is all too likely to find himself the proprietor of a public convenience.

Irrespective of the client's sales concept, the practicalities of public house planning are as follows:

1. Cellarage planned to serve sediment draught beers within 6 m and top pressure beers within 12 m of storage location: and sited to permit direct off-loading of kegs and casks or direct discharge into tanks, either by doors not less than 9 m clear opening, or cellar flaps and barrel skid not less than 12 m clear width. The substitution of mechanical for gravity pumps has eliminated the need for cellarage to be sited at basement level.

On the rare occasions where an urban location implies a high site value and maximum utilisation at street level, cellars can be planned at first floor level provided unobstructed access is given to a delivery hoist located to stock the cellar from the delivery point and the servery from the cellar. The cellar must be furnished with a cold water bib tap for washing down, and a sink with h & c water for equipment cleaning.

The floor must be laid to falls and crossfalls to trapped gulley and where necessary, a sump with submersible pump fitted with float switch.

2. In the case of bottled beer, minerals etc, and crate storage, the same criteria for siting relative to delivery point and servery apply. Separate wines and spirits and tobacco storage is frequently formed by a lockable stud and expanded metal enclosure entered from the crate store, to afford added security for high value stock. Tobacco storage, however, requires natural ventilation to prevent stock deterioration.

3. To facilitate security, a single delivery point should be planned for and a single access route from storage to servery. Neither must be readily apparent to the public. All access doors should be fitted with security locks, and windows and louvres to storage areas should be kept to the minimum commensurate with adequate ventilation, and furnished with burglar bars.

4. The Manager/Tenant will normally be resident and a three bedroom flat or maisonette should be planned for, furnished with its own private entrance. The accommodation should be so arranged that a resident Relief Manager can be restricted to one bedroom, of adequate size to serve as a bed-sitting room, the bathroom and the kitchen, if the catering kitchen is unsuitable, enabling the permanent Manager to lock up the remainder of his quarters when going on leave.

5. There is an increasing tendency for Licensing Justices to take into account in granting licences, the extent to which houses have been planned to facilitate use by the disabled. This is by no means a universal attitude, and in many cases it therefore remains for the client to decide on the extent of such provisions. It is usually acceptable and more economic to provide a separate 'uni-sex' semi-ambulant compartment rather than one in each toilet. Doors used by the public for access should open a full 90° and provide not less than 787 cm clear width, and the main entrance should have a ramped approach to a gradient n.e. 1 in 12.

6. Many small houses serve a restricted selection of food. Demand for snack service peaks at lunchtime, although if food service is advertised it must under the Trade Descriptions Act, be available during all opening hours. Neither Licensing Justices nor Public Health Officers will today accept the use of the domestic kitchen for the preparation of food for sale in the bar, and it is therefore necessary to provide a separate catering kitchen adjacent to the servery. The size and equipment of the kitchen is so intimately related to the type and standard of service to be offered that it is impossible to generalise. A section of the servery will normally be devoted exclusively to the display and sale of snacks.

SPACE REQUIREMENTS

Different styles of catering, the provision of different levels of entertainment and different methods of beer storage and dispensing are examples of the variables affecting the planning of public houses. Ideal situations must be tempered by the capital outlay justifiable, and for this reason alone it is essential that the Architect secures a full brief from his client at an early stage. In general, however, if the provision of adequate storage is sacrificed to maximise income generating sales space, the Manager or Tenant is likely to find himself embarrassed at time of peak demand.

The areas needed are as follows:
Customer space (Bar).
Customer space (restaurant): optional.
Off sales: optional.
Games area: optional.
Servery.
Toilets for public.
Toilets for staff.
Catering kitchen or snack preparation.
Storage: liquor, food, cleaning materials.
Boiler and/or plant room.
Service yard.
Managers and/or staff living accommodation.

At the end of this section there is a typical schedule of allocation of areas in a recent design by the Architects Department of a major Brewery Company (page 5–6).

BARS

Bars are normally measured to exclude serveries and entrance lobbies, from the front edge of the bar counter to the perimeter walls. The average bar area in a new public house totals 140–149 m² and may or may not include a catering operation. It is difficult to avoid an atmosphere of impersonality in a larger area, and if more customer space is required, it is preferable to provide it by an additional bar.

The following rule of thumb assessments can be taken as typical overall space requirements per customer excluding provision for games:

Drinking bars without catering	0.6 m²
Catering bars	0.9 m²
Grill style restaurants	1.1 m²
A la carte restaurants	1.4 m²

Playing areas for typical public house games are given under 'Data' (see page **5**–19).

The 1974 DOE Draft Design Code for 'Means of Escape in Case of Fire' gives the following alternative method of assessment.

For occupancy multiply the floor area in m², by the following occupant load factors:

Bars (including public and lounge bars)	0·5
Assembly Halls without fixed seating	0·5
Restaurants, cafes and canteens	1·0

When Local Authorities have a site available, usually put out to rental tender, requirements are invariably set down as a condition of tender. Lessors of 'in-built' public houses in a development may also do this.

OFF-SALES

Separate Off-Sales shops are seldom provided. In the first place sales for consumption off the premises are permitted over the bar of fully on-licensed premises and in the second the competition of other retail outlets has reduced the importance of this trade.

SERVERY

All bars should have a common servery to facilitate economic staffing and proper bar supervision with adequate storage and display space so that stocks do not have to be replenished during trading hours. Counter and back fittings should be long enough, in addition to glass and bottle storage, to accommodate:

Cash tills: number dependent on layout.
Glass washing machine or double sink with drinking water supply.
Bottle openers and empty bottle baskets.
Cool shelves, beer dispense points.
Spirit optics.
Flap and wicket for access to bar.
Space for the display of statutory notices.
Overhead glass rack: where frontage is restricted and subject to the agreement of Public Health Officer.
Tape machine for background music: optional.

Dimensions of typical items of this equipment are shown under 'Data'. A separate staff wash hand basin is required readily accessible from the servery. Dispense counters adjacent to restaurants where service will continue outside licensing hours will require to be fitted with security grilles.

PUBLIC TOILETS

Minimum standards for toilets should be:
Males: 0·3–2·4 m urinal or four bowls
1 w.c.
1 basin with hot and cold water supplies
Hand drying facilities
Females: 2 w.c.'s
2 basins with hot and cold water supplies
Hand drying facilities

These standards are in excess of the minimum legislative requirement under the Offices, Shops & Railway Premises Act.

It is preferable that entrances, by way of ventilated lobbies, should lead directly off the bars and be visible from the servery to ensure proper supervision. Services should be ducted to prevent vandalism. This is particularly important where the toilets are sited not under direct supervision.

STAFF TOILETS

In the average sized public house 1 w.c. and 1 basin will be adequate. Catering operations will require a minimum of one staff toilet for each sex and other provisions under the Offices, Shops and Railway Premises Act of 1971.

STORAGE

Separate storage is required for:
Draught beer (cooled).
Bottled beer (not cooled).
Wines and Spirits store.
Food (optional).
Cigarettes and sundries.
Cleaning materials.
Empties store and/or service yard.

For areas to be allocated, it is necessary to question the client and liaise with his supplier's cellar service technicians on the estimated trade, storage period, type of dispensing equipment and cooling. Wines and spirits need to be enclosed in a secure area, and local refrigerated storage may be necessary.

Food storage areas vary with the type of operation but in the main will consist of dry goods and either deep freezers and refrigerators or built-in cold rooms. Dry and well ventilated conditions are needed for storage of cigarettes and sundries.

Storage for cleaning materials and equipment can easily be underestimated and is becoming particularly important as bulk purchases are made for reasons of economy, and large stocks may be carried.

Particular attention should be given to storage of empty containers and crates under cover within a service yard pending collection. A separate refuse bay should also be provided. At an early stage the Architect must ascertain from the Local Authority the means of refuse collection and make adequate provision for any mechanical method. Whilst smoke emission usually precludes the installation of an incinerator, balers or compactors are worth considering for large multi-bar catering houses.

MECHANICAL SERVICES

The choice of heating method will be dictated by the relationship between capital and running costs. Because a public house operates during limited hours and with widely varying levels of trade, a system capable of quick response and cut-off is essential.

The selection of central heating is not therefore automatic, since local fan convectors and hot water immersion heaters can adequately service the simple public house at a lower installation cost. A domestic boiler will be required for the Manager's accommodation.

MANGER'S ACCOMMODATION

This should be at least to Parker Morris standards with its own fire escape.

SCHEDULE OF NET AREAS IN TYPICAL PUBLIC HOUSES

The following schedule is drawn from a recent design brief for a major brewery company and can be regarded as typical.

CUSTOMER SPACE

	m²
Lounge Bar/Snacks	88.5
Saloon Bar	68.0

SERVERY

(Drinks) Lounge Bar	15.4
(Dispense) Saloon Bar	15.4
(Snacks) Lounge Bar	13.4
(Counter length to Bars 20 ft run to each with additional 17 ft run snacks counter to Lounge Bar only).	
Snacks preparation area and storage	18.3

PUBLIC CIRCULATION

Entrance lobbies and corridor	12.1

BOILER ROOM

	4.3

TOILETS

Male: Public	14.0
Female: Public	11.6
Staff	1.8

STORAGE

Draught beer	40.0
Bottled beers and minerals	34.7

Empties and yard	24.3
Wines and spirits	9.8
Cigarettes and sundries	0.9
Cleaning	0.9
Total Trading	373.4

MANAGER'S ACCOMMODATION

Living/Dining Room	23.2
Kitchen	12.1
Bathroom	5.4
W.C.	2.0
Bed/Sitting Room	20.6
Bedroom 1	14.0
Bedroom 2	11.6
Bedroom 3	8.4
Entrance Hall, staircase and circulation	26.8
Total Private	124.1

SUMMARY

Trading	373.4
Private	136.3
Total	509.7

(Plus Manager's Garage)

DATA

The schedules and data given below embody typical examples of the equipment used by one major brewer which affects the planning and design of public houses and other clients may have variations in some details.

Delivery vehicles

The dimensions given in Table 5.4 relate to the three largest types of delivery vehicle in common use.

Liquor packages

Tables 5.5 to 5.12 detail the overall dimensions of packaging units and containers in common use, and can be used as the basis for the assessment of storage capacities.

Hoists and bottle disposal

Under the Hygiene Act, an impervious lining is required to the hoist car. Care should be taken to ensure that the hoist design complies with the provisions of the Building Regulations in respect of fire resistant construction or fire protection, and ventilation. Top motor hoists are normally the most reliable, economic and efficient. Where possible, planning should avoid calling for access to adjacent sides of the car at different levels, which increases the installation cost. The Offices, Shops & Railway Premises Act requires the enclosure of all types of hoist. Typical service hoist details are given in Figs 5.1 to 5.3 and Table 5.3.

Bottle disposal units may, where the service is above cellarage be used to transfer bottles direct from a disposal point in the service to a receiving point in the cellar below. Fig. 5.4 illustrates a typical unit.

Bar equipment

Fig. 5.5 gives typical dimensions of glass washing machines, bottle cooling units and cash register (see also Table 5.11,

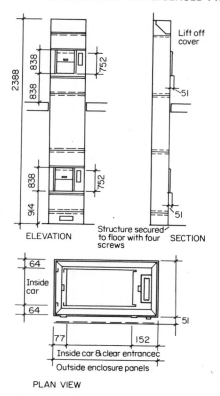

Fig. 5.2 *Typical light service lift details. This lift can be supplied in a self-contained unit thereby reducing overall building costs*

5.12 and 5.13). The cash till must by law be placed in a position where the customer can see the amount registered. The dimensions given in Table 5.13 are for both manual and electric models, the latter requiring an adjacent power unit.

Tables 5.14 and 5.15 give dimensions of the two forms of local servery cooling in common use, the cooled shelf for bottles and the flash cooler for reducing the temperature of beer in lines at point of sale. The latter are not normally installed in public houses with cooled cellars. Table 5.16

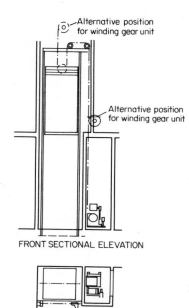

Fig. 5.1 *Typical goods service lift details*

Table 5.3 TYPICAL GOODS SERVICE LIFT DETAILS

Standard Travel

Load (kg)	152.4	254.0	355.6	508.0	762.0	762.0	101.6
Travel (m)	9.75	7.16	12.19	6.71	3.81	6.4	3.81
Speed (mph)	11.28	8.23	14.02	11.28	8.23	11.28	9.14
Car size (m)	0.6 wide	0.76	0.91	0.91	0.91	0.91	0.91
	×	×	×	×	×	×	×
	0.76 deep	0.91	1.07	1.07	1.07	1.07	1.07

Long Travel Single Fall

Load (kg)	50.8	101.6	159.4	203.2	330.2	279.4	406.8
Travel (m)	16.45	14.32	24.38	13.41	7.62	12.8	7.62
Speed (mph)	22.5	16.45	28.04	22.5	16.45	22.5	15.24
Car size (m)	0.45 wide	0.6	0.76	0.76	0.91	0.91	0.91
	×	×	×	×	×	×	×
	0.6 deep	0.6	0.76	0.91	1.07	10.7	1.22

gives dimensions of bottle skips which are plastic or g.r.p. buckets on castors to receive empty bottles for removal, sited adjacent to bottle openers.

Figs 5.6 and 5.7 detail the integration of typical equipment into the bar carcass and typical arrangements and dimensions of serveries relative to the bars they serve. Such details in individual houses will vary with the volume and type of trade anticipated and the number of lines stocked for sale, this diagram should be regarded as providing guidelines only.

There is of course, no more annoying detail mistake than for the client to find that bar shelving has been fixed to centres which will not accommodate stock or glassware. Tables 5.17 and 5.18 detail dimensions of the full range of bottles and glasses in common use.

Catering

The extent and type of catering to be provided will govern the selection of equipment. The equipment required is listed in Table 5.19, and Table 5.20 details equipment dimensions and requirements for typical catering operations ranging from bar snacks to full 'a la carte' service. This schedule should also be regarded as a guideline only for establishing a brief with the client.

Typical seating and table layouts at various density levels are detailed in Figs 5.8, 5.9 and 5.10. Seating layouts for function catering are governed by the style of the function and the furniture used to an extent that makes generalisation very difficult. For full meal functions a minimum area of 0.93 m² per person should be allowed, which converts to 0.8 m² per person for lecture style layouts. In a general purpose hall, adequate space should be provided to clear all furniture to store.

Games

Table 5.21 details dimensions of equipment and playing areas for a number of games commonly installed in public houses. Games classed by law as 'games of pure chance' are

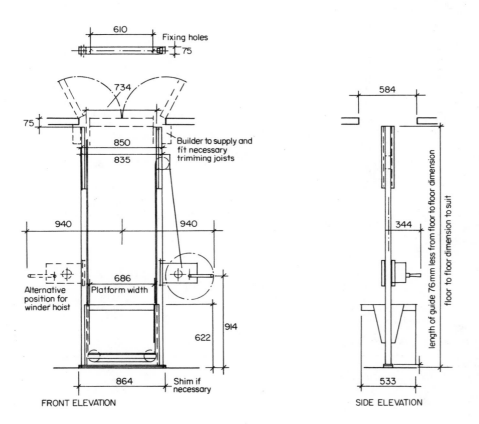

Fig. 5.3 *Typical hand-operated cellar hoist. (Enclosure omitted for clarity)*

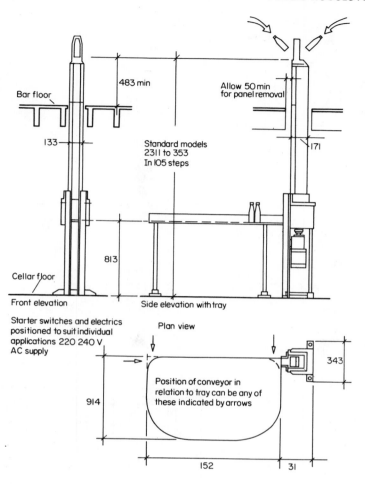

Bar floor

483 min

Allow 50 min
for panel removal

133

Standard models
2311 to 353
In 105 steps

171

Cellar floor

813

Front elevation

Side elevation with tray

Starter switches and electrics
positioned to suit individual
applications 220 240 V
AC supply

Plan view

343

914

Position of conveyor in
relation to tray can be any of
these indicated by arrows

152   31

Fig. 5.4   Typical bottle dispense unit

illegal in public houses under the Licensing Act of 1964, and the provision of machine games requires a Justice's exemption from that Act, as provided for by the Gaming Act of 1968, unless the machine merely returns stake money or offers a free turn.

Cellar planning

Separate storage provision is necessary where both 'bright' keg beers are served under pressure and sediment draught beers by beer engines, the former requiring to be stored in controlled temperature conditions with maximum variance of 10°–12.7° C. Only sediment draught beer requires the provision of 'stillions' to store horizontally off the floor allowing space for tilting behind the casks. Wall surfaces must either be impervious or treated to protect against condensation and fungus growth. The floor finish should

be impervious and the floor should fall to a trapped gully. A clear headroom of 2 m is adequate: a larger cube, by increasing the duty of cooling equipment, adds to both installation and running costs. Equipment emitting heat by exchange, e.g. compressors, icemakers, wine refrigerators, should not be sited in cooled cellars.

Fig. 5.11 gives a typical cellar layout with separate storage for top pressure beer. Fig. 5.12 gives typical wine and crate storage details. Optimum wine storage temperatures are: red wine, 14.4–15.15° C; white wine, 10.0°–11.6° C. Figs 5.13 and 5.14 provide typical top pressure beer cellar installation details.

Planning for the disabled

For data on premises which may be used by the disabled, refer to Section 3 in the volume *Planning; Buildings for Health, Welfare and Religion*.

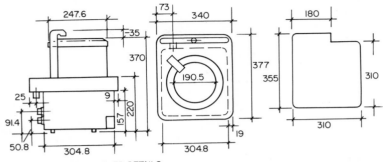

TYPICAL GLASSWASHER DETAILS

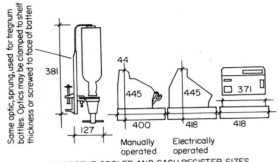

Fig. 5.5   Glasswasher, optic, bottle cooler and cash register details

Compressor
Bottle cooler
72½ pint bottles
1118x457x241 allow 330

Manually operated   Electrically operated

OPTIC, BOTTLE COOLER AND CASH REGISTER SIZES

Shelving for cigarettes etc   Adjustable shelves

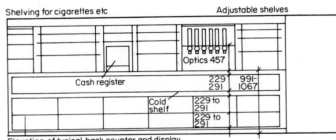

Optics 457
Cash register
Cold shelf

Elevation of typical back counter and display

Fig. 5.6   Typical front and back bar

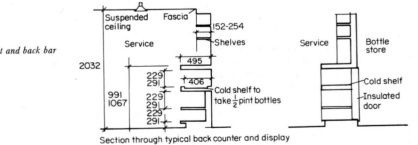

Suspended ceiling   Fascia
Service   152-254
            Shelves
495
Service   Bottle store
406
Cold shelf to take ½ pint bottles
Cold shelf
Insulated door

Section through typical back counter and display

Stainless steel sink sealed at junction (or glasswasher)   Beer engine in groups or separately   Flap retainer
Dispensers   Bottle opener   457-610
                            flap

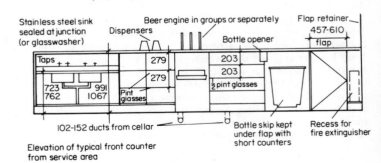

Taps
Pint glasses   ½ pint glasses   Bottle skip kept under flap with short counters   Recess for fire extinguisher
102-152 ducts from cellar

Elevation of typical front counter from service area

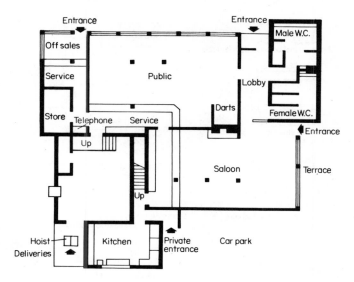

TYPICAL BAR PLAN LAYOUT AND RELATED AREAS

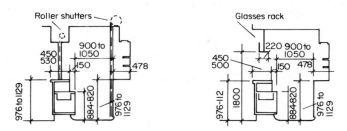

TYPICAL BAR COUNTER SECTIONS AND SIZES

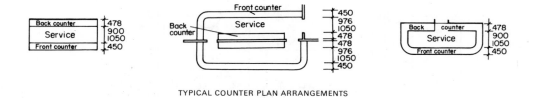

TYPICAL COUNTER PLAN ARRANGEMENTS

Fig. 5.7   Service and circulation layouts

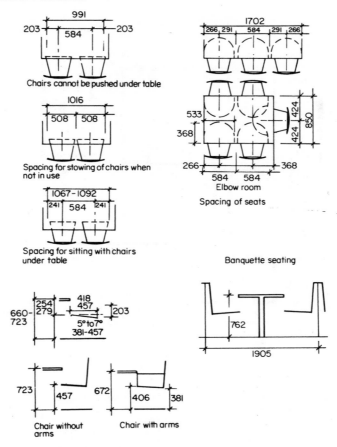

Fig. 5.8 *Seating dimensions and spacing*

Table for drinking	610	610	914	1143	1372
Table for eating	762	864	1067	1219	1524
Circular	1 seat	2 seats	4 seats	6 seats	8 seats
Square & oblong	1 seat	2 seats	4 seats	6 seats	8 seats
Table for eating	762	762	914 1143 x 762	1372x914 1676x762	1753x914 2286x762
Table for drinking	457 510	610	762		

Fig. 5.9 *Recommended table sizes to number of seats*

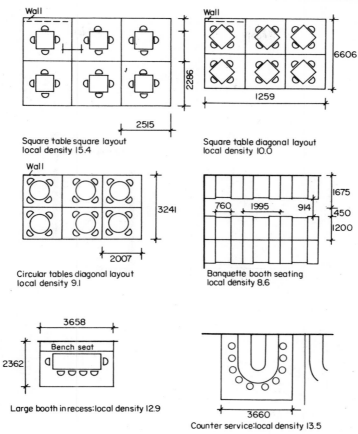

Square table square layout
local density 15.4

Square table diagonal layout
local density 10.0

Circular tables diagonal layout
local density 9.1

Banquette booth seating
local density 8.6

Large booth in recess: local density 12.9

Counter service: local density 13.5

Fig. 5.10   *Seating layouts arrangements and densities*

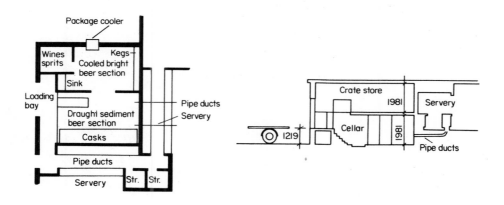

Fig. 5.11   *Typical cellar layout with special cooled bright beer storage section*

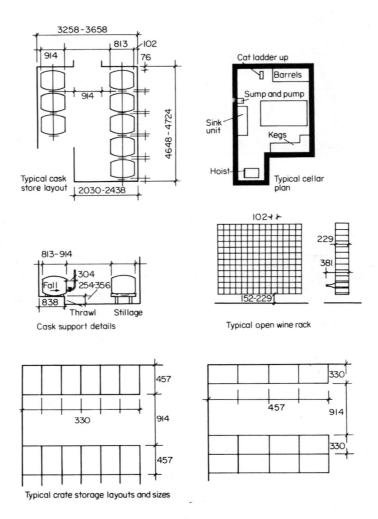

Fig. 5.12   Cask, wine and crate storage details

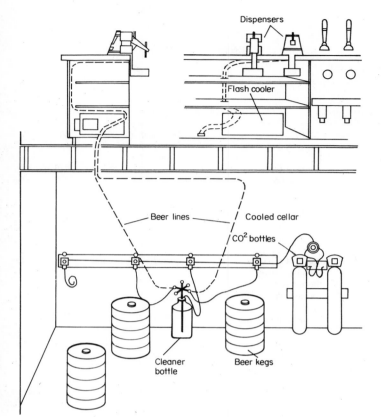

Fig. 5.13   Typical keg beer installation

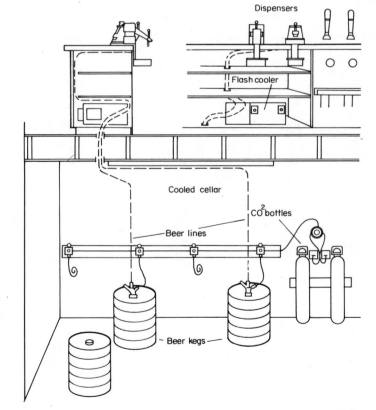

Fig. 5.14   Five-head cleaning bottle installation

Table 5.4 DIMENSIONS OF DELIVERY VEHICLES

4-wheel – 2-wheel drive
General delivery vehicle

Overall length	7.010 m
Platform length	4.877 m
Width	2.515 m
Clearance height	3.638 m
Platform height	1.118 m
Turning circle	14.021 m
Gross weight	10,000 kilos
Max. axle weight	6,500 kilos

6-wheel – 2-wheel drive
Bulk beer delivery vehicle

Overall length	8.230 m
Platform length	6.096 m
Width	2.513 m
Clearance height	3.638 m
Platform height	1.118 m
Turning circle	17.374 m
Gross weight	15,000 kilos
Max. axle weight	7,000 kilos
Bottom discharge at rear of vehicle	

Large delivery vehicles

Overall length	8.687 m
Platform length	6.553 m
Width	2.515 m
Clearance height	3.658 m
Platform height	1.118 m
Turning circle	20.726 m
Gross weight	14,500 kilos
Max. axle weight	7,500 kilos

Table 5.5 LIQUOR PACKAGES

Crates: universal crate	No. of bottles (dozens)	L	W	H
			(in mm)	
Bottle 10 fl oz	2½	418	279	305
Split 6 fl oz	4	418	279	305
Baby 4 fl oz	6	418	279	305
Malvern Crate:				
Malvern Water	1	418	279	305
Canned table water can:				
Can 12 fl oz	2	415	279	127
Fruit juice crate:				
Bottle 4 fl oz	3	469	226	178
Squash carton:				
Bottle 26 fl oz	1	327	247	285
Wine carton:				
Bottle 26 fl oz	1	362	273	324
Soda water syphon case:				
Syphons	1	483	356	356
Syphons	½	356	254	356

Side or tail loading and unloading in all cases, when working at the side of the vehicle a minimum width of 1.2 m is desirable.

Table 5.7 DRAUGHT BEER CONTAINERS

Beer barrels (Wood)	Capacity (gall.)	Length	Diameter Centre	Diameter End
Hogshead	54	914	762	584
Barrel	36	864	692	559
Kilderkin	18	672	559	457
Firkin	9	545	457	368
Pin	4½	457	368	305
Beer Barrels (Metal)				
Barrel	36	762	660	469
Kilderkin	18	610	533	432
Firkin	9	533	406	293
Pin	4½	412	330	248
Keg beer containers				
Beer barrels (Metal)				
Kilderkin	18	604	533	393
Firkin	9	520	418	293
Guiness Keg (Metal)				
Firkin	9	571	444	393

Table 5.6 TYPICAL OVERALL SIZES OF CANNED BEER CARTONS

Packs and cartons canned beer	Capacity of can	L	W	H
			(in mm)	
2 cans	7 pt	330	178	260
4 cans	7 pt	330	330	260
6 cans	16 fl oz	206	133	158
6 cans	10 fl oz	206	133	108
24 can	16 fl oz	426	293	175
24 can	10 fl oz	426	293	117

Table 5.8 TYPICAL OVERALL SIZES OF BEER CRATES

Crate	No. of bottles (dozens)	L	W	H	Weight full (kilos)	Weight empty (kilos)
			(in mm)			
Nip bottles	2	431	291	226	14.25	9.75
½ bottles	2	437	330	260	22.5	15.75
1 pt bottles	1	396	285	308	18.0	11.75

Note all dimensions in above tables are in mm

Table 5.9 BEER AND ALE MEASURE

	Pin	Firkin	Kilderkin	Barrel	Hogshead	Puncheon	Butt	Tun
Gallons	4½	9	18	36	54	72	108	216
Type of bottle								
Imp ½ pt	72	144	288	576	864	1,152	1,728	3,456
Imp 1 pt	36	72	144	288	432	576	864	1,728
Imp Quart	18	36	72	144	216	288	434	864

Equivalent measures in dozens of bottles:

	Pin	Firkin	Kilderkin	Barrel	Hogshead	Puncheon	Butt	Tun
Gallons	4½	9	18	36	54	72	108	216
Type of bottle								
Imp ½ pt	6	12	24	48	72	96	144	288
Imp 1 pt	3	6	12	24	36	48	72	144
Imp Quart	1½	3	6	12	18	24	36	72

Equivalent measures in capacity of crates:

		Pin	Firkin	Kilderkin	Barrel	Hogshead	Puncheon	Butt	Tun
Gallons		4½	9	18	36	54	72	108	216
Type of bottle	*No. of Bottles*								
Imp ½ pt	2 doz	3	6	12	24	36	48	72	144
Imp 1 pt	2 doz	3	6	12	24	36	48	72	144
Imp Quart	1 doz	–	3	6	12	18	24	26	72

Table 5.10. CO² BOTTLES

Weight (kilos)	Length (mm)	Diameter (mm)
12.75	1.600	152
6.375	838	152
2.25	533	152

Table 5.11 GLASSWASHER

	W	D	H	Weight
		(mm)		(kilos)
18 mm	285	323	359	12
25 mm	314	381	378	12.5

Location Preference. Installed in service counter in convenient position to receive dirty glasses, but not opposite till or cool shelves to avoid congestion.
Power 65 W
Consumes 2–3 pints of water per running minute
Services: hot water 12 mm dia
       cold   12 mm

Table 5.12 OPTIC UNITS

Sizes	Wall mounted		Free standing	
No. of bottles	H	W	H	W
	(in mm)		(in mm)	
1	457	102	—	—
2	457	178	824	178
3	457	279	816	279
4	457	406	816	406
5	457	484	816	584
6	457	711	816	711
4 rotary stand	—	—	635	254
6 rotary stand	—	—	635	279
7 rotary stand	—	—	635	305

Table 5.13 CASH REGISTERS

Electric   Width 412 mm   Depth 426 mm   Height 444 mm
Power 240 V AC 50 Hz, 3 A plug
Allow 164 mm on right hand side for handle.
Allow 178 mm on left hand side for till rolls 1, 2, 3 and 4 total models.

Manual   Width 412 mm   Depth 426 mm   Height 444 mm
Allow 50 mm on left hand side for key.

Location preference. The cash register should be centrally located, not behind the pumps or dispensers or where washing up takes place.

Table 5.14 BOTTLE COOLING SHELVES

Capacity	W	L	H	Use
		(in mm)		
144 $\frac{1}{2}$ pt bottles	431	838	762	Two tier back bar fitment
72 $\frac{1}{2}$ pt bottles	444	1.067	203	Back bar fitment
72 $\frac{1}{2}$ pt bottles	451	502	279	Underslung cooling unit
41 $\frac{1}{2}$ pt bottles	495	457	672	Free standing. Weight 25 kilos

Power 210/240 V AC 50 Hz.

Table 5.15 FLASH COOLER

Use	W	D	H	Weight
		(in mm)		(kilos)
1 beer cooler single coil	508	375	539	27
2 beer cooler double coil	559	375	539	30
4 beer cooler four coil	654	375	254	32
2 beer cooler double coil extra output	426	375	215	28

Power 210/240 V AC 50/60 Hz

Location preference. Below counter in prepared space and preferably not situated on a built in shelf to avoid unit vibration registering in bar counter.

Table 5.16 SIZES OF BOTTLE SKIPS
(Plastic containers on castors situated under the counter to receive and cart away empty bottles)

L	W	H
	(in mm)	
686	457	723
571	571	520
825	823	727
825	457	787

Table 5.17 DIMENSIONS OF GLASSES *(in mm)*

Type	H	Dia
Port	82	45
Sherry	88	43
Liqueur	99	43
Small Goblet	114	70
Large Goblet	127	76
Champagne	108	88
Brandy	139	82
Wine Goblet	152	79
Hock	181	60
$\frac{1}{2}$ pt mug	94	76*
1 pt mug	120	94†
$\frac{1}{2}$ pt tumbler	114	76
1 pt tumbler	152	96
$\frac{1}{2}$ pt ($9\frac{1}{2}$ fl oz) bottle	178	76
Tankard (Pewter)	127	92

*including handle, 111 mm + including handle, 133 mm

Table 5.18 DIMENSIONS OF BOTTLES *(in mm)*

Type	H	Dia
Whisky Tregnum	432	102
Champagne Magnum	381	114
Rhine Wine	356	76
Soda Syphon	381	108
Vermouth	317	88
Squires Tregnum	305	114
Whisky	305	76
Jumbo Port or Sherry	342	108
Burgundy	294	88
Claret	291	76
Chianti	279	127
Cider	317	91
Cordial	257	76
Beer 1 pt	279	76
Beer $\frac{1}{2}$ pt	203	57

The table shows the sizes of glasses and bottles commonly in use in public houses, slight variation may occur depending upon manufacturer. These sizes accommodate imperial measures, and can be expected to change with the universal introduction of metric measure.

Table 5.19 CATERING
Equipment required for up to 40 customers:

Domestic refrigerator
Cold display case
Washing-up sink
Hand-wash bowl
Stand, brackets and taps
Pie warmer or hotplate

For larger houses the following additional equipment will be required:

Convection oven
Boiling rings
Deep freeze cabinet
Valentine fryer
Hot cupboard
Refrigerated display cabinet
Coffee maker

Table 5.20 REQUIREMENTS FOR TYPICAL CATERING OPERATION
Seating allowances including circulation space

	m²
Table service	0.93–1.3
Counter service	1.2–1.86
Cafeteria service (tables of 1–6)	1.1–1.4
Cafeteria service (tables of 8 or over)	0.74–0.93
Banqueting rooms (long tables)	0.74–0.93

Table 5.21 GAMES

	L	W
Pool Table		
Standard	1829	914
Space required	3658	1829
Small	1524	762
Space required	3533	1676
Spot black table		
Hexagonal shape	1372	1219
Space required	2591	2438
Bumper Pool	1219	762
Space required	3048	1676

Ric-o-chet (2 or 4 players)

width (mm)	depth (mm)	height (mm)	weight (kilos)
749	698	1694	100

Space required 1372 × 1295 mm

The average acceptable plan size for gaming machines is:
762 × 686 mm

Darts	
Size of board	437 mm
Height centred at	1727 mm
Throwing line	2743 mm
at (max)	2591 mm
	2438 mm

Games such as chess, dominoes, draughts, bagatelle, cards, shove ha'penny require normal tables and present no space problems.

LEGISLATION

Table 5.22 is taken from the report of the Erroll Commission on Liquor licencing, Cmnd 5154, December 1972, and sets out the scope of the Acts and powers of the Justices. The majority of these Statutes are common to the design and construction of all premises used by the public and their procedures should be well known to the Architect. It is however recommended that the various Officers concerned with their enforcement should be consulted at sketch stage on those specific to licensed premises.

The law relating to the sale by retail of intoxicating liquor is contained in the Licensing Act 1964 which sets out in detail the procedures in applying for either a full on license or restaurant license. Application is made by the proposed Licensee, usually a multiple license holder of the Brewery Company responsible for building the new premises. The application is presented to the Licensing Justices (known as a Committee) at any Transfer Session by a Solicitor, with the proposed Licensee and the Architect in attendance. Transfer Sessions are held not more than eight times a year and Notice of Application must be submitted to the Justices Clerk not less than three weeks in advance. Plans for the premises are submitted to the Justices with the Notices and to Police and Fire Authorities. Notice of Intention to apply for a licence must be posted on the site and in the local Press.

The Justices require to be satisfied that there is a need for a public house in the area and that the proposed premises are suitable in all respects for drinking intoxicating liquor on the premises ('on-sale'). Due consideration by the Justices will be taken of recommendations by Police and Fire Authorities, and other Licensees, organisations, or the public at large, have a right to object at the Transfer Session. The applicant has the right of appeal against a refusal by the Justices.

The receipt of Planning Permission is not a condition for the granting of a Justices' Provisional licence. Equally, the Justices are in no way bound to grant a licence by its previous receipt. In some cases it may be necessary to obtain a decision in principle, for instance when the purchase of the site is subject to the grant of the licence. The procedure in these cases is very similar to an Outline Planning Application, being made on a site plan only with a written description of the proposed premises.

The licence then granted, is conditional on detail plans being submitted and approved within twelve months of the original grant by the Justices, (known as 'Affirmation'), otherwise the license is automatically nullified and all procedures must be repeated.

Justices approval must be sought for any amendment made for any reason to the plans submitted to support the provisional licence: on completion of the premises application is made for what is known as the Final Order, three weeks notice again being required, and if the Justices, having inspected the premises, are satisfied, the Final Order will be granted and the Public House can open immediately for trading.

A Music and Dancing Licence is granted only at the final hearing but since its requirement will have an important effect on both planning for means of escape, and equipment by entailing the installation of emergency lighting, smoke detectors and fire alarm systems, the Architect must ascertain his client's intentions in this respect at an early stage. Those provisions of part 2 of the Fire Precautions Act 1971 which affect licensed premises are now being enforced and if there are six or more staff living in a Fire Certificate will be required.

Public Health Inspectors are very much concerned under various legislation with the hygiene and sanitary conditions for both public and staff, accent being on adequate inside washing and toilet facilities and the provision of snack preparation areas separate from the domestic kitchen.

Compressor and other mechanical equipment has to be sited and suitably sound-proofed not to cause local objection and thereby the attention of the appropriate Local Authority officials.

Table 5.22 PRINCIPLE FUNCTIONS OF LOCAL AUTHORITIES IN RELATION TO LICENSED PREMISES

Subject	Type of Licensed Premises concerned	Statute	Scope	Present Enforcement Authority (New authorities after local government re-organisation—outside Greater London—in brackets)	Powers of Justices in Similar Fields
1. Planning	All types	Town and Country Planning Act 1971. The General Development Order 1963 (as amended by the 1964, 1968 and 1969 Orders.) Town and Country (Amendment) Planning Act 1972.	Planning permission is required for development of land (i.e. the carrying out of building, engineering, mining or other operations, in, on, over or under land, or the making of any material change of use of any buildings or other land.) The following works or uses are excluded from this requirement: Works of maintenance, improvement or alteration which affect only the interior of a building or do not materially effect its external appearance (other than additions below the ground); the use of buildings or land within the curtilage of a dwelling house for any purpose incidental to the enjoyment of the dwelling house as such; the use of land for the purpose of agriculture or forestry; and where land or a building is used for a purpose within a class defined in the Schedule to the Town and Country Planning (Use Classes) Order 1963, change to another use within the same class. In considering an application for planning permission to build a public house or to change the use of an existing building to use as a public house, the local planning authority are bound by the terms of the 1962 Act to "have regard to the provisions of the development plan and to any other material considerations". The latter must be planning considerations and these would include the effect of the proposal on road safety and the amenities of the locality. The question of "need" would only be relevant if there were basic planning objections to the proposed site, and might in such circumstances be weighed against the objections. Authorities would normally give publicity locally to a planning application and would take into account representations received insofar as they affected planning interests.	County Boroughs County Councils County Districts London Boroughs City of London (Metropolitan Counties Metropolitan Districts Non-metropolitan Counties Non-metropolitan Districts)	On application for a new justices' licence, a plan must be deposited with the application. Justices have power on grant of a new on-licence to impose such conditions governing the tenure of the licence *or any other matters* as they think proper in the public interest. On application for renewal of a licence, justices can require a plan of the premises and can make an order that, within a fixed period of time, such structural alterations as they require shall be carried out. Alterations affecting the public parts of the licensed premises require the consent of the justices unless required by order of some lawful authority (e.g. local authority).

	Premises	Act	Description	Local Authorities	Conditions
2. Planning (Sanitation)	All On-Licensed Premises	Public Health Act 1936	Local authorities have power to reject plans for new buildings (including licensed premises), if provision of sanitary accommodation is insufficient. They also have power to serve notices as regards existing buildings if facilities are inadequate or prejudicial to health or a nuisance. Disputes about standard of provision are settled in a magistrates court. (Toilets for staff are covered in the section on employment conditions—see 3 below).	County Boroughs London Boroughs County Districts (Metropolitan Districts, Non-metropolitan Districts)	The powers to impose conditions on a licence enable justices to control the provision of toilet facilities, etc.
3. Employment conditions	All types	Shops Act 1950 (Section 74(1) of the Act includes sales of intoxicating liquor in the expression 'retail trade or business'. A shop is defined as premises where any retail trade or business is carried on).	Part II of the Act contains provisions relating to hours of employment of shop assistants under 18 years of age, Sunday employment, meal breaks and weekly half holidays for all shop assistants. (Licensed House Managers would probably be included in this expression.) Employers in catering establishments (including those selling intoxicating liquors) can elect to have alternative conditions applied to their employees which guarantee them a prescribed number of holidays on Sundays and weekdays.	County Boroughs District Councils with a population of at least 20,000. District Councils with a population of less than 20,000 to whom responsibility has been delegated by the County Council. Elsewhere the County Council. (Metropolitan Districts Non-metropolitan Districts).	Although the powers of licensing justices to apply conditions to new licences are theoretically unlimited, they have not in practice generally extended to these matters.
		Offices Shops and Railway Premises Act 1963.	This Act contains provisions regarding the health, safety and welfare of employees. The provisions which apply to those parts of the premises in which employees work, require provision of sanitary convenience, washing facilities, drinking water, seats and first aid equipment for employees, and also apply standards of cleanliness.	County Boroughs London Boroughs County Districts (Metropolitan Districts Non-metropolitan Districts)	See above
4. Food Hygiene	All licensed premises where open foods are stored, prepared or exposed for sale.	The Food Hygiene (General) Regulations 1970 (Made under the Food and Drugs Act 1955).	Regulations covering cleanliness of premises and equipment, storage of food, dress of employees, toilets and washing facilities, refuse disposal.	Borough and District Councils, London Boroughs Common Council of City of London (Metropolitan Districts Non-metropolitan Districts)	Conditions imposed by justices.
5. Noise	All types	Noise Abatement Act 1960.	Noise or vibration which is a nuisance or a statutory nuisance for the purpose of Part III of the Public Health Act 1936. Local authorities have powers to make abatement orders.	County Councils GLC County Boroughs London Boroughs Common Council of City of London County Districts. (Metropolitan Districts Non-metropolitan Districts)	The general powers of justices to impose conditions on new licences could be used in this field, as could their power to refuse to renew a licence.

Table 5.22 PRINCIPAL FUNCTIONS OF LOCAL AUTHORITIES IN RELATION TO LICENSED PREMISES

Subject	Type of Licensed Premises concerned	Statute	Scope	Present Enforcement Authority (New authorities after local government reorganisation—outside Greater London—in brackets)	Powers of Justices in Similar Fields
6. Safety	All types	Licensing Act 1964.	Paragraph 5 of Schedule 2 to the Act provides that on an application for a new licence or a removal the fire authority should be given notice of the application. The fire authority can oppose grant of a new licence or removal if they consider the premises dangerous.	County and County Borough Councils (Metropolitan Counties Non-metropolitan counties)	Justices have general power to refuse a licence if they consider the premises unsuitable or to impose conditions, or to require either on grant or renewal of a licence that certain structural alterations be carried out.
	Public Houses and Licensed Restaurants	Offices Shops and Railways Premises Act 1963.	Section 28 of the Act requires all premises to which the Act applies to be provided with such means of escape in case of fire as may reasonably be required in the circumstances of each case. Section 29 requires premises in which more than 20 persons are employed or where more than 10 are employed elsewhere than on the ground floor to be covered by a certificate ('a fire certificate') that the premises are provided with such means of escape in case of fire as may reasonably be required in the circumstances of the case.	County Boroughs London Boroughs County Districts (Metropolitan Districts Non-metropolitan Districts)	See above
	Hotels and clubs	Fire Precautions Act 1971.	Premises require to be covered by a fire certificate issued by the fire authority for the area, dealing with the means of escape from fire and other related precautions (including, for example, fire alarms and training of staff). (The Act has not yet been brought into force as regards licensed premises.)	The authority responsible for discharging in the area the function of fire authority under the Fire Services Act 1947 (i.e. normally County and County Borough Councils). (Metropolitan Counties Non-Metropolitan Counties)	See above (When the 1971 Act comes into force any conditions of licence or registration certificate relating to fire precautions will be superseded.)
	Registered clubs	Licensing Act 1964.	Part II of the Act provides the fire authority and local authority with power to inspect club premises on first registration or renewal.	(Metropolitan Counties Non-Metropolitan Counties)	Magistrates in considering an application can have regard to the nature of the club premises. Objections to the grant or renewal can be made on the grounds that the premises are not suitable. (Such powers would be superseded by implementation of Fire Precuations Act 1971 in relation to registered clubs.)

	Premises	Statutes	Description	Authorities	Notes
7. Music and dancing	Public houses, Hotels, clubs and other Licensed Premises providing public music and dancing (in areas covered by statutes)	1. London Government Act 1963. 2. Home Counties (Music and Dancing) Licensing Act 1926. 3. Local Acts.	In London, parts of the Home Counties and certain areas covered by local Act powers, premises providing public music, singing and dancing are required to be licensed by the local authority. Local authorities have general power to refuse a licence if they consider the premises unsuitable or to impose whatever conditions they think fit.	1. GLC 2. Essex, Hertfordshire and so much of the administrative counties of Kent and Buckinghamshire as lies within 20 miles of the City of London or the City of Westminster, whichever may be nearer to them. 3. County, County Borough or District Councils depending on terms of local Act.	A public music and dancing licence is required before a special hours certificate can be granted under the Licensing Act 1964. In some parts of the country where section 51 of the Public Health Acts Amendment Act 1890 is in force, justices are the licensing authority for places for public music and dancing.
8. Weights and Measures	All types	Weights and Measures Act 1963.	The Act prescribes the quantities in which certain intoxicating liquors may be sold. The provisions are enforced by the weights and measures authorities through an inspectorate.	County and County Borough Councils, and certain County District Councils, and Non-County Borough Councils, London Boroughs and City of London. (Metropolitan Counties, Non - Metropolitan Counties).	The scope of the justices' general discretion is wide enough for them to concern themselves with weights and measures, but in general practice, they do not do so.
9. Building Regulations	All types	Public Health Act 1963, Public Health Act 1961.	Regulations made under the Acts govern the construction of buildings in the interests of public health and safety. (For example, certain structures must be sound, and certain materials used must be fire-resistant).	County Borough, Non-County Borough, and County District Councils. Outer London Boroughs. (Inner London Boroughs and City of London are covered by London Building Acts 1930–39). (Metropolitan Districts Non-Metropolitan Districts).	The justices' discretion is that described under 'Planning and Safety'.

EXAMPLES

1. Southend Electricity Board Dining Room
Architects: Edgington, Spink & Hyne
Building (16 Feb 1973)

2. The Wheatsheaf, Camberley, Surrey
Architects: John & Sylvia Reed
Architects' Journal (9 June 1971)

3. Cake House, St. James' Park, London.
Architects: Ministry of Building & Public Works
Building (20 March 1970)

4. Queen's Public House, Queen's Market, Newham, London
Architects: Covell, Matthews & Partners
Architects' Journal (18 April 1970)

5. The Lord High Admiral, Charlwood House, Vauxhall Bridge Road, London
Architects: Darbourne & Darke
Architects' Journal (18 April 1970)

BIBLIOGRAPHY

JOURNAL ARTICLES

Bradbeer, F., 'Public house buildings'. Design guide and technical study. Incl. information sheet on the relationship of spaces in public houses. *Architects' Journal*, pp 785–801; information sheet 1488 (March 29, 1967).

Curl, J. S., 'The vanished gin palaces'. *Country Life*, pp 1598–1600 (June 22).

Curl, J. S., 'Whatever happened to the London pub?' *Archt & Bldg. News,* pp 59–61 (Nov 19, 1970).

'Design for hospitality: pubs.' *The Designer*, pp 7–11 (Nov 1971).

'Eating and dinking spaces: dining-room equipment'. *Archts Jnl. information sheet* 1258 (May 13, 1964).

'Eating and drinking spaces, fixtures and equipment: Briefing guide.' *Archts Jnl.,* pp 931–948: information sheet 1257, pp 931–948 (April 22, 1964).

Edleston, W. E., 'Drink storage and bar service spaces, fixtures and equipment Briefing guide'; information sheets by A. S. Hunt *et al. Archts Jnl.* pp 1209–28 (May 27, 1964) information sheets 1259 and 1260 (June 3, 1964), information sheet 1261 (June 10, 1964).

Nairn, I. and Browne, K., 'Pub in focus'. *Archtl. Review,* pp 401–4 (Dec 1962).

'Public houses, inns and taverns'. *Interior Design,* pp 96–110 (Feb 1972).

'Public houses, inns and taverns: recent developments'. *Interior Design,* pp 21–42 (Jan 1971).

'Pubs and restaurants'; two architects well known in these different fields of design—David Brookbank and Peter Jordan. Article by J. Chisholm. *The Architect*, pp 28–30 (June 1972).

Salmon, G., The post-war pub. A Survey of 77 British pubs. *Archts Jnl.* pp 1143–68 (May 20, 1964).

Sugden, B. H., 'The British pub—its history, current developments and future trends'. *Era,* No. 25, pp 14–15 (March/April 1972).

Two London pubs: (1) Queens public house, London borough of Newham; Architects, Covell, Matthews and Ptnrs. (2) The Lord High Admiral, Charlwood House, Vauxhall Bridge Road, London borough of Westminster; Architects Darbourne and Drake. *Archts Jnl.* pp 925–940 (April 15, 1970).

BOOKS

The Architects' Journal (Ed) *Principles of hotel design.* Arch. Press, London (1970).

Architectural Record, *Motels, hotels, restaurants and bars,* 2nd ed. F. W. Dodge Corpn., N.Y. (1960).

Batchelor, Denzil. *The English inn.* Batsford, London (1963).

Fengler, Max, *Restaurant architecture and design,* Leonard Hill, London (1971).

Goldsmith, Selwyn, *Designing for the disabled,* 2nd ed. R.I.B.A. London (1967).

Hattrell, W. S., *Hotels, restaurants, bars,* Batsford, London (1962).

Home Office, *Report of the Departmental Committee on Liquor Licensing* (Chairman: The Rt. Hon. Lord Erroll of Hale), Command Paper 5154, HMSO (1972).

Housing & Local Government, Ministry of, *Homes for today and tomorrow. Report of a committee* (Chairman: Sir Parker Morris), HMSO (1961).

Hutt, Christopher, *The death of the English pub,* Hutchinson, London (1973).

IHVE Guide 1970. Book A: *Design Data;* Book B: *Installation and Equipment Data;* Book C: *Reference Data.* IHVE (1970).

Lawson, Fred, *Principles of catering design,* Arch. Press, London (1973).

Lawson, Fred, *Restaurant planning and design,* Arch. Press, London (1973).

Miles, J. G. (ed.) *Innkeeping: a manual for licensed victuallers,* Barrie & Jenkins (for the National Trade Development Association), London (1972).

Monckton, H. A. A., *History of the English public house,* Bodley Head, London (1969).

Oliver, Basil, *The renaissance of the English public house,* Faber, London (1947).

Richards, Timothy M. and Curl, J. S., *City of London pubs: a practical and historical guide,* David and Charles, Newton Abbot (1973).

Spiller, Brian, *Victorian public houses,* David and Charles, Newton Abbot (1972).

C. John Main *Degree of B. Arch., Liverpool University, 1957: A.R.I.B.A. 1959. Present appointment: Assistant Director of Architecture, London Borough of Camden. From 1957–58 was Assistant, G.L.C. Architect's Department, Housing Division and Senior Assistant to Miss Nadine Beddington, Chief Architect of Freeman Hardy Willis, from 1959 to 1961.*

During period 1961–73 was Design Architect and subsequently Deputy Chief Architect, Trust Houses Forte Limited. Chief Architect, Whitbread London Ltd, 1973–74. John Main was lecturer in part-time evening courses in History of Architecture and studio at Thames Polytechnic, from 1960–72. Has contributed various articles for 'The Architect' and has interests in music, (piano playing and composition), landscape design, history. Mr Main has travelled in the U.S. and Europe on study tours of hotel and restaurant operations.

6 SPORTS CENTRES AND SWIMMING POOLS

GERALD A. PERRIN,
Perrin Associates

INTRODUCTION

Sports halls and their later counterparts, indoor sports centres, have evolved in the UK largely as a result of findings in the Wolfenden Report published in 1960, which drew attention to the growing need for a wider range of sports facilities, and in particular for the greater provision of indoor facilities.

This need stemmed from a number of changing requirements. Schools' physical education teaching methods were placing more emphasis on game diversification and skill learning, which rapidly outdated the traditional wall-barred gymnasium. Society was more settled than at any time in the preceding forty years, and was looking for different ways in which it could spend its growing leisure time. People were becoming more mobile and could see how other countries were also beginning to provide for recreation. As living standards rose throughout Europe, people were becoming increasingly accustomed to expect higher environmental standards.

Early sports halls in the UK were often little more than 'barns', sometimes only three-sided, and frequently unheated and unventilated. Players soon expressed their dislike of these conditions and the first fully enclosed and properly heated halls began to appear between 1962 and 1967.

Many variations were experimented with in this period including circular domes (Lightfoot Centre Newcastle and Perth Sports Centre), glass 'boxes' (Hull University and Crystal Palace), and a combination of solid wall and partial fenestration (Harlow and Bracknell). A completely window-less box soon came to be preferred by most players and the first major example at the University of Kent, Canterbury became the prototype for many subsequent projects.

From a planning and economic point of view it became clear that where a sports hall and swimming pool were proposed for the same town, it was better to combine them in the form we have now come to associate with the indoor sports centre. Many recently completed centres have extended this range to include indoor bowls halls (Dunstable, Bletchley, Picketts Lock Centre in the Lea Valley, London) and ice skating rinks (Grimsby Leisure Centre and Sobell Centre, Islington, London).

Ancillary facilities are invariably included and normally consist of squash courts, smaller games halls, target-shooting galleries, leisure-conditioning suites, sauna suites, weight-training rooms and practice climbing walls. Refreshment and bar services are always included, to rising specification standards which allow for indoor landscaping, fitted carpets, purpose built furniture, well-designed bar optics, curtains, and tape recorded music.

With these rising standards, user participation has veered away from the active competitive atmosphere of early sports centres, to a more relaxed and in many respects more enjoyable form of involvement which has appealed to a much wider public. This is reflected most clearly in the design of many recent swimming pools, where former rectangular (and therefore competitive-based) pools have been replaced by irregular shaped pools, some equipped with wave-making apparatus, indoor trees, carpeted surrounds, poolside creches, and children's sandpits. Probably the best examples at the present time may be seen at Bletchley, Dunstable and Rotherham (The Herringthorpe Centre).

Future trends will probably develop this movement away from 'pure' sport still further—and if they follow current practice in western Europe, where development in many respects is probably five to ten years ahead of our own—we will probably see more facilities sited in urban parks. In these circumstances they will be more closely associated with other, more passive, forms of recreation such as the arts, exhibition halls, zoos and museums.

SITING

SUB REGIONAL

In a number of cases sports centres have been sited in small towns easily reached by car or public transport and serve sub regions of up to 15–20 miles radius from the centre (see Fig 6.1).

Examples are Bingham (Nottinghamshire) and Blaby (Leicestershire).

CENTRAL AREA – TOWN CENTRE

Generally referred to as a 'Generator' unit due to the demand stimulated by a central area location. Usually a combination of Sports Hall and Swimming Pool known as a Sports Centre (Fig 6.3). This unit would be the normal centre for major events, tournaments, galas and crowd-pulling attractions.

Examples are the Billingham Forum, Sobell Basingstoke, Guildford, Cambridge, and Newton Aycliffe.

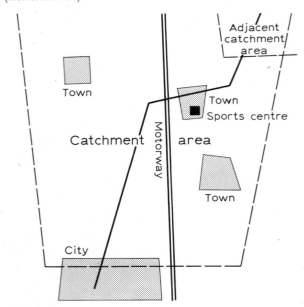

Fig. 6.1   Sub-regional sites

TOWN CENTRE PERIPHERY

This is possibly the most popular choice of any to date, as access is normally easy both by car and public transport. Unlike the central area location future expansion sets no particular problems (see Fig 6.2).

Examples are Harlow, Dunstable, Eastleigh, Bletchley, Ashford, Bracknell and Slough.

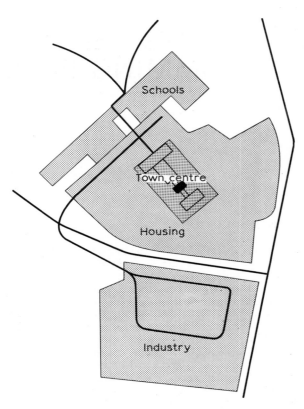

Fig. 6.3   A town centre site

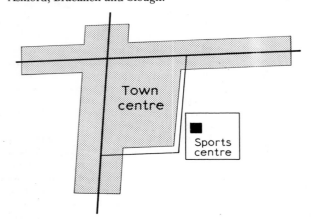

Fig. 6.2   Town centre periphery site

PERIPHERAL – NEIGHBOURHOOD CENTRE

This is a dispersal arrangement based upon the neighbourhood principle in Mark One New Towns (see Fig 6.4). Each unit is designed to serve a community of between 20 000 and 30 000.

Some units form part of a secondary school campus as joint provision facilities (jointly sponsored by Local and Education Authorities).

In theory, units 1–4 could be designed to accommodate specific specialist facilities, e.g. unit 1, a ski slope, unit 2, a target shooting gallery, unit 3, six squash courts, and unit 4, a bowls hall. Unit 5 represents a central area location which may also house the administrative headquarters for all other units.

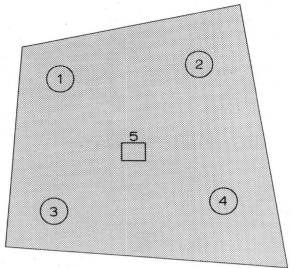

Fig. 6.4   A neighbourhood centre site

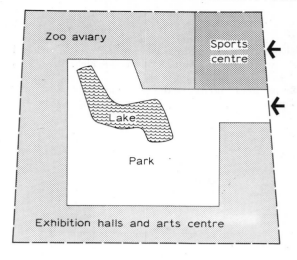

Fig. 6.6   Urban park location

Note. Access to the sports centre must be separate to that of the park

SCHOOL OR UNIVERSITY CAMPUS

Sports centres built adjacent to schools or universities are generally referred to as joint use projects where use can be shared by both school and the public. The latter obtain access via a completely separate entrance from that used by the school, (see Fig 6.5).

Examples are Bingham, Carlton Forum and Balderton, all in Nottinghamshire, Cheetham Crumpsall Centre, Manchester and Lancaster University.

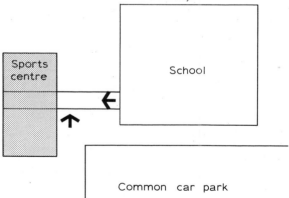

Fig. 6.5   School or university campus site

Note. This example is being actively encouraged by Government Policy and it is intended to extend it to industrial and commercial premises

URBAN PARK LOCATION

This is a relatively untried concept in the UK but is widely seen on the Continent particularly in West Germany. The sports centre shares the urban park with a wide range of other facilities such as those suggested in this example (see Fig 6.6).

Examples are in the Gruga Park, Essen, and the Bundesgarten Park in Cologne.

PLANNING

GENERAL CIRCULATION

Fig 6.7 illustrates a typical combined example showing entry at ground level leading to changing rooms (left) and a self-contained Sauna Suite (right).

Separate changing rooms are indicated for the Sports Hall and Swimming Pool, although the trend is towards combined areas.

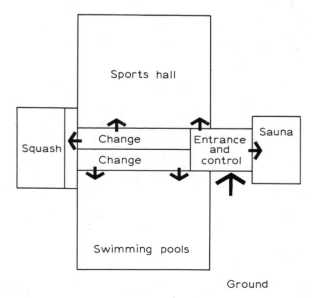

Fig. 6.7   Showing general circulation

FIRST FLOOR VIEWING

Formal viewing (through glass screens) is normal to the Swimming Pool, informal viewing (from open galleries) to the Sports Hall and Squash Courts (see Fig 6.8).

Lifts for a maximum of six persons are usually installed for paraplegic users, and dry goods supplies to food preparation areas.

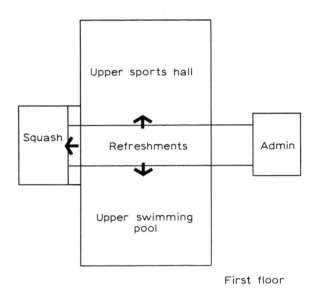

First floor

Fig. 6.8   First floor arrangement

SOME TYPICAL PLANS

Fig 6.10 shows the general arrangment of main elements at the Eastleigh Sports Centre. Refreshment rooms and administrative offices are positioned over the central changing room spine. Entrance is at first floor level leaving ground floor circulation free for players and swimmers only. Viewing galleries overlook all indoor activity areas, and outdoor pitches. Low level entry for paraplegic users and school parties. There is a lift to the first floor.

Main activity areas at Bletchley Leisure Centre are shown in Fig 6.11. Entrance is at first floor level above central changing room spine, for the same reasons as above. Viewing facilities to Sports Hall and Swimming Pool. Refreshments and social facilities positioned above changing rooms. Youth wing below Bowls Hall. There is a lift to all floors.

Fig 6.12 illustrates the arrangement of the Grimsby Leisure Centre showing general disposition of main areas. Viewing and eating facilities at first floor level overlooking pool and ice rink.

DATA

Recommended constructional dimensions for various indoor activities are shown in Figs 6.20 to 6.23. For basketball the recommended space required about the court is 32 × 17 m.

Minimum height is 7.6 m. Five-a-side football (Fig 6.24) will occupy the entire hall. Near square halls are mainly preferred to rectangular. Penalty area sizes vary with users. Likewise, six-a-side hockey will also occupy the entire hall.

Figs 6.25 (a) and (b) illustrate typical Sports Stadia data showing arrangements for stands, soccer pitch, running track, athletics arena etc. Figs 6.26 to 6.30 give recommended data for outdoor athletics facilities and individual sports pitches.

SCHEDULE OF ACCOMMODATION

Sports Hall	Squash Courts
Ancillary Hall(s)	Main Swimming Pool
Combat Room(s)	Learner Pool
Weight Training Room	Diving Pool
Leisure Conditioning Suite	Thermal Pool
Gallery Hall	Paddling Pool
Reception Office/Control	Pre Cleanse Areas
Shop	Basket/Locker Rooms
Administration Suite	Dry Land Training Area
First Aid Room	Sunbathing Areas/Solarium
Sauna Suite	Unit
Changing Rooms	Spectator Areas/Viewing
Instructors Rooms	Galleries
Bar and Bar Lounge	Equipment Store
Refreshment Lounge	Poolside Supervisor's Office
Meeting Rooms	Display/Notices Area
Creche	Laundry
Staff Rest Room	Plant Room and Boiler House
Equipment Store	Toilets
Bar Store	Changing Rooms
General Store	Showers
Dry Good Store	Rowing Basin
Plant Room	Refreshment Lounge
Water Storage Area	Bar and Bar Lounge
	Control Areas

SPORTS HALLS

Sports hall. Should be suitable for tennis, badminton (4 or 5 courts), netball, basketball, volleyball and five-a-side football. Normally described as a one court hall. A two court hall doubles the above accommodation. The most common units are:

	33.6 × 18.2 × 7.6m (120 × 60 × 25ft)
One Court Halls	33.5 × 21.3 × 8.5m (110 × 70 × 28ft)
	32.0 × 25.9 × 8.5m (105 × 85 × 28ft)
Two Court Hall	36.6 × 32.0 × 9.1m (120 × 105 × 30ft)

Ancillary Hall. For activities more suitably accommodated outside the Sports Hall, e.g. trampolining, table tennis, yoga, etc. Often used as a disco area, or for large public meetings, conferences etc.

Combat Room. Designed to accommodate the combat group of activities, e.g. boxing, judo, karate, fencing, etc. Ideally, Judo should have a separate room to avoid frequent dismantling of apparatus.

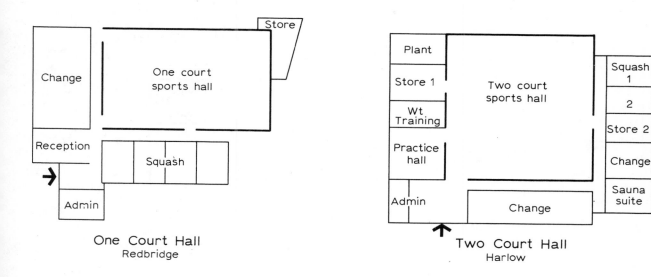

One Court Hall
Redbridge

Two Court Hall
Harlow

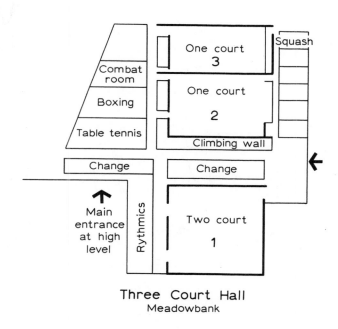

Three Court Hall
Meadowbank

Fig. 6.9 Planning arrangement for 3 typical sports halls

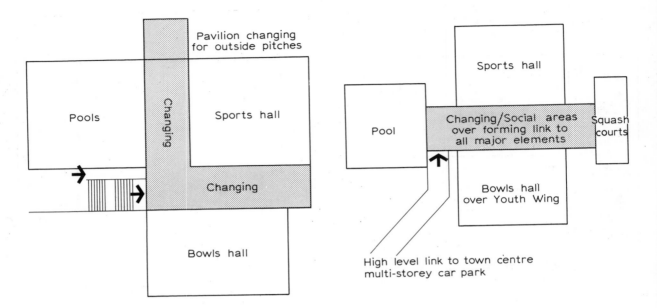

Fig. 6.10   Eastleigh Sports Centre

Fig. 6.11   Bletchley Leisure Centre

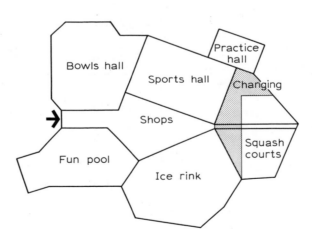

Fig. 6.12   Grimsby Leisure Centre

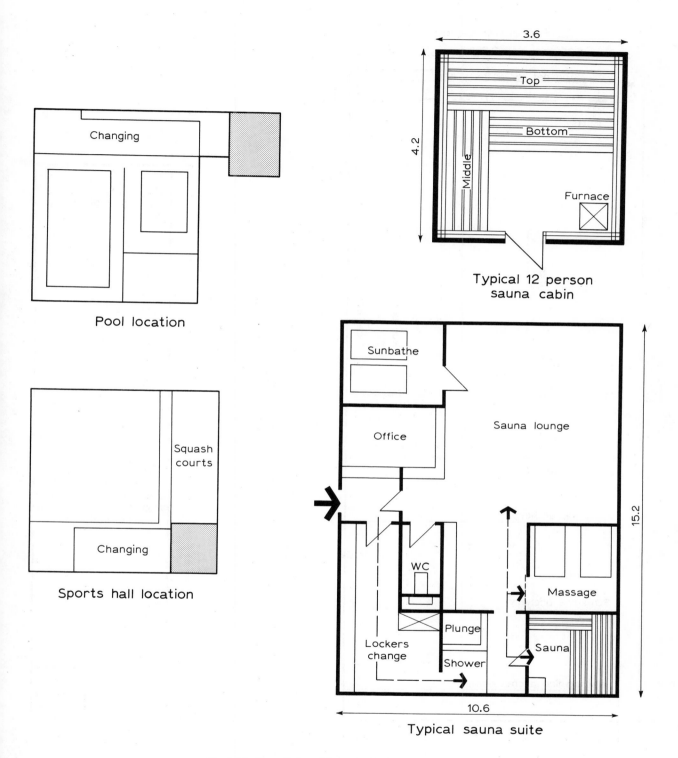

Pool location

Sports hall location

3.6

4.2

Top

Bottom

Middle

Furnace

**Typical 12 person
sauna cabin**

Sunbathe

Office

Sauna lounge

15.2

WC

Massage

Lockers
change

Plunge

Shower

Sauna

10.6

Typical sauna suite

Fig. 6.13   Sports Halls and Swimming Pools: secondary spaces

Projectile gallery

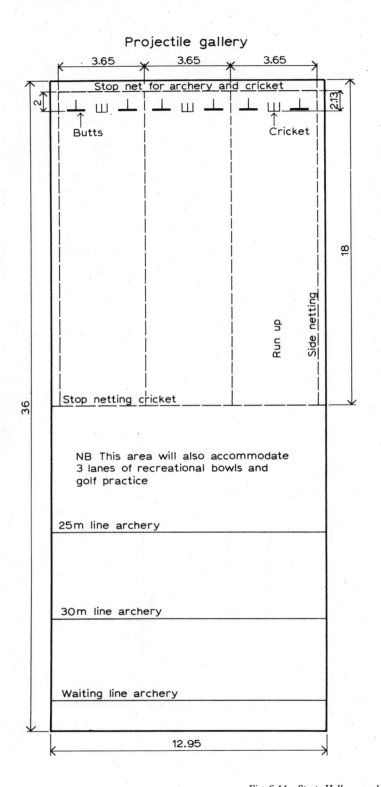

Target shooting

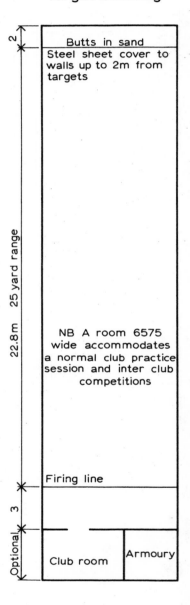

Fig. 6.14   *Sports Halls: secondary spaces*

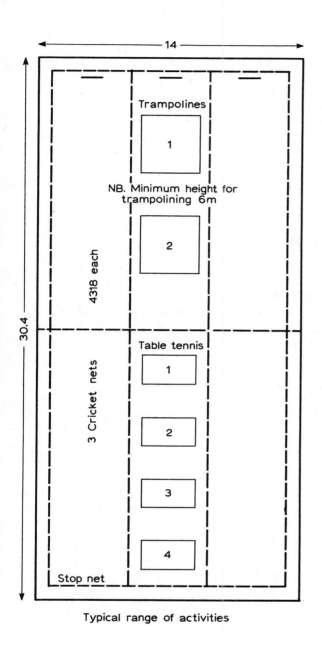

Typical range of activities

Single unit 1

Single unit 2

Double unit

Fig. 6.15   Sports Halls: secondary spaces (continued)

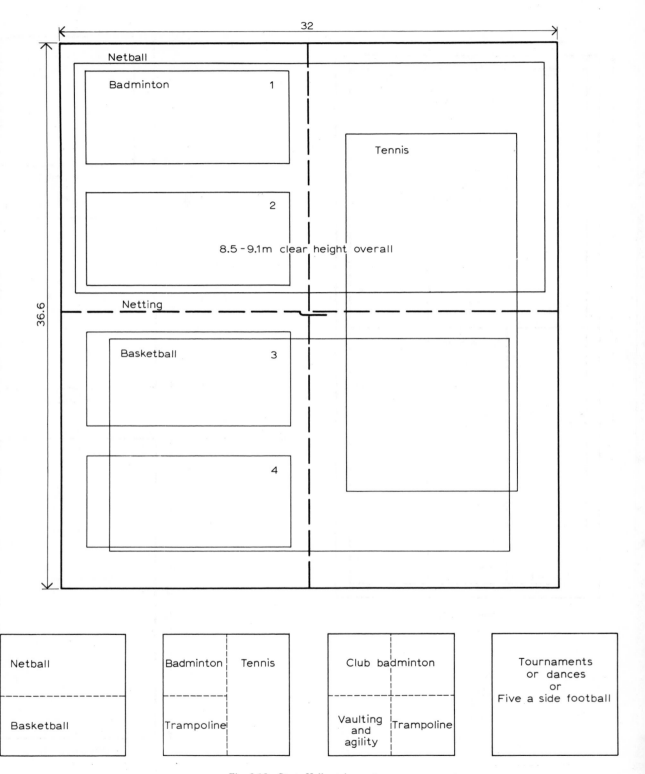

32

36.6

Netball

Badminton   1

2

Tennis

8.5 - 9.1m clear height overall

Netting

Basketball   3

4

Netball		
Basketball		

Badminton	Tennis	
Trampoline		

Club badminton		
Vaulting and agility	Trampoline	

Tournaments or dances or Five a side football

Fig. 6.16   Sports Halls: primary spaces
(See also Technical Unit for Sport recommendations contained in the publication
'Sports Halls – a new approach to their dimensions and use')

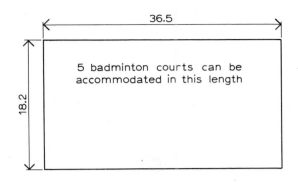

36.5

18.2

5 badminton courts can be accommodated in this length

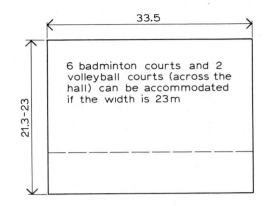

33.5

21.3–23

6 badminton courts and 2 volleyball courts (across the hall) can be accommodated if the width is 23m

Note. Sports Council recommended sizes are:
32 × 26 × 7·6 m
32 × 23 × 7·6 m
29 × 23 × 7·6 m

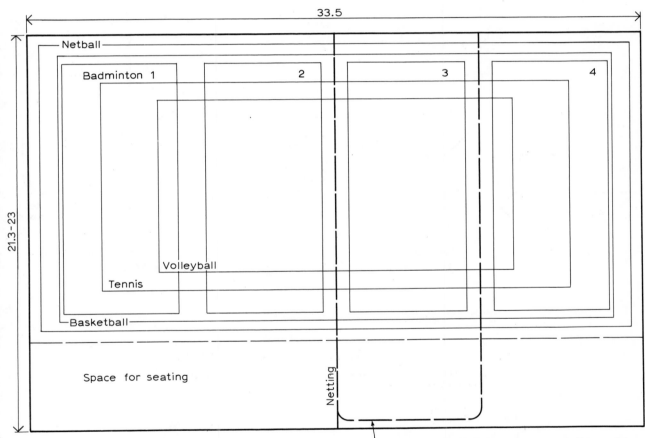

33.5

21.3–23

Netball

Badminton 1   2   3   4

Volleyball

Tennis

Basketball

Space for seating

Netting

NB. With this netting arrangement the end bay can be used for trampolining, table tennis, vaulting and agility, etc. at the same time as 3 badminton courts are in use

Fig. 6.17   Sports Halls: primary spaces (continued)
(See note under Fig 6.16)

6–11

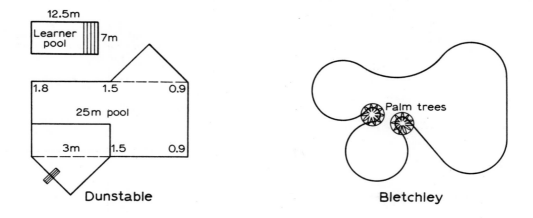

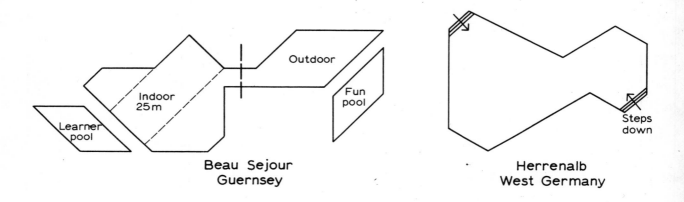

Fig. 6.18 Swimming Pools: primary spaces. All examples have a top deck water level

Note. The Dunstable and Beau Sejour examples can accommodate district and county competitions over 25 m length.
Planning priorities tend to be as follows:
1. Recreational swimming;
2. Teaching and water safety;
3. Competition and training.

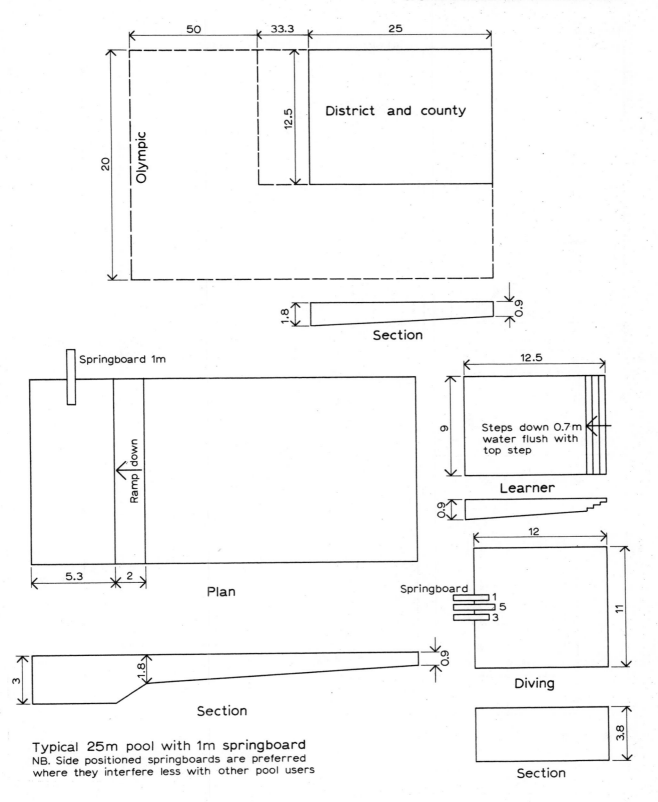

Fig. 6.19 Swimming Pools. Primary spaces.

Netball

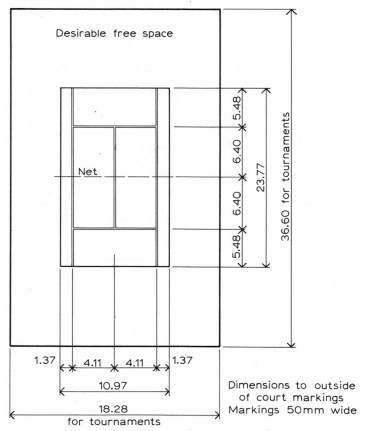

r 457mm

r 4.87

Space about court

30.48
33.48
10.16
10.16
10.16

15.20
18.20

Dimensions to outside
of court markings.
Markings 50mm wide

Volleyball

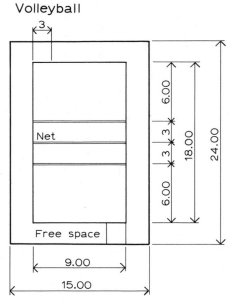

3

Net

Free space

6.00
3
3
3
6.00
18.00
24.00

9.00
15.00

Dimensions to outside of court markings.
Markings 50mm wide

Tennis

Desirable free space

Net

5.48
6.40
23.77
6.40
5.48
36.60 for tournaments

1.37   4.11   4.11   1.37
10.97
18.28
for tournaments

Dimensions to outside
of court markings
Markings 50mm wide

Badminton

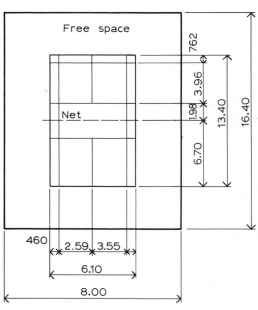

Free space

Net

762
3.96
1.98
6.70
13.40
16.40

460   2.59 3.55
6.10
8.00

Dimensions to outside of court.
Markings 38mm wide

Fig. 6.20   Sports Halls. Netball, volleyball, tennis and badminton courts.

Squash

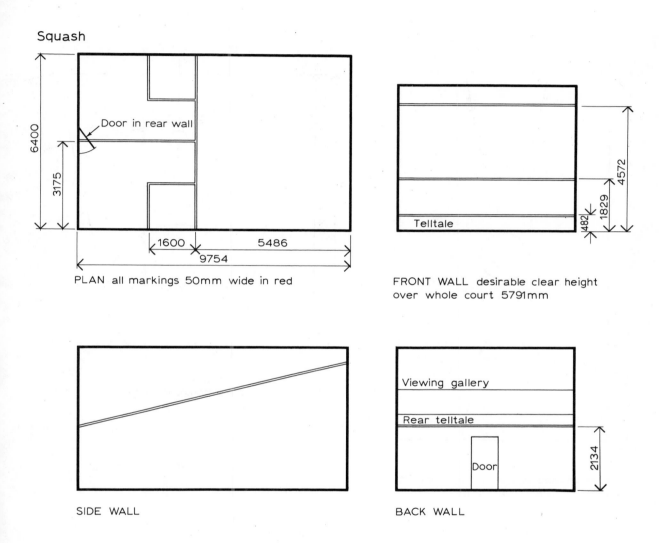

6400

3175

1600

5486

9754

PLAN all markings 50mm wide in red

4572

1829

482

Telltale

FRONT WALL desirable clear height over whole court 5791mm

SIDE WALL

Viewing gallery

Rear telltale

Door

2134

BACK WALL

Fig. 6.21   Squash court

Note. Glass walls are being increasingly used for spectator viewing and group coaching. Pull-out courts for exhibition matches are also on the market

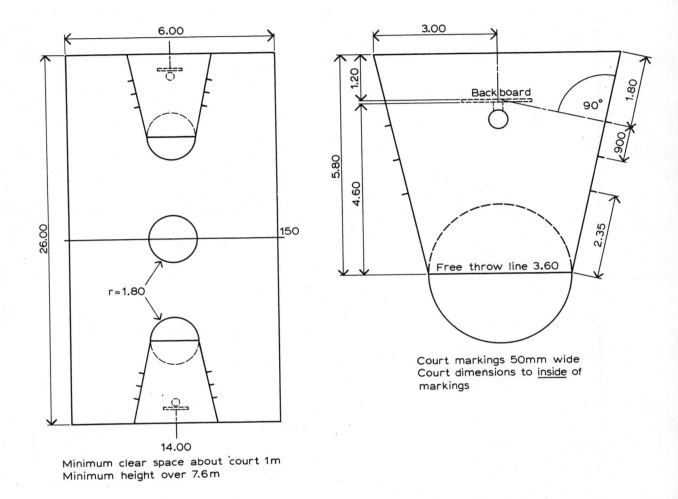

6.00

26.00

150

r=1.80

14.00

Minimum clear space about court 1m
Minimum height over 7.6m

3.00

1.20

5.80

4.60

Backboard

90°

1.80

900

2.35

Free throw line 3.60

Court markings 50mm wide
Court dimensions to inside of
markings

Fig. 6.22   Basketball court

Note. Many continental backboards are free standing (on 'periscopes' retracting into the floor) in preference to being wall or ceiling mounted

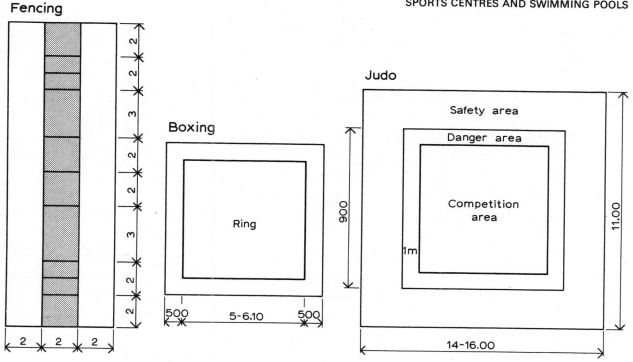

Fencing

Boxing

Judo

Safety area

Danger area

Competition area

Ring

Fig. 6.23   Combat group of activities

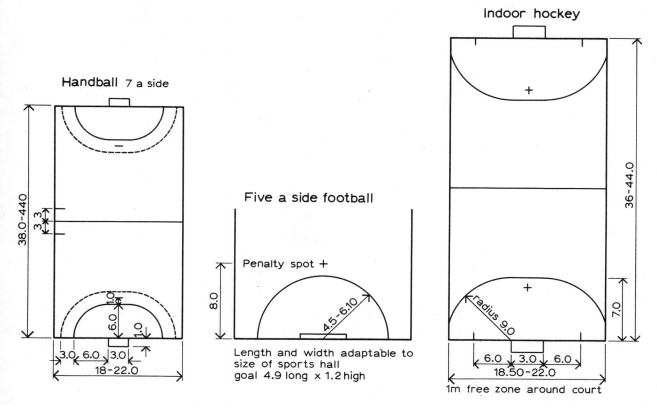

Indoor hockey

Handball 7 a side

Five a side football

Penalty spot +

Length and width adaptable to size of sports hall
goal 4.9 long × 1.2 high

radius 9.0

1m free zone around court

Fig. 6.24   Courts for handball, indoor hockey and five-a-side football

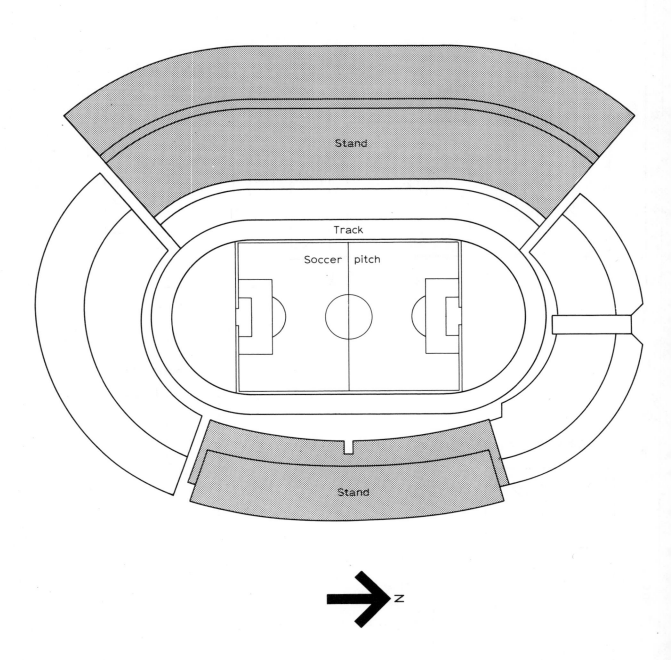

Fig. 6.25 (a)   Typical stadium for 10–15 000 showing arrangement for stands, etc. Details of track and field events are shown in Fig. 6.25(b)
Note that rugby and hockey pitches may also be accommodated in the 'Soccer pitch' area.

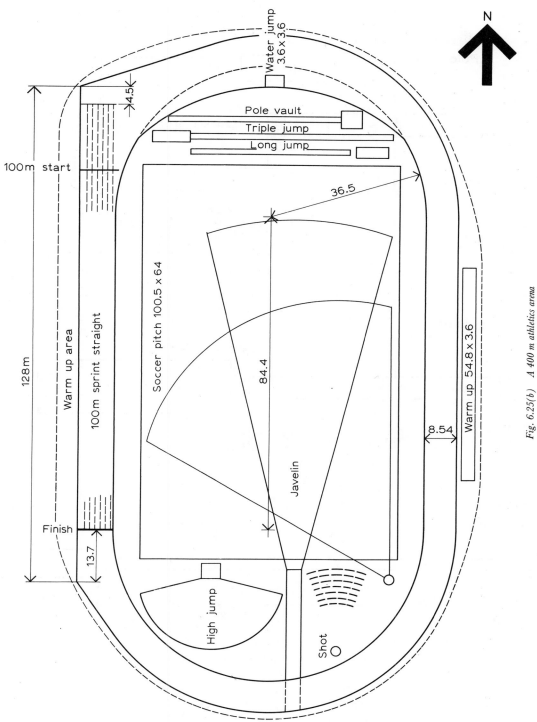

Fig. 6.25(b)   A 400 m athletics arena

Pole vault

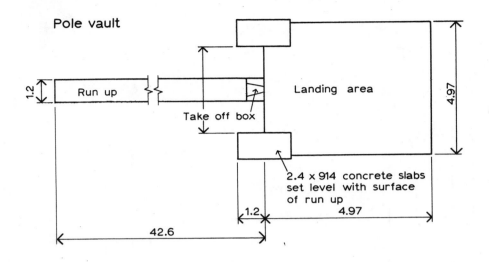

Long jump

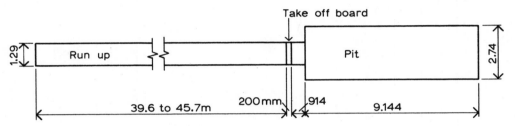

Triple jump

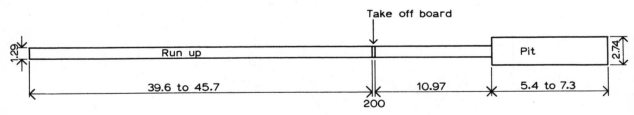

Fig. 6.26 Outdoor athletics facilities

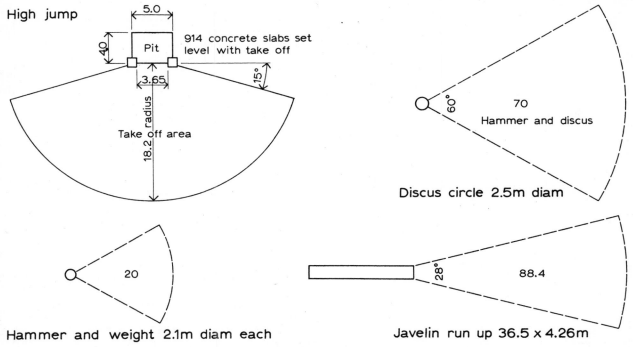

Fig. 6.27   Outdoor athletics facilities (continued)

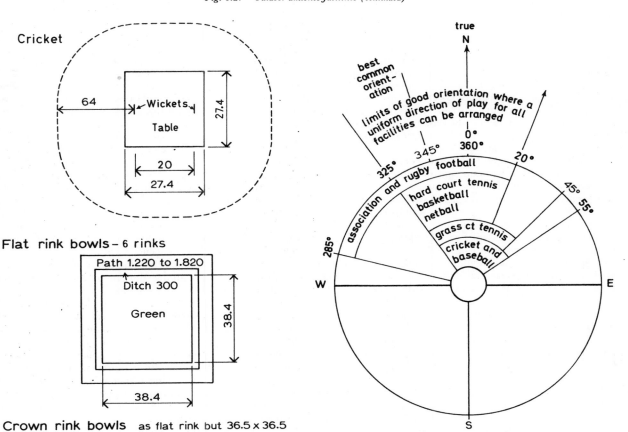

Fig. 6.28   Bowls and cricket pitches

Fig. 6.29   Orientation of sports fields and courts

6–21

Soccer

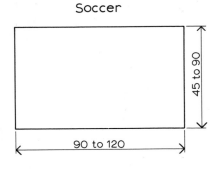

Rugby

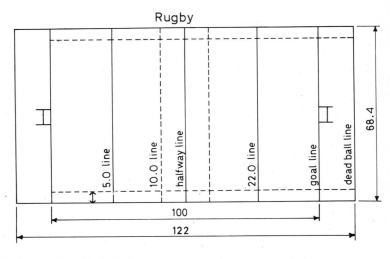

Hockey

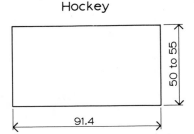

Fig. 6.30   Soccer, rugby and hockey pitches

Weight Training Room. Cannot be used for any other activity as much apparatus is fixed to the walls and ceilings.

Leisure Conditioning Suite. A sophisticated keep-fit room, usually fitted out with rowing/bicycling apparatus etc. Walls often lined with curtains. Carpet on the floor.

Gallery Hall. For 'long narrow' activities, e.g. cricket, archery, and recreational indoor bowls. Not to be confused with a target shooting gallery which must be self-contained to meet Home Office regulations.

Reception/Control Office. The main check point in the main entrance. Also the main control point for all internal communications and lighting. Usually manned by two receptionists. Often contains a small wall safe or has direct access to one. Should display a clock, and be equipped with ticket issuing machines and audio apparatus.

Shop. Often franchised. For the sale of goods such as rackets, shuttles, track suits etc.

Administration Suite. Should contain separate rooms for management staff, secretarial staff, typists, and staff toilets. Ideally located close to the main reception office.

First aid room. A mandatory requirement. Should be equipped with a couch bed, lavatory basin, medicinal cabinet, stretcher, and blanket cupboard. Should be kept to 25°C.

Sauna Suite. Common to both the Sports Hall or Swimming Pool. It is usually sited near the main entrance as a self-contained unit. The cabinet suite normally comprises a sauna cabin, changing room, shower area and plunge bath, toilet, attendant's office, massage room, sunbathing area, and sauna lounge. A 12–14 person cabin is most commonly seen. Several examples have two cabins. Single cabin units require a rota booking arrangement for alternate days. The sauna lounge should be equipped with hairdrying apparatus, powder table, mirror, and a coffee-making machine. The attendant's office should have shelving for towel storage, a sink for washing up beverages served in the lounge, and facilities for valuables storage.

Changing Rooms. Mass changing is normal in both male and female changing areas. Women usually prefer shower curtains and shower nozzles at a lower height (1524 mm above floor level) than men. The standard normally worked to is 0·7 to 0·8 m^2 per person, although in practice a spacing of 305 mm between hat and coat hooks is normally accepted. The provision of lockers is optional. Mechanical ventilation is desirable. A mirror is essential. Notices should be prominently displayed stating 'No Smoking', 'Leave no valuables', 'Glasses should not be brought into this area', etc. Changing accommodation is not required by bowls players. Automated systems of control requiring minimal staffing are being introduced to the UK from the continent.

Instructors' Rooms. Coaches usually prefer to change separately to their classes and provision should be made for both sexes.

Bar and Bar Lounge. These are often common to both Sports Halls and Swimming Pools. Preferably sited overlooking indoor activity areas. Normal lounge capacity is 50–70 people at peak periods of use. Should be well furnished with curtains, carpets, wall paper, attractive light fittings etc. A public toilet should be positioned nearby. Also public telephone(s) should be adjacent.

Bar Store. Best sited below the Bar when beer can be pumped upwards via tubing, thus eliminating the necessity to transport barrels to the first floor.

Refreshment Lounge. Common to both the Sports Hall and Swimming Pool. Should be large enough for 140–150 people, seated. Ideally overlooking indoor activity areas. Standard of service, meals, etc. optional but dictates the size of the food preparation room adjacent. Should be mechanically ventilated. Public Health requirements must be met.

Meeting Rooms. Common to both the Sports Hall and Swimming Pool. For club annual general meetings (most centres rapidly form 70–100 clubs/societies), film shows, tactics talks, conferences, etc.

Creche. An optional facility. Often required where womens' group activities are encouraged.

Staff Rest Room. A mandatory requirement in local authority sponsored centres, common to both the Sports Hall and Swimming Pool. Should be equipped with coffee/tea-making facilities, powder table, mirror etc.

Equipment Store. An area of approximately 144m² is considered essential and rectangular shapes are preferred to square. Access doors should be high enough to allow easy passage of trampolines (2·3 m). Access should be directly into the Sports Hall and other ancillary play areas via either sliding or up and over doors.

General Storage. Facilities should be provided for refuse disposal under cover, cleaning equipment, dry goods associated with the food preparation area, and stationery required by the administrative suite.

Plant room. Size will depend upon the method of heating, which is usually oil or gas-fired. As temperature requirements are much lower than in the Swimming Pool, minimum plant is necessary. For example, a Sports Hall with a 36·6 × 21·3 × 8·5 m hall, four squash courts, single ancillary hall, refreshment room, bar and bar lounge, and normal changing and toilet facilities, will require a plant room of approximately 18·5 m².

Water Storage Area. Usually contains the main water storage tank supplying the Showers and central heating system. A room of approximately 3 × 1·5 m is adequate for this purpose.

Squash Courts. It is normal for two, four, or six courts to be built as a self-contained unit adjacent to the Sports Hall or Swimming Pool. Viewing galleries with glass-walled rear walls are considered essential, but may be optional for up to 40–50 spectators. Background heating only in the viewing galleries. Mechanical ventilation desirable. Several centres have separate changing room facilities for squash members in order that use may continue if the main building is closed or being used for another event.

SWIMMING POOL

Main Pool Hall. The most frequently seen pools are 25, 33⅓, and 50 m in length; 12·5 or 20 m in width; with 2–3 m surrounds. Heights over normally range between 5·4 and 6 m. Pools of other shapes are gradually superseding conventional rectangular-shaped pools where recreational swimming is given preference over competitive. It is normal to provide separate learning and diving facilities. Permanently fixed spectator seating is not now considered desirable, and is being replaced by informal high level viewing galleries which can accommodate 200–300 seats for occasional gala night events.

Learner Pool. Normal dimensions are 12·5 × 7·5 or 9 m with 2 m surrounds on three sides; 3 m on one side for class instruction. Height over the pool is optional. Steps (457 mm wide) are required along one side of the shallow end, to allow very young users to enter the water gradually.

Diving Pool. The Sports Council suggests a policy of regional provision for facilities of 3 m and over. Diving into the main pool is now actively discouraged apart from 1 m springboards. Space requirements are shown in the diagram for the Dunstable swimming pool in Fig 6.18.

Thermal Pools. These are more frequently seen on the Continent where therapeutic bathing is more popular. However, as the tendency for recreational bathing increases so will the demand for special brine baths, paraplegic facilities, continuously moving water baths etc. continue to grow.

Paddling Pool. Often associated with sunbathing facilities adjacent to the main pool hall in a self-contained area not normally accessible to the non-swimming public. Toilets should be located nearby for the very young.

Changing Rooms And Pre-Cleanse Area. Opinion is divided between the use of baskets or lockers for clothes storage. As full time supervision is required in such areas, a basket system appears preferable, for the storage of 200–250 baskets (25 m pool); proportionately larger for larger pools. Mass changing is preferred in men's changing areas and cubicles in womens. Several 'modesty' cubicles are desirable in men's changing rooms. A system of interchange rooms between male and female changing areas is considered desirable to accommodate periodic all-male or all-female events. Self-contained toilets are required on the way to the pools, including paraplegic facilities. A pre-cleanse area between the changing room and pool is essential consisting of a sunken footpath and continuously-flowing showers. Public spectator access to the pools is usually via a separate dry route.

Dry Land Training Area. A number of instructors require space adjacent the main pool for dry land training, including instruction in capsize dinghy drill. Classes are normally no larger than 12–14 persons.

Sunbathing/Solarium Areas. Indoor sunbathing under lamps is growing in popularity usually associated with the side of the main pool. Provision should be made for 3–6 beds, overhead lamps, and screening facilities if required. Outdoor sunbathing terraces are popular during summer months, with access only through pre-cleanse footbaths from the main pool hall. Toilet facilities and portable refreshment stands are desirable ancillary features.

Spectator Facilities. As previously stated, formal fixed seating arrangements are no longer considered desirable. Viewing galleries overlooking both main and learner pools are generally preferred, wide enough to accommodate 200–300 spectators for occasional gala events. This may be provided by 'bleacher' units, or by stacking chairs. The latter are also often provided at pool surround level for additional spectator viewing and for judges.

Equipment Store. Accommodation is required for floats/booms, vacuum-cleaning equipment, starting blocks, backstroke-warning apparatus. life-saving equipment, etc. Separate storage is required for cleaning and maintenance equipment.

6—23

Poolside Supervisor Office. An office usually located between main and learner pools is considered essential for general poolside supervision and for broadcasting public announcements.

Plant Room and Boiler House. Accommodates water-treatment equipment, plenum system, filtration tanks, and boilers, etc. Minimum height 2896 mm. Plan area approximately 300 m², if gas fired. Access from the outside is required to the electricity substation and chemical storage room(s). Cold water storage is required separately at high level of approximately 81 m².

Rowing Basin. These are occasionally provided where local demand is high, and generally sited in a basement location.

Facilities for refreshments, administration, toilets, and control are as described under Sports Halls.

STATUTORY REQUIREMENTS

CHECK LIST

Public Health	Kitchen/Food preparation layout and finishes.
	Bar Stores layout and finishes.
	Refuse Stores layout and finishes.
	Sauna Suite refreshment services and washing up facilities.
	Bar washing up facilities.
	Provision of Staff Rest Room and toilet facilities: also refreshment services.
	Plant Room safety devices and warning systems.
	Poolside supervisors—numbers, and safety devices.
Building Regulations	Structural stability of building.
	Standards of insulation.
	Zones of open space containment.
	Fire rating of structural members and division screens/doors/staircases, etc.
	Means of escape in case of fire.
	Waivers, i.e. in respect of exposed steelwork in roof of sports hall.
	Fire rating of finishes i.e. ceilings.
	Drainage and external works.
Town Planning	Advertisement in local press (21 days notice).
	Car Parking provision and access.
	Scale and massing.
	Noise factors.
	External signs.
	Landscaping requirements around building.
Licensing Authority (Local Magistrates or County Court)	Provision of Bar and Bar Lounges for the sale of alcoholic drinks.
	Display of warning notices.
	Selection of bar manager and staff.
	Toilet and basin facilities.
	General use levels at peak periods.
	Limitation on numbers using the building for dances, concerts, etc.
	Licensing hours.
Statutory Undertakers	Location of services into building.
	Size of services.
	Necessity for sub stations, etc.
	Access to same.
	General plant room services and filtration systems.
Fire Service (At present non mandatory)	Escape service via staircases, door openings, etc.
	Fire warning systems and notices.
	Smoke control screens/doors, etc.
	Emergency lighting arrangements.
	Means of escape from sports hall and or swimming pool hall and ancillary facilities.
Police (In consultation— non mandatory)	General security arrangements to external doors and licensed areas of the centre.

EXAMPLES

Some Sports Centres completed within the last eight years are as follows.

Herringthorpe Centre, Rotherham (see Fig. 6.31)
  Architects: Gillinson Barnett & Partners

Newton Aycliffe Town Centre (see Fig. 6.32)
  Architects: Robert Turner Associates

Dunstable Park Recreation Centre (see Fig. 6.33)
  Architects: G. A. Perrin, Perrin Associates

Huddersfield Sports Centre (see Fig. 6.34)
  Architects: Faulkner Brown, Hendy, Stoner and Partners

Bletchley Leisure Centre (see Fig. 6.35)
  Architects: Faulkner Brown, Hendy, Stoner and Partners

Bingham Sports Centre, Notts (see Fig. 6.36)
  Architects: Notts County Architects Department

Billingham Forum (see Fig. 6.37)
  Architects: Elder Lester & Partners

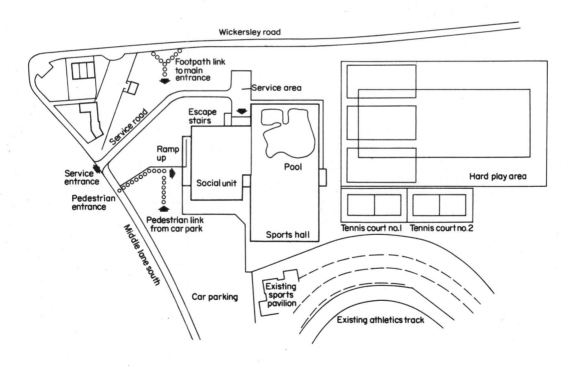

Fig. 6.31   Herringthorpe Centre, Rotherham

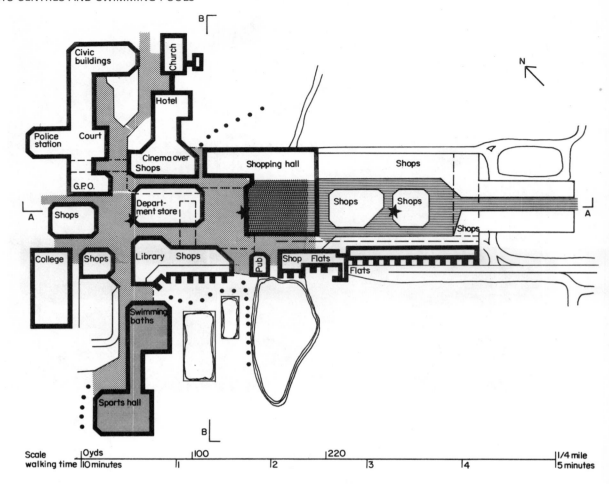

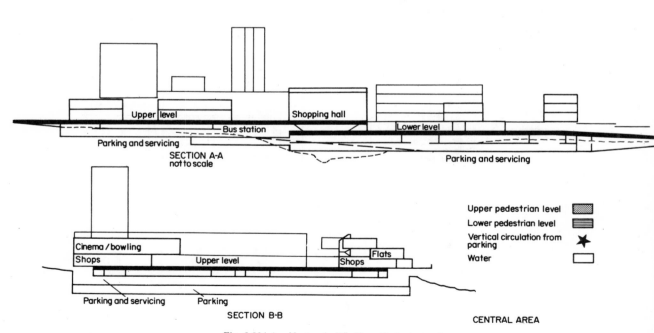

Fig. 6.32(a) *Newton Aycliffe Town Centre proposals*

Fig. 6.32(b)   Newton Aycliffe expansion—central   area—General view of model from SW. Architects: C. Edmund Wilford & Son with Robert Turner (Copyright: Robert Turner)

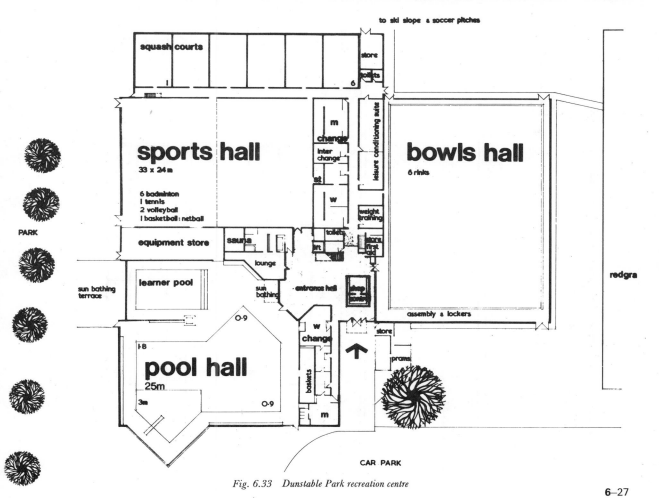

Fig. 6.33   Dunstable Park recreation centre

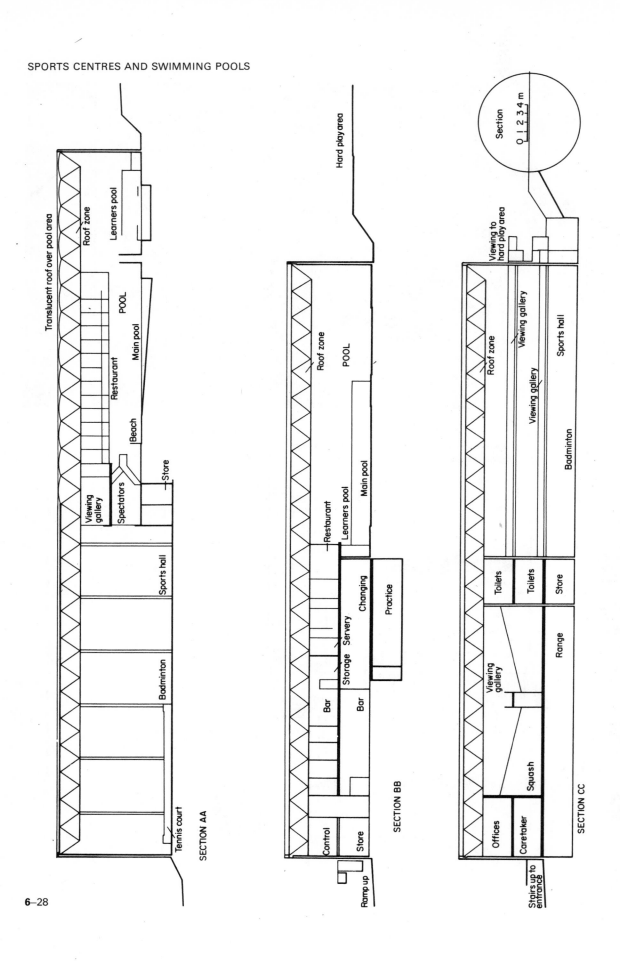

Fig. 6.34 Huddersfield Sports Centre

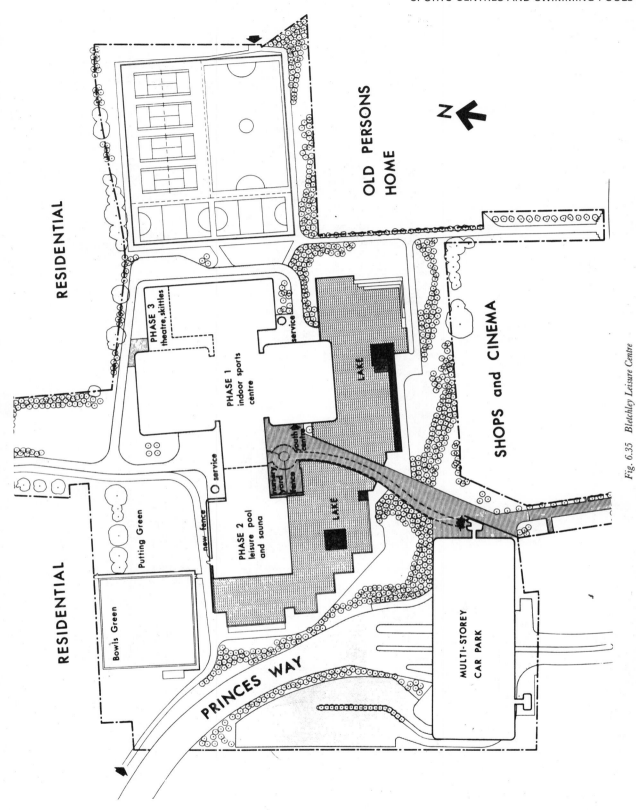

Fig. 6.35 Bletchley Leisure Centre

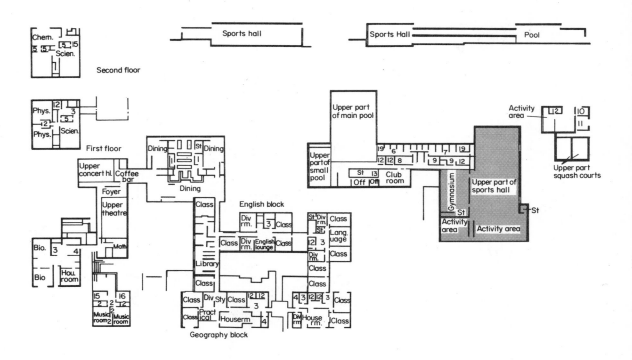

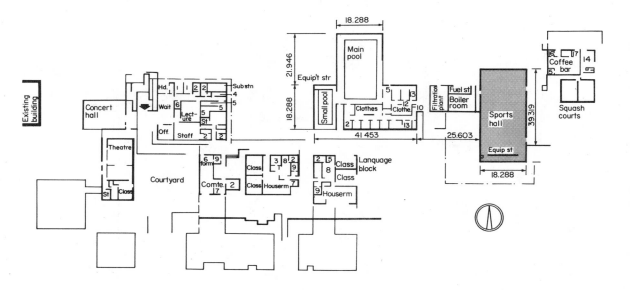

Fig. 6.36   Bingham Sports Centre

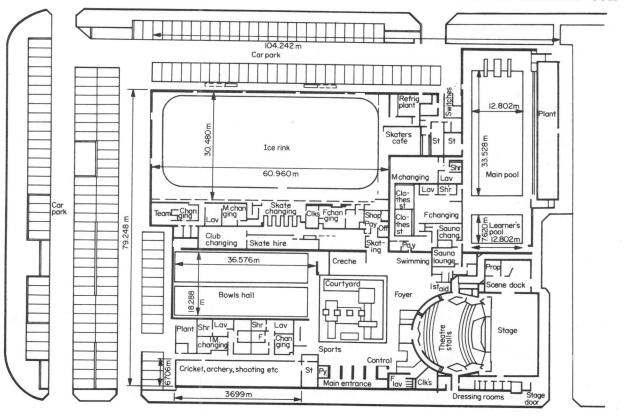

Fig. 6.37   Billingham Forum

BIBLIOGRAPHY

The following appraisals of Sports Centres and Sports Halls have been published in the Architects' Journal. The date of the issue is given in brackets.

Keele University Sports Centre (6.3.1968)
Exeter University Sports Centre (21.2.1968)
The University of Kent Sports Hall (30.10.1968)
Billingham Forum (27.8.1967)
Harlow Sportcentre revisited (26.4.1967)
Crystal Palace National Sports Centre (26.4.1967)
Bracknell Sports Centre (15.5.1968)
St Andrews University P E Centre (11.3.1970)
Totnes Grammar School Sports Hall (7.5.1969)
Worthing Aquarena (24.9.1969)
Bingham Joint Use Sports Centre (18.6.1969)
Bletchley Leisure Centre (11.7.1973)
Picketts Lock Centre (21.11.1973)
Merton College Oxford (4.9.1974)

IMPORTANT PUBLICATIONS

Planning for Sport. A report by a Working Party set up by the Sports Council to assess and recommend standards of provision for sports grounds, swimming pools, sports halls, and multi-purpose sports centres. Central Council of Physical Recreation (1968).

Community Sports Halls. A textbook on sports hall design planning and construction. The National Playing Fields Association (Revised 1971).

Indoor Sports Centres. A study undertaken for the Sports Council, HMSO (1972).

Indoor Recreation Centres. A report on combinations of indoor swimming pools, and sports halls. The National Playing Fields Association (1972).

Aquatic Buildings. A well documented book by Dr. Dietrich Fabian on swimming pools throughout Europe. Verlag GDW Callweg, Munich.

Planning for Leisure. 'An enquiry into the present pattern of participation in outdoor and physical recreation, and the frequency and manner of use of public open spaces, among people living in the urban areas of England and Wales'. HMSO (1969).

Design Notes 1 and 2. Notes prepared by the Technical Unit for Sport on the design of low-cost swimming pools. TUS (1971 and 1972).

AJ Metric Handbook. Section 22 gives metric details on sports and swimming facilities. Architectural Press (1971).

AJ Urban Landscape Handbook. Contains a section on sports facilities and standards of provision among more general landscape details. Architectural Press. (1972).

Building Research Station Current Paper 16/70. Case studies of local authority covered swimming pools. BRS (April 1970).

Sports Ground Construction. NPFA (1965).

Sports Pavilions. A report of a research project sponsored and pulished by the NPFA and Polytechnic of Central London (1970).

Local Recreation Centres. Research study sponsored by the NPFA, (1974).

Public Indoor Swimming Pools. TUS Bulletin 1. Gives general guidance for the construction of swimming pools. The Sports Council (1974).

Facilities for Squash Rackets. TUS Bulletin 2. Gives general guidance for the design, planning and construction of squash courts accompanied by good illustrations. The Sports Council (1975).

Sports Halls—a new approach to their dimensions and use. A revision of chapter 4 of Planning for Sport 1968, a report of a Working Party on scales of provision. The Sports Council (1975).

Converted Buildings. Suggestions for converting railway stations, drill halls, warehouses, hangars, etc into buildings for sport and recreation. The Sports Council (1975).

JOURNALS

Sport + Baderbauten (Sports & Aquatic Buildings). A bi-monthly journal in German with English summaries. Verlag A Krammer & Co, Dusseldorf Hermannstrasse 3.

Sportstättenbau + Bäderanlagen (Sports Facilities and Swimming Pools). Another bi-monthly journal. IAKS Organisation (international working group for the construction of sports and leisure facilities), 5 Köln 41, Postfach 450 568.

Recreation Management. A bi-monthly journal. Kernan Publishing Co. Camberley, Surrey.

Architectural Review (October 1974). An appraisal of UK Sports Centres.

Recreation Management Yearbook, 1975. Edited by the Institute of Recreation Management. E. & F. N. Span Ltd.

Gerald A Perrin. *Trained at Brighton College of Art (Architecture) and the Regent Polytechnic (Town Planning). Worked with Harlow Development Corporation from 1955 to 1961 when he joined Sir Donald Gibson's War Office Army redevelopment group at Chessington. He was awarded a Research Fellowship for the study of sports halls and other indoor sports facilities by the National Playing Fields Association and Regent/Polytechnic in 1962, and published a report 'Community Sports Halls' in 1965.*

Appointed to the full time teaching staff at the Regent/Polytechnic in 1965 and made head of the Recreation Research Unit until 1970. The unit was responsible for publishing reports on 'Sports Pavilions' (1970), 'Indoor Recreation Centres' (1973) and 'Local Recreation Centres' (1974). Gerald Perrin has been in private practice since 1970 and was responsible for the Sports Centres at Redbridge, Eastleigh, Folkestone (with David Cadman his associate), Dunstable, Harlow (stages 2, 3 and 4), Blaby, Epping & Chigwell. He acted as Consultant for Sports Centres at Grimsby, Carn Brea (Camborne), the University of Kent, Bracknell (stage 2) and Cheltenham College.

Appointed UK representative to the International Union of Architects Working Party on Sport & Leisure in 1971. Has contributed frequently as appraiser to the Architects' Journal and was author of the section on recreation facilities in the 'Urban Landscape Handbook' (1973).

7 GRANDSTANDS

MICHAEL DIXEY, Dip. Arch. ARIBA

INTRODUCTION

Sport is now of international status. World-wide coverage by television of the Olympic Games, motor racing, and tennis has ensured that the results of these competitions are now regarded as matters of national importance. As a consequence, no grandstand, swimming pool or sports complex can be conceived without a detailed awareness of international demands for competitors, newsmen, commentators and spectators alike.

The prime functions of the grandstand are:
1. Clear and unobstructed viewing.
2. Economical structure.
3. Minimised structural maintenance.
4. Speed of initial construction.
5. Spectator safety (fire and panic hazards).
6. Spectator comfort (dining, banqueting, bar and other facilities).
7. Press and broadcasting facilities.

To these may be added
8. Car and coach parking.
9. Competition facilities.
10. Betting facilities (horse- and dog-racing).

These aspects must be integrated into an overall design concept which must dramatise the event, symbolise the sport, and create an immediacy of spectator/competitor impact. This has been a continuing characteristic from Greek and Roman amphitheatres to the present-day football stadium during World Cup events. It is equally evident and expressive in the cool elegance of new swimming pool structures and horse-racing grandstands.

SITING

Before considering the ten items listed above, the siting of the grandstand in relation to the sport must be examined. This will vary from racing grandstands which require views of starting post, far side of the course and winning post, to ice hockey where spectators need absolute clarity of vision for a fast-moving puck. Each case, though differing greatly from the other, requires calculation of maximum spectator/action distance on the same formula. This is based on the premise that the smallest object that can be seen by the human eye is one that subtends an arc of one minute. However, for it to be recognisable, this arc has to be increased to four minutes. The maximum distance between spectator and object to be recognised (jockey's silks, football, puck, etc.) is given by the formula:

$$r = 0.86\,s$$

where r is the distance in metres, and s is the size of the object in mm.

International football diameter is 220 mm, and therefore the greater distance of spectator from the far side of the football pitch is $0.86 \times 220 = 190$ m. Empirically, it has been found that viewing at such limits has to be classified as poor, and a more acceptable working formula should effect a 40% improvement. The formula should be modified to the following:

$$r = 0.52\,s$$

This should be followed for all working calculations, and will reduce the example of a 190 m viewing distance to 115 m, giving perfect viewing.

In a grandstand, the limiting factor governing viewing distance will be the back row of seats. Table 7.1 gives maximum viewing distances for objects of varying size.

Table 7.1 VIEWING DISTANCES

Object size (mm)	Max. viewing distance (m)
40	20
60	31
80	41
100	52
120	62
140	73
160	83
180	94
200	104
220	115
240	125

These maximum distances may limit the extent of a single rake grandstand. If accommodation does not meet requirements, double or multi-rake grandstands will be required.

SIGHT LINES AND RAKE SLOPE

Fig 7.1 shows the accepted distance between the eye and the top of the head. To include allowance for a hat, increase to

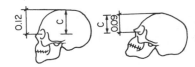

Fig. 7.1   Accepted distance between eye and top of the head

150 mm. Where momentary interruption of viewing can be accepted, dimension C can be used as 90 mm.

Viewing steps in raking stands are of three main classes:
1. Straight line, constant going.
2. Series of straight lines, with changed going.
3. Curved rake.

Type 1 is first choice for simplicity of construction and economy but limited to 20 m, for total depth of rake. Beyond this, savings in height and width justify other geometry. Type 3 is the theoretical ideal, but expensive and difficult to construct due to the progressive adjustment of each step.

Type 2 can therefore be the ideal compromise for all cases beyond the limits of Type 1.

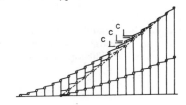

Fig 7.2   Profile comparisons of straight and curve rake

Fig 7.2 gives profile comparisons of straight and curved rake and illustrates the application of the c dimension of Fig 7.1.

Detailed examinations of a straight line profile are given by the formula $n_1 = x_1/d_1$ $n = x/d$ $p = l/d$ (for references, see Figure 7.3).

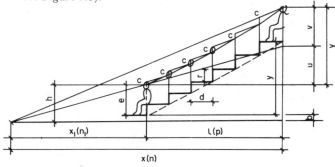

Fig 7.3   Straight-line profile

Standard parameters are as follows:

c = Distance from eye observing object F and the point on the head where a line joining F and the eye of the spectator behind is tangential.
d = Tread of step (750 mm for seating, 600 mm for standing).
e = Height of spectator's eye above step (1·200 m seating, and 1·400 m standing).

A summary of the c value for different uses can be made as follows:

c empirical standard 120 mm
c with head error 150 mm
c for athletic stands 90 mm (momentary vision loss)
For football, rugby, cricket, tennis, the full c value of 150 mm should be maintained.

Full parameters for Fig. 7.3 are:

F = Focal point. This could be near edge of a playing pitch, or the centre line of the closest lane of an athletic track.
b = Feet level, first spectator row. This can be positive or negative value (boxing, negative but should not be greater than e).
$h = (b + e)$. A major influence on value of u in the formula $y = u + v$. May be negative, zero or positive. For athletic stands, not less than zero.
x_1 = Horizontal distance (metres) between F and first spectator.
x_2 = same distance, but expressed as x_1/d.
l = Horizontal distance between spectators of the first and last rows (in metres).
$p = l/d$.
$X = x_1 + d$. Horizontal distance between F and a spectator in any row other than the front.
$n = x$ but expressed as multiples of rows in terms of d, i.e. $n = x/d$ or $n = n_1 + p$.
Z = height of spectator in back row above Focal point, F.
u = constant, as long as x_1 is constant. Value of h should be kept within 700 mm, especially in large stands, as this can dramatically affect the stand height, and cost.

The cross section of the rake is affected primarily by the dimensions x_1 and n. As x_1 increases, stand height decreases. The world's largest single rake grandstands do not exceed 30 m. These factors govern the central and critical design decision which is the choice between reducing the arena/spectator distance, involving steep rake and high cost, and increasing that distance to lower the stand height and its construction costs.

The values of l and p affect the capacity of the stand, determined by viewing distance limits, excessive and dangerous rake slope, and construction costs which escalate rapidly with stand height. An absolute practical limit is 90 rows in a rake.

Requisite parameters for evaluation are:

r = riser—constant for straight rake, and variable on a curved rake. (Seat height, however, will remain a constant, at some chosen figure between 300 and 450 mm.)

y = vertical distance between the eye level of first and last row spectators, a measure of the height of rake and therefore of the cost.

u = relative value—zero, negative or positive, depending on h, since $U = h.l/x_1$.

v = constant, always positive.

The 'ideal sigh curve' propounded by Bogoslowski can be used to obtain values of the above parameters:

$$y = h.l/x_1 + c.l(x_1 = 1)/d.x_1$$

When x is a multiple of d, then

$$x_1/d = n_1 \text{ and } 1 = n - n_1$$

hence,

$$y = (n-n_1)/n_1 h + (n-n_1)/n_1 nc.$$

If r is known the profile can be determined by the equation:

$$r = h + nc/n_1$$

Profiles composed of straight line slopes can be analysed by using the above formulae, provided y is determined separately for each slope.

An alternative analysis of a curved profile can also be made by a simplified Daniluk equation:

$$y = (n-n_1)/n_1 h + 2.3026 \, nc \log(n-0.5)/(n_1 - 0.5)$$

This equation assumes d is a multiple of x_1.

FUNCTIONAL REQUIREMENTS

The above formulae may then be applied as appropriate to the precise nature of the sport being dealt with. Broadly, this will be of three categories:

1. *Static crowd.* Typified by rugby, football and some athletics, on the assumption that no other diversfied activities occur during intervals.

2. *Circulating crowd.* Typified by betting activities at horse- and dog-racing events, between a succession of events.

3. *Combination of 1 and 2.* Cases where one part of a stand may have a static crowd, while others have circulating spectators.

Category 1 will generally involve very large crowds (football etc.) while Categories 2 and 3 will involve smaller, more leisurely crowds, the latter requiring greater space for dining, betting and bar amenities. A direct comparison between the cross sections of Cardiff Arms Park and Sandown Park (Figs. 7.4 and 7.5) will give an immediate illustration of this point.

The areas behind the viewing stands are dramatically different. As these must be brought into the calculation of space per person (spectator), and are taken into account in the figures given in Table 7.2.

Table 7.2 SPACE PER PERSON

Category	Grandstand	m^2 per person
1	Manchester United Old Trafford	0.68
	Meadowbank, Edinburgh	0.835
2	Ascot Racecourse Grandstand	2.04
	Sandown Park Grandstand	2.60
	Doncaster Grandstand	2.96
3	Calgary Grandstand U.S.A.	1.42

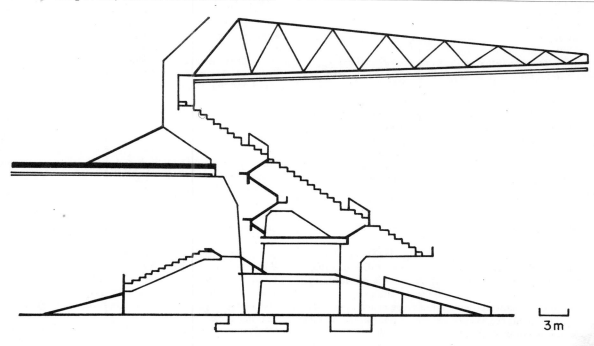

Fig 7.4   Cross-section of Cardiff Arms Park Grandstand

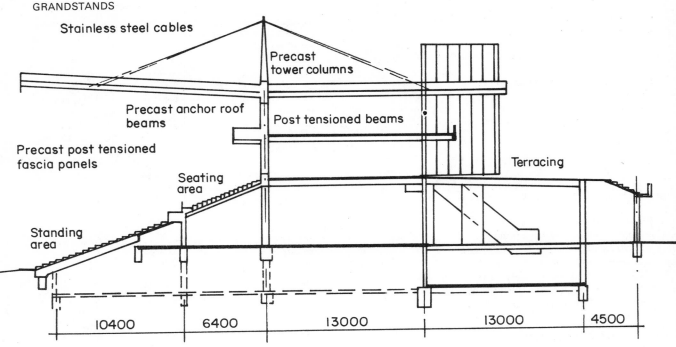

Stainless steel cables

Precast tower columns

Precast anchor roof beams

Post tensioned beams

Precast post tensioned fascia panels

Terracing

Seating area

Standing area

10400   6400   13000   13000   4500

Fig 7.5   Cross-section of Sandown Park Grandstand

AMENITIES

These can vary widely and will be the subject of a particular design brief from the Client. Typical elements of the brief may be as follows.

1. Desirability for seating to be provided for all, or the maximum number of spectators. By this, standards of safety are increased.
2. Special facilities for disabled.
3. Provision for emergency evacuation and easy exit. After an event spectators want to leave early.
4. Ample toilet facilities, with provision for disabled.
5. Bar, restaurant, banqueting facilities. Catering and cooking require specialist discussion.
6. Functional catering, etc. for non-event days, i.e. Board Rooms, small-scale attendances for special purposes, with associated restricted catering/kitchen facilities.
7. Possible betting facilities, requiring specialist discussion.
8. Telephone, Press and Broadcasting facilities.
9. Royal/distinguished visitors' accommodation.
10. Possible judge's viewing position, etc, dependent on use.

CROWD SAFETY

Paramount in the designer's responsibility is the securing of crowd safety. Not only is this true because of disasters that have occurred, but because in Britain there is no statutory control or legislation on whose provisions the designer may rely. Pending legislation, the designer has a crucial personal contribution to make. Whatever the rssponsibility of the owners and executors of the grandstand, the designer cannot be free of a moral and legal onus to safeguard against accidents to his full ability.

The Building Acts and Regulations do not apply to terraces nor to escape routes from them, although they will apply to the building structures. *Local Acts* vary widely, but none assists materially on Crowd Safety. The *Fire Precautions Act 1971* can, by Order of The Secretary of State, be made to apply. *The Public Health Act 1936* can empower a Local Authority under S.59 to require 'adequate' means of ingress and egress. *The Occupiers' Liability Acts* (1957 England and Wales; 1960 Scotland) refer to obligations of occupiers and visitors to premises, but provide no basis for a safety code. *The Offices, Shops and Railway Premises Act 1963* has only a minor bearing on the problem.

Proposals for new statutory legislation have been put forward by the Wheatley '*Report of the Inquiry into Crowd Safety at Sports Grounds*' (H.M.S.O. 1972). In the interim, reference should be made to the recommendations of the Report.

Some salient extracts from Appendix A of the Report are given below, but it cannot be stressed too highly that the whole Report should be assimilated, and every recommendation applied.

(a) Each exit should evacuate its section in 8 minutes.
(b) Exit widths governed by above, but minimum 1.220 m. (Flow rate governed by *a* and *b* factors, should be assessed at 40 persons per minute per unit of exit width of 550 mm).
(c) Turnstile admission rate (guide) 750 persons per hour.
(d) Stairs: treads, 300 mm min; risers, 190 mm max; flights, not more than 16 steps and not less than 3 steps; hand rails ideally spaced 1·220 m apart, not less than 1·070 m height 240 mm (unvaryingly).
(e) Ramps: gradient to be constant, maximum 1:10, and not broken by steps.
(f) Terrace steps: minimum 280 mm, but ideally 375 mm for treads, relevant risers being 90 mm and 190 mm respectively. Above 190 mm, crush barrier essential at top of riser.

Table 7.3 CRUSH BARRIER DATA

Terrace gradient		Maximum horizontal distance in metres between barriers			
		Peak Viewing		Other areas	
	Riser : Step width	A	B	A	B
05°	1:11·4	4·725	3·200	7·770	7·180
10°	1:5·7	4·270	2·900	6·700	4·420
15°	1:3·7	3·810	2·590	5·640	3·600
20°	1:2·7	3·500	2·290	4·880	3·200
25°	1:2·1	3·200	2·135	4·265	2·745
30°	1:1·7	2·900	1·980	3·810	2·440

(g) Gangways: No spectator to be more than 6 m from a gangway.

(h) Penning: Should be arranged to prevent major migrations of crowd, but to allow minor migrations.

(i) Crush barriers: See Table 7.3. Peak viewing areas are such as behind a goalmouth/penalty area. Column A are maximum distances between barriers when safety is the sole consideration. Column B will add greater comfort for spectators. Column A barriers should resist a force of 4·96 kN per metre run, and Column B barriers 3·36 kN per metre run. All barriers should be 1·1 m high as standard, but in any case never outside the limits of 1·0 m and 1·12 m. Top rail should be 100 mm vertically.

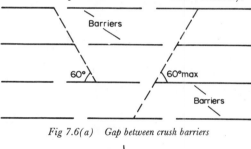

Fig 7.6(a)   Gap between crush barriers

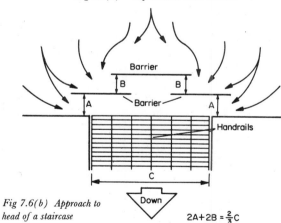

*Fig 7.6(b) Approach to
head of a staircase*

$$2A + 2B = \tfrac{2}{3}C$$

(j) Spacing arrangements of crush barriers should be as in Figs. 7.6(a) and 7.6(b). Barriers should be capable of withstanding an overturning moment of twice the designed load on the rail.

(k) Viewing slopes (non-stepped terraces) should be of non-slip finish (e.g. packed ash), and of a desirable maximum gradient of 1:6. Anything steeper must have

continuous crush barriers between gangways.

(l) Seating area per person: mimimum, 457 mm wide × 610 mm deep; preferred, 550 mm wide × 762 mm deep. Included in the 610/762 mm dimension is an allowance of 305 mm minimum space between the back of one seat and the front of the next row behind.

(m) Fire warning systems should be provided for all buildings to which public or staff have access, with a central control point containing an indicator panel showing position of outbreak. Full discussion is needed with local Fire Brigade.

(n) Lighting must be of a high standard, especially in escape routes all of which must be covered by a standby system separate from the mains supply. Generator delay must not exceed 10 seconds. Battery standby should have a minimum period of 3 hours life. Either system must be fully automatic in operation.

(o) Fire-fighting installation and equipment should be to local Fire Brigade requirements.

Reference may also be made to the Association of Consulting Engineer's Draft Code of Safety at Sports Grounds. This is a document which gives practical implementation to the recommendations of the Wheatley Report previously referred to.

BIBLIOGRAPHY

Bobrowski, Bardhan-Roy and Maciag. 'The design and analysis of Grandstand Structures'. *The Structural Engineer* (Feb 1972)

'Code of Safety at Sports Grounds'. The Assoc. of Consulting Engineers (1973).

Lord Wheatley. *Report of the enquiry into crowd safety at Sports Grounds*. HMSO (1972).

Merton College Sports Pavilion, Oxford. Architectural Press Ltd.

Michael Dixey, *Dip. Arch. RIBA, Educated at the Northern Polytechnic School of Architecture. Joined Playne and Lacey in 1955 and Sudell and Partners in 1958. He formed his own practice in 1968 and is currently with the Department of the Environment. Michael Dixey is Architect for a number of sports pavilions and recreation centres including the new sports pavilion for Merton College, Oxford. Researcher for the National Playing Fields Association and spent 2½ years with the Technical Unit for Sport at The Sports Council. He has conducted research into most types of recreational building including facilities for Squash. Author of 'Local Recreation Centres' published by The National Playing Fields Association.*

8 MARINAS

STEPHEN L. WAGSTAFFE, R.I.B.A., M.R.S.H.

INTRODUCTION

The marina is a product largely of the last two decades which has come into being to cater for the specific needs of leisure boating. The growth of private boating over this period has completely outstripped the meagre facilities that were previously available in harbours where the rich private boat owner had to compete with commercial interests for services. Likewise, the virtually non-existent services of the river banks and the tidal creeks were also rapidly outgrown.

Shorter working hours and higher pay, coupled with overcrowding of other leisure activities have encouraged people to the water for recreation. The growing demand has led to the development of centres catering for the private boating world in a similar manner to caravan parks which have evolved for the exclusive use of the land tourists. Public demand for boats has been advanced by the advent of laminated glass-fibre boats, whose one-piece hulls are quick to manufacture, are strong and resilient, easy to repair and require negligible maintenance. These hulls can be moulded into almost any shape and size and can therefore be tailor-made for any particular activity.

Three basic kinds of leisure boating have evolved, each of which has specific types of craft and requires suitable facilities and locations.

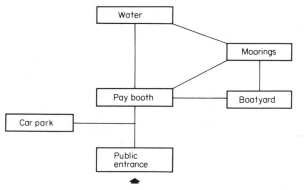

Fig. 8.1 Casual and by-the-hour boating

CASUAL BOATING

Casual or by-the-hour boating comprises of hired rowing, paddle, sailing and motor boats on lakes in parks, trips round the bay in speedboats at seaside resorts and conducted tours in river buses at tourist centres. There is a need for good public access, a paybooth, a public address system (either ashore or on the boats) overnight moorings for the boats and provision for out-of-season overhauls on dry land (see Fig 8.1).

DAY AND WEEKEND BOATING

This involves privately owned and individually hired boats ranging from one-man canoes to sailing dinghies, motor boats for fishing, sailing and motor cruisers, to water-skiing boats, power boats and racing yachts.

This kind of boating can be found at seaside resorts, in river estuaries and on rivers, lakes and gravel pits near centres of population. It requires, as a minimum, a slipway with all-day access to the water, adequate parking for cars, boat trailers and caravans and large areas of boat hard-standings close to the slipway. A clubhouse with changing rooms, refreshment facilities, administration offices and some maintenance services, should also be provided. A typical arrangement is shown in Fig 8.2.

HOLIDAY BOATING

Full-scale holiday boating (see Fig 8.3) again involves privately owned and individually hired boats and includes both sailing and motor cruisers.

The facilities required are basically as those for day and weekend boating except that, as most of these boats are kept afloat during the season, easy access to the water is not as important as the provision of adequate secure moorings. These vessels will only leave the marina when cruising or racing, so extensive on-site maintenance facilities should be provided for overhauls. Provision should also be made for chandlery and provisions sales.

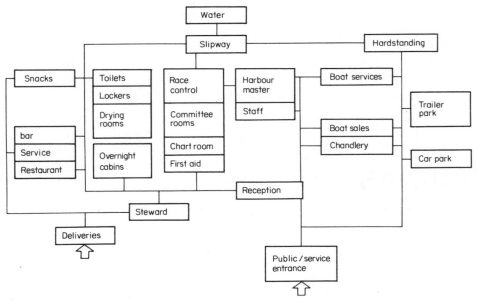

Fig. 8.2   Day and weekend boating (offshore cruising, all racing)

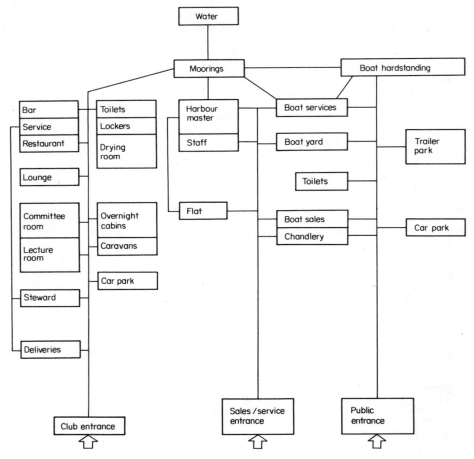

Fig. 8.3   Full scale holiday cruising (upriver, inland waterways)

SITING

In Britain every available stretch of water supports some kind of boating activity. There are, however, basic differences between sea and coastal sailing and boating on inland rivers, lakes, gravel pits, canals and the redundant docks that are now being used.

A major factor in the utilisation of these water areas is climatic; whether they can be used all year round; whether there is a tidal range which prevents access to the water at low tide; and whether the prevailing winds are favourable or not. Other factors are whether the site is in a rural or urban area which affects the amount of facilities provided and whether the complex is for one class of boats only, or several types.

The space requirements for each type of marina are different, both in the water and on land. In the water the extent of the moorings required controls selection of sites, while on land car parking, yacht and dinghy parking, hard-standing, ramps and slipways differ greatly with different classes of boats, and therefore affect land utilisation. In some instances the clubhouse may be so remote that it would have to provide sleeping accommodation with washing and toilet facilities, as well as supplies, chandlery and a boat maintenance workshop.

With powerboats, particularly the smaller racing boats and water-skiing boats, the siting of centres is very sensitive and locations must be selected where the noise and wash will not disturb the local population or other water sports such as swimming and fishing.

COASTAL SAILING

At coastal locations the prime requirement is for protection from strong winds and the tides. Protection from strong winds can only be achieved by selection of sheltered sites, but the tides can be coped with by dredging natural harbours to provide adequate water at all states of the tide, or by building artificial harbours in deep water. Within these harbours there will still be a rise and fall of water level, so unless boats are moored fore and aft to piles by slip-moorings, they must be on individual swinging moorings that have sufficient cable length to allow for the tide variation. Thus boat densities will be low and extensive dredging must be undertaken to provide more moorings. As an alternative, especially on tidal rivers where swing moorings would be an obstruction, pontoons on long moorings secured to piles can be provided to which boats can be moored direct. This will allow higher densities of boats and simpler moorings, but the capital and maintenance costs for the pontoons are high and the major part of the boat owners' yearly sailing expenses is the cost of mooring.

Where it is not economically viable to provide protected harbours in tidal waters, there is no alternative to the use of swinging moorings. But, whereas the cost of these is usually low, usage of the boats is severely limited and access to them has to be by tender craft, which in turn need launching facilities and storage on land.

The adoption of the container system of cargo carrying in recent years has meant that many existing port facilities on tidal estuaries have been superseded by larger deep water ports nearer the sea. Where these old ports are enclosed with lock gates impounding water at the high-tide level it has been possible to adapt them for use as marinas. However, they are usually only suitable as home bases for cruising vessels, as casual day-use boats would not be able to function due to the limitations imposed on them by the lack of access to open water through the locks.

INLAND SAILING

Away from the coast and tides, the problems of marina siting resolve themselves to those of access and available land space, as the constant water levels in rivers and canals allow all-year round-the-clock use of the water.

There must be either good public transport facilities, roads and local amenities, or adequate space to develop car parking, service facilities and accommodation. Likewise there must be sufficient space for enough boats to cover the costs of any facilities which are considered necessary. Gravel pits adjacent to rivers, and redundant canal basins, are typical examples of easily adaptable mooring sites.

WIND CONDITIONS

In addition to the above requirements, sites used primarily for sailing should have steady wind conditions, while at the same time there should be sufficient natural shelter to allow racing to continue in strong winds so that regattas are not disrupted by changes in the weather and educational sailing is not endangered.

PLANNING AND ACCOMMODATION

When planning a marina, consideration should be given to the needs of the administration offices, the members clubhouse and the boat sales and service division.

The Administration services could require provision for:

Marina Manager's office.
Harbour Master's office.
General office.
Reception.
Staff Rooms—lockers, toilets, rest rooms and mess room.
First-Aid room.
Harbour Master's accommodation.
Chartroom (for coastal locations).
Race Control/Starters' and Timekeeper's box (for coastal locations).

The Members Clubhouse could require provision for:

Car parking.
Snack Bar, restaurant, bar, kitchen and storage.
Committee and lecture rooms.
Race Control/Starters' and Timekeeper's box (for upriver locations).
Lockers and changing rooms, showers, toilets and drying rooms.
Hostel or overnight accommodation with its own toilet and washing facilities. This could take the form of a caravan park.
Launderette.

The Boat Sales and Service Division could require provision for:

Mechanical spare parts store and workshop.

Boat-builder's yard with hoist or slipway into the water.

Boat hardstandings with hoist or slipway into the water.

(It could be possible with careful planning to amalgamate the hoist or slipway for the boat yard with that for the boat hardstandings. This would not be desirable where racing forms the main activity at day and week-end marinas as water access must be generous and not obstructed by other activities.)

Boat trailer park adjacent to the boat park and slipway or hoist.

Storage and sales facilities for petrol, diesel oil, lubricants and bottled gas.

Sail measurement hall, sail store and spar store.

Boat moorings.

Boat services, including water points, power points, fire fighting points, waste-disposal and toilet sluices.

Boat chandlery and general store dealing in protective clothing, lifejackets, navigational aids, cordage, tackle, new and used boats, food, drink, tobacco, newspapers, confectionery and postal items.

THE ADMINISTRATION SECTION

This controls both the sales and services division and the general usage of the marina, and must be situated in such a way that all activities can be conveniently supervised. As a minimum, the harbourmaster would require an office and the staff would need toilets, a wash room, locker and changing room and a mess room. With a larger marina, the management would be supported by a secretariat which would include a receptionist to deal with the booking and reservation of berths and general enquiries such as lists of approved hotels restaurants and taxi services.

For marinas in coastal situations, the management would also directly control the clubhouse and the membership. Off-shore cruising and racing requires competent organisation and the sale and storage of equipment is very complex. The clubhouse can be more efficiently run by full-time professional management than by part-time club officials, though of course the latter would be entitled to some share of the responsibility.

Staff facilities could include workshops for the maintenance of the marina buildings and moorings and living accommodation for the Harbourmaster and his family.

THE CLUBHOUSE

The clubhouse would be provided for the members for the weekend and the full scale holiday marinas and it would fulfil both the social and racing needs of the boat owners. As has been mentioned above with off-shore boating, the clubhouse would be closely integrated with the Administration section and would be run by the management who would employ a steward, organise all racing and control services.

With up-river marinas and those on other non-tidal sites, the function of the clubhouse is more social and would almost certainly involve itself with out-of-season activities such as dances, parties, film shows, etc. This would not concern the Administration in anyway and, because of the likelihood of non-boating members of the public attending such functions, it is desirable for the clubhouse to have its own facilities such as parking, access, toilets and accommodation completely independent of the marina on the grounds of security. A club pier within the basin or marina separate from all other shore facilities would, of course, be necessary and desirable.

Toilets, showers, locker rooms and drying rooms should have direct external access from the moorings. Likewise, where there is racing, it is of value to provide a snack bar with access from the slipway so that competitors can come ashore for a break without having to change before going into the clubhouse. The main rooms of the clubhouse are the bar and the restaurant. These should be provided with large observation windows and terraces overlooking the water to encourage the feeling of involvement even when not actually boating.

Racing requires rooms to be set aside for course briefings, committee meetings and lectures, whilst the more remote locations call for the provision of sleeping cabins away from the main clubrooms. These would be used to provide overnight accommodation for members whose boats lack bunks and for guests. Although the Harbourmaster would be in overall charge of all Marina activities, the clubhouse, whether management- or member-run should have a full-time steward to supervise day-to-day running. As with other marina activities, the seasonal nature of boating would mean that most of the clubhouse staff would be either part-time daily or seasonal only.

SERVICES

Boat services on land are directly concerned with the boat basins, so the workshops should be situated close to the slipway or hoist and the boat hardstandings. There should be sufficient headroom in the workshops to allow boats to be worked on under cover and for engines to be lifted out.

In all kinds of marina the call on the service facilities will be seasonal consisting of attention to running repairs and breakdowns during the season and overhauls, stripdowns, major services on engines, anti-fouling painting of hulls and general repainting in the winter. This means that unless there is a full-scale boat building yard included in the marina, there is no justification for installing a full range of service equipment or the employment of full-time specialist staff. Sufficient general tools should be provided to facilitate the above activities, but the fitting out of new boats, repairs of badly damaged hulls and major engine work would be contracted out to specialists who would either remove the boats to their own yards, or bring in their own equipment.

Fuel and oil sales machinery, the sluice pump and the hauling-out and launching equipment, which can be slipway, travelling 'drot' hoist or crane depending on the class of boat being handled and the amount of space available, should be situated in a position central enough to allow convenient access for service vehicles, easy control from the administration offices and good accessibility from the moorings without causing disturbance to other boats.

Where boats are moored in basins to systems of piers, services such as drinking water standpipes, refuse collection bins and fire-fighting equipment should be brought to the landward end of each pier.

It is not considered necessary to take these services out onto the piers themselves to each individual berth, except where berths are provided for larger sea-going craft equipped with a large number of auxiliary services. This is especially the case where electrical services are concerned and many marina authorities forbid the use of electric tools on boats moored in basins. They do, however, usually provide a coin-meter controlled outlet position near the servicing facilities to enable owners to use electrical equipment where they will not disturb the general moorings.

As mentioned above, there are however instances where all services have to be taken out onto the piers. Where the piers are fixed this presents few problems except for the final connections to the boats where it becomes necessary to avoid damage by chaffing whilst still allowing sufficient slack in the connecting cables and hoses to cope with the differing movements of the boats relative to the piers. Where the piers are in fact floating pontoons, movements between the shore and the pontoons and between the pontoons themselves should be allowed for. This adds to capital and maintenance costs and restricts adaption of the piers at later dates to meet changing requirements.

In addition to power requirements for boats there is a need for general lighting to the basins, car parks, hard-standings and buildings. A main switchboard controlling the entire installation should be situated in a readily accessible location. In order to reduce hazards that might be caused by the failure of supplies, the system should be designed in such a way that, in the event of a fault occurring, the area isolated is relatively small.

When installing sewage sluices the full approval of the local Public Health Authority must be obtained to the proposed system. If direct connection to a public sewer is possible, provision must be made for diluting the toilet waste with several volumes of water or ten times its volume of domestic sewage to reduce the strength of the accumulated chemicals additives that are used in the boat tanks.

Where cesspits or holding tanks are used, the method of construction is controlled, but there is no limit on the size of the tank itself which should be at least large enough to contain double the amount of sewage collected weekly by the local authority as a safeguard in the event of a breakdown in the collection service.

SALES AND CHANDLERY

The Sales and Chandlers Division supplies the equipment needs of the boat owners, but at the same time, can act as a shop-window and a wider source of income to the marina that the club members alone could provide. As has already been noted, with coastal marinas the Management usually runs the equipment sales because of its specialised nature. This is also true of the smaller inland marinas where boating needs are comparatively few and turnover is low. In most other marinas, it is now the general practice of the management to sublet space to a separate organisation which runs the sales service.

Sales activities are twofold and are divided accordingly. One side deals with the sale of boats, dinghies and outboard motors, whilst the chandlery sells everything from navigational aids and cordage to life-jackets, pennants and special clothing. Depending on the proximity of the marina to the nearest built-up area, it could be necessary with the more remote situations to also provide a general shop selling groceries, dairy produce, bread, confectionery, tobacco and newspapers.

SPACE REQUIREMENTS

The amounts of space that can be allocated to the various sections of a marina complex are initially controlled by the usable land and accessible water available at the time of development, but consideration must always be given to later expansion to cope with increasing demand. This is usually achieved by planning a basic core of buildings covering the prime functions which can be built onto as further land is acquired and profits can be turned to more development.

When planning items such as offices, toilets, kitchens, restaurants, bars, hostels and shops, minimum requirements are laid down (as with all buildings) by public health regulations, various building acts and specific local authority regulations which cover all aspects of public safety, means of escape in case of fire and general public health. These should be observed in the same way as with any other building.

With regard to the special items such as workshops, petrol sales, showrooms, slipways, hoists and parking areas various advisory documents and booklets are available. These are listed in the Bibliography at the end of this section.

SPECIFIC SPACE DATA

The following are recommended minimum allowances that should be made in marinas for specific types of boat:

Dinghies
   Boat park 6·50 × 3m hardstanding per boat.
   Trailer park. Allowance equal to one third area of boat park, adjoining the boat park.
   Car park. Allowance of one car per boat, plus 50% extra for visitors and spectators.
   Launching ramp. As wide as possible and accessible at all states of the tide.
   Lockers. One per boat at 1 m³ each.

Keel Boats
   Boat park. 16·0 × 3·5 m hardstanding per boat.
   Trailer park. Not necessary as Keel Boats rest on their trailers when ashore.
   Car park. Allowance of two cars per boat, plus 100% extra for visitors, spectators and crews.
   Launching. By crane direct to water or to cradle on slipway. Allowance of 100 m² working space per crane.
   Moorings. As for Boat park, subjected to allowances made for types of mooring used—to floating pontoon, fore and aft to piles, or swing moorings.

Motor Cruisers (up to 10 m length)
Boat park. 10 × 3 m hardstanding per boat.
Trailer park. Not necessary as cruisers are seldom trailed
    to other marinas, and where they are equipped with
    trailers they usually rest on them when ashore.
Car park. Allowance of one per boat, plus 50% extra for
    visitors. It is usual to locate the boat park and car park
    adjacent to each other so that extra cars can be accom-
    modated in the boat park in the summer and extra
    boats in the car park in winter. Provided there is no
    hindrance of the different activities the boat park and
    the car park may be combined, with considerable
    saving of space.
Launching. As for Keel boats.
Moorings. As for Boat park, allowing one mooring for
    every boat in the fleet plus 25% extra for visiting
    boats. Motor cruisers are able to turn 90° in one and a
    half times their own length, therefore when setting out
    floating pier moorings 15 m clear water must be allowed
    between opposite berths.
Lockers. One per boat at 1 m^3 each if necessary.

Motor Cruisers (Over 10 m length)
Boats up to 15 m in length can be handled as for the
smaller cruisers, and a limited number can be accommodated in the same berths, but no specific data can be
given for larger craft. These generally only enter and leave
the water at a boat-builder's yard and must be transported
on land by low-loader lorries. Likewise berthing and
manoeuvring requirements will be larger, so the usual
practice in marinas is to locate boats over 15 m across
the ends of the piers or stern on to the shore itself so that
manoeuvring is simplified and servicing access more
direct.

DATA

Table 8.1 and Fig 8.4 show recommended dimensions for
berths and piers. When calculating actual berth widths
where fixed pier systems are used, the half-widths of the pier
support piles on one side of the berth only may be deducted
from the minimum boat beam clearance. When piles project
on both sides of the berth, the full minimum boat beam
clearance must be provided between the piles. A mooring
arrangement using a loose mooring ring on a traveller iron
is shown in Fig 8.5. This arrangement is widely used in
tidal waters Figs 8.6 to 8.14 show various types of construction of types of pier and access ramp, including materials,
i.e. timber and aluminium, which can be used. Figs 8.15
and 8.16 illustrate a marine hoist and pier and Fig 8.17
shows an installation for sewage disposal from boats.

Table 8.1 RECOMMENDED DIMENSIONS FOR BOAT BERTHS AND PIER SYSTEMS
(to be read in conjunction with Fig. 8.4)

Length groups for boats	Beam to be provided for	Minimum clearance for boat beam-total	Minimum clear width of boat berth	Allowance for half of fender pile	Allowance for half of finger pier	Gross berth width type **A**– fixed and floating piers	Gross berth width type **B**– fixed and floating piers	Gross berth width type **C**– fixed and floating piers	Gross berth width type **D**– floating piers	Total length of finger pier-**E**	Total length of boat berth-**F**
Up to 4.250	2.000	690	2.690	250	600	3.540	2.940	3.290	2.940	3.660	5.180
Over 4.250 to 4.900	2.240	710	2.950	250	600	3.800	3.200	3.550	3.200	3.660	5.790
Over 4.900 to 5.500	2.440	740	3.180	250	600	4.030	3.430	3.780	3.430	4.250	6.400
Over 5.500 to 6.100	2.600	760	3.360	250	600	4.210	3.610	3.960	3.610	4.900	7.010
Over 6.100 to 6.700	2.800	760	3.560	250	600	4.410	3.810	4.160	3.810	5.500	7.600
Over 6.700 to 7.600	3.120	860	3.980	250	600	4.830	4.230	4.580	4.230	5.500	8.500
Over 7.600 to 9.150	3.430	910	4.340	250	600	5.190	4.590	4.940	4.590	6.100	10.060
Over 9.150 to 10.670	3.740	1.040	4.780	250	600	5.630	5.030	5.380	5.030	6.700	11.590
Over 10.670 to 12.200	4.040	1.120	5.160	250	600	6.010	5.410	5.760	5.410	7.300	13.100
Over 12.200 to 13.720	4.300	1.170	5.470	250	600	6.320	5.720	6.070	5.720	7.900	14.630
Over 13.720 to 15.250	4.550	1.250	5.800	250	600	6.650	6.050	6.400	6.050	8.540	16.150
Over 15.250 to 18.300	5.030	1.370	6.400	250	600	7.250	6.650	7.000	6.650	10.360	19.200
Over 18.300 to 21.350	5.500	1.500	7.000	250	600	7.850	7.250	7.600	7.250	10.360	22.250
Over 21.350 to 24.390	6.020	1.575	7.595	250	600	8.445	7.845	8.195	7.845	10.360	25.300

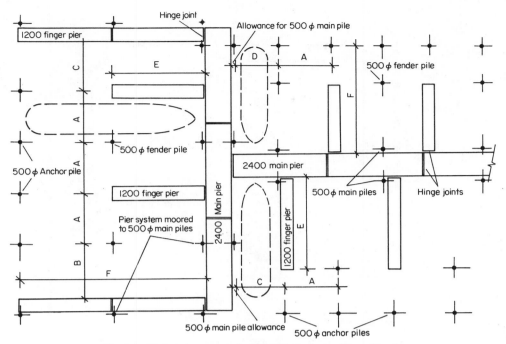

Fig. 8.4   Typical pier system indicating maximum berth widths and lengths
obtainable with various pier arrangements using 2400 and 1200
wide piers.

Notes: Floating piers

1. Where pier system is floating, boats will be moored direct to cleats on the edges of the pier sections, and the piers will be anchored to the main piles by one of the various pier guide systems.
2. Use of this system results in considerable savings in piling.
3. Clear widths of berths will be reduced by full width of pile in some locations.

Fixed piers

1. Where pier system is fixed, piers are supported on piles at between 2400 and 3600 centres, depending on size of pier and the nature of the bed of the basin.
2. The boats would be moored fore and aft to the anchor piles and main piles by way of traveller irons.
3. Clear widths of berths will be reduced by half width of piles supporting piers where piles are not fully recessed into pier decks.

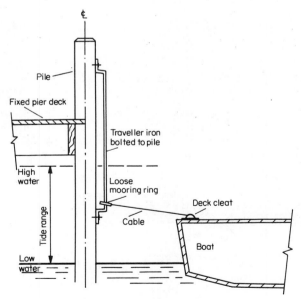

Fig. 8.5   Typical traveller iron mooring arrangement

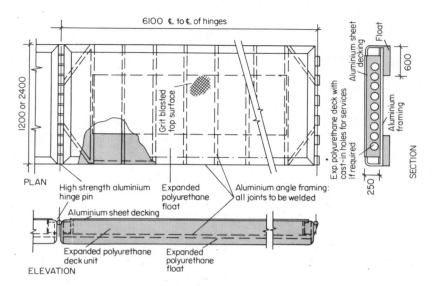

Fig. 8.6 Pier fabricated from aluminium sheeting and expanded polyurethane float

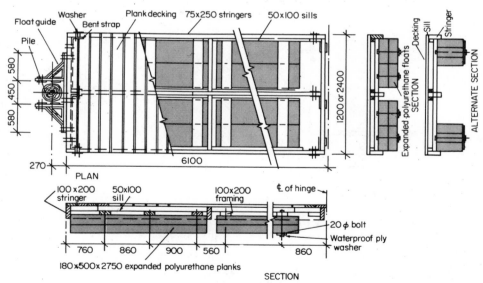

Fig. 8.7 Timber framed pier using cellular polyurethane plank floats

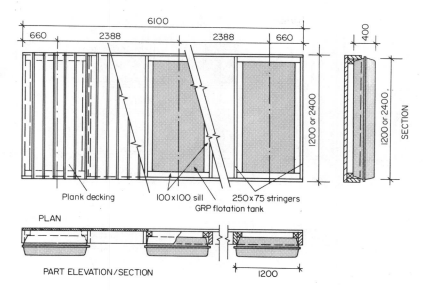

Fig. 8.8   Timber framed pier using hollow GRP floatation tanks

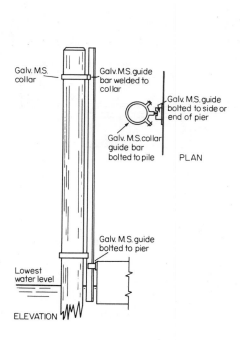

Fig. 8.9   Pier guide using MS collar and guide bar

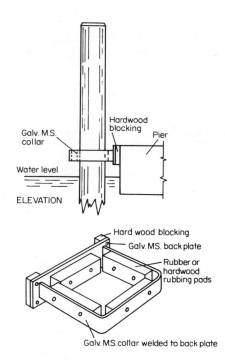

Fig. 8.10   Pier guide using MS collar bolted to pier

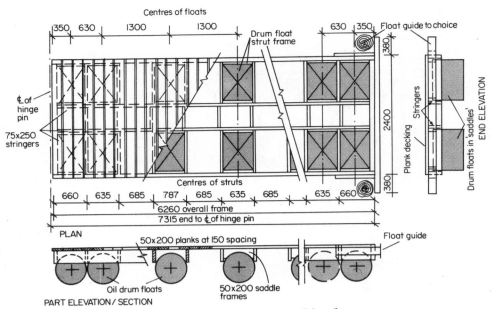

Fig. 8.11 Timber-framed pier using oil drum floats

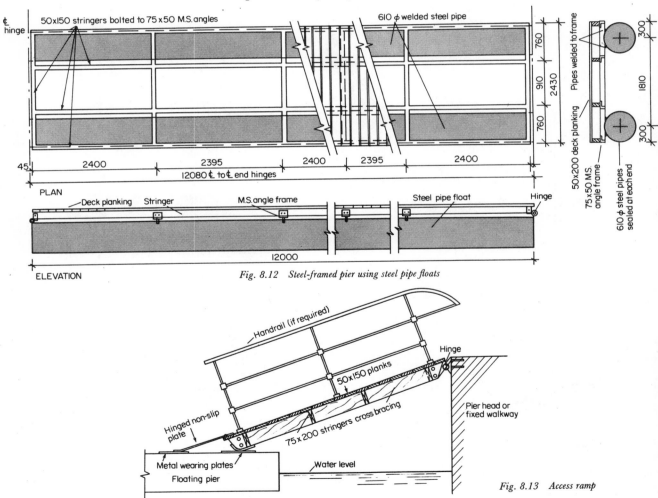

Fig. 8.12 Steel-framed pier using steel pipe floats

Fig. 8.13 Access ramp

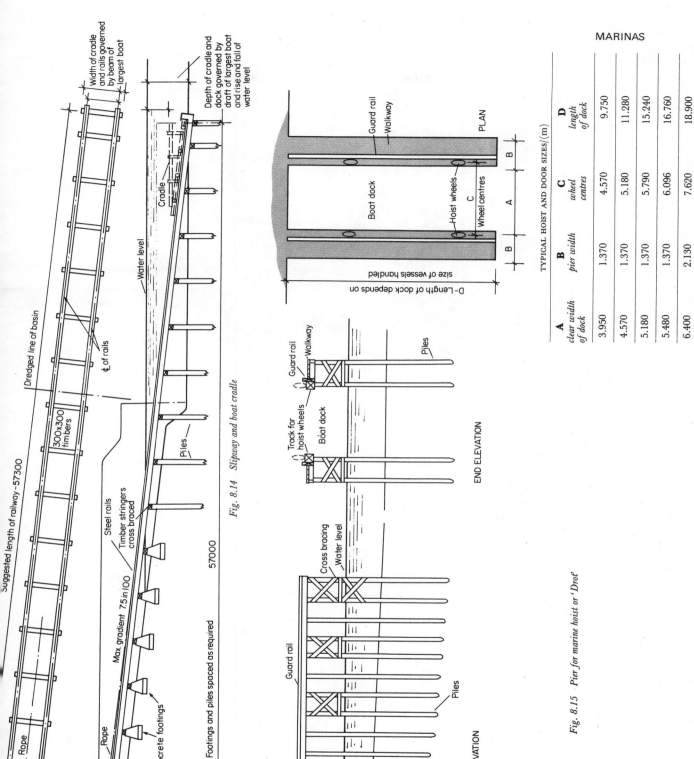

Fig. 8.14 Slipway and boat cradle

TYPICAL HOIST AND DOOR SIZES/(m)

A clear width of dock	B pier width	C wheel centres	D length of dock
3.950	1.370	4.570	9.750
4.570	1.370	5.180	11.280
5.180	1.370	5.790	15.240
5.480	1.370	6.096	16.760
6.400	2.130	7.620	18.900

Fig. 8.15 Pier for marine hoist or 'Drot'

8–11

Fig. 8.16   Typical travelling marine hoist
Lifting capacity 18000 lb. Adjustable wheelbase

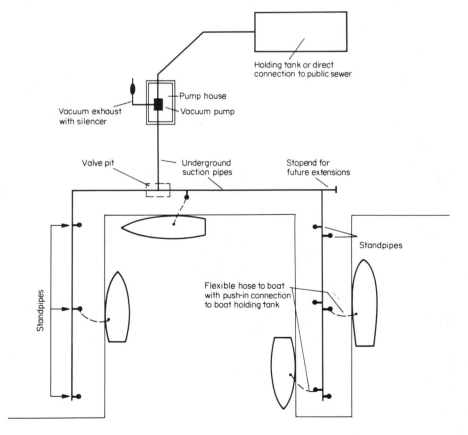

Fig. 8.17   Centralised disposal of sanitary sewage from boats

STATUTORY REQUIREMENTS AND LEGISLATION

The following permissions are normally required for development of marinas in addition to the normal building permissions.

LANDOWNERS

It is necessary to obtain the permission not only of the owners of the actual land on which the marina buildings are to be erected, but also the owners of the foreshore and sea-bed below high-water mark, including any dredged channels with tidal and coastal sites, or the local Water Authority with inland sites.

In some instances the developer is able to purchase the sea-bed or foreshore, but usually it remains the property of the Crown Estate Commissioners, the local Harbour Commissioners or some other authority.

AREA PLANNING AUTHORITY

The consent of the Planning Authority is required for all aspects of the scheme. The Planning Authority is the District Council or Greater London Borough, and its concern is with:

County planning. Each Authority has an overall development plan for its area defining in general terms how the land under it is to be used. The construction of a Marina must conform with the overall plan.

Access and parking facilities. Both the access to the Marina and the car-parking facilities within it must be adequate for the size of the harbour. With developments in isolated locations this could also involve the developer in the making up or improving of considerable lengths of access roads outside the actual marina.

Sewerage and Sewage Disposal. Adequate toilet facilities must be provided ashore and sewage treated before being discharged. In addition the authority may insist on lavatories on board boats not being used whilst they are in harbour, particularly in the case of locked basins.

Diversions of Rights of Way. Very often properties bordering water have highways, footpaths or bridle-ways crossing them. In the case of bridle-ways and footpaths the local authority can make a public diversion order and with highways an application must be made to two Justices of the Peace. In both cases the ultimate authority is the Department of the Environment.

The standard procedure of inserting a notice in a local newspaper in order that representations may be made by interested parties is usually required by the Planning Authority. This will then be followed by consideration of any representations by the Authority and the granting of consent, with or without conditions, or by the refusal of permission. Following the Authority's decision, the aggrieved party may appeal to the Department of the Environment which will then appoint an inspector to hear the case, either in private or at a public enquiry. The inspector is only employed to assist the reaching of a decision and his findings may not be inplemented in the final decision.

OTHER INTERESTED PARTIES

It will also be necessary to obtain the approval of any local Water Authority, Harbour Board, or Riparial Interest in whose area the proposed development lies. With regard to fresh water supply a licence must be obtained from the local Water Authority to extract an agreed amount of water daily from the mains or from a well. In the case of the former a meter with a cut-out will be installed and, with the latter, the pump will be adjusted to cut off after the agreed amount of water has been drawn. In both cases it will be necessary to have the installation tested and approved by the local Public Health Department.

COAST PROTECTION AUTHORITY

Under the Coast Protection Act, each area of coast is under the control of a Coast Protection Authority.

The Act provides that no work involving coastal protection shall be carried out without the Authority's consent and also that no materials should be removed from the sea-shore or shallow sea-bed.

BOARD OF TRADE APPROVAL UNDER THE COAST PROTECTION ACT

The approval of the Board of Trade is necessary before any works are undertaken below high-water mark. They will not normally give their approval until the approval of the other parties (such as the Harbour Board and Water Authority) have been given. If there is not a harbour board who have satisfied themselves that the scheme is structurally and hydrographically sound, the Board of Trade will investigate these aspects themselves.

Before giving approval, they also require that the scheme should be advertised in the local press and local interests consulted. Any points raised by the public are investigated and, if necessary, a public enquiry held. The Board of Trade has statutory power to order such an enquiry but may be prepared to forgo this or to permit the points with which they are concerned to be dealt with at any enquiry initiated by the Planning Authority.

MINISTRY OF TRANSPORT APPROVAL UNDER THE HARBOURS ACT, 1964

If the cost of the project exceeds a certain limit (see chapter 40, Clause 9) the approval of the Ministry of Transport is necessary.

ACT OF PARLIAMENT

In some instances, where there are many interests involved, it may be necessary or advantageous to obtain an Act of Parliament, which has the advantage of giving the developer statutory authority. The disadvantage of this is the time and cost of obtaining such an Act.

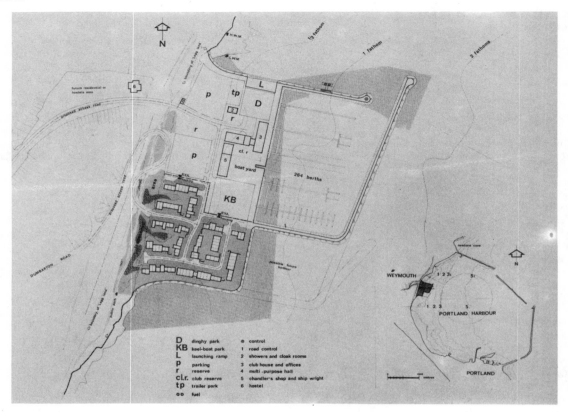

Fig. 8.18   Development plan for R.Y.A. National Centre
Architect: Howard V. Lobb & Partners, ARIBA, AMTPI

D	dinghy park	o	control
KB	keel-boat park	1	road control
L	launching ramp	2	showers and cloak rooms
p	parking	3	club house and offices
r	reserve	4	multi-purpose hall
cl.r.	club reserve	5	chandler's shop and ship wright
tp	trailer park	6	hostel
oo	fuel		

OTHER AUTHORITIES

In addition to the above statutory requirements, due attention must be given to the regulations and by-laws of the boating associations and authorities governing the classes of boats using the marina, and of the Marina Company itself.

Approvals must also be sought from the local Public Health Authority and other statutory bodies such as the Electricity Board.

EXAMPLES

COASTAL SITES

Newhaven	Sussex
Brighton	Sussex
Hamble	Hampshire
Lymington	Hampshire
Weymouth Harbour	Dorset (See Fig. 8.18)

TIDAL RIVER SITES

Bucklers Hard	Hampshire

Burnham-on-Crouch	Essex (Royal Corinthian Y.C.)
Bradwell-on-Sea	Essex (Bradwell Y.C.)
Chelsea Embankment	London (The general waterfront)

ENCLOSED BASINS (TIDAL SITES)

Maldon	Essex (Tulsbury Basin)
St. Katharine's Marina	London (St. Katharine's Dock)
Maidenhead	R. Thames, Berkshire (Bray Marina)
Staines	R. Thames, Surrey (Penton Hook Marina)
Henley-on-Thames	Oxfordshire (the General waterfront)

CANAL BASINS

Hampstead Road Locks	Regent's Canal, London
City Road Basin	Regent's Canal, London
Little Venice	Grand Union Canal, London
Wooton Wawen	South Stratford Canal, Warwickshire
Market Harborough	Leicester Canal, Leicestershire

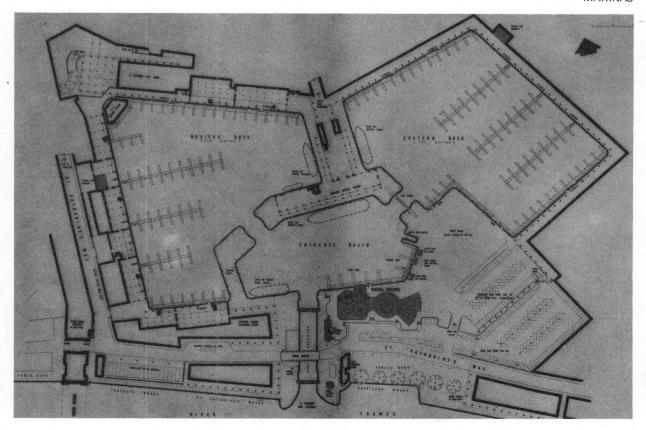

Fig. 8.19   Proposal for Marina at St. Katherine's Dock, London
Architect: Stephen L Wagstaffe, RIBA, MRSM

BIBLIOGRAPHY

BOOKS AND PAMPHLETS

Adie, Donald, *Marinas – a working guide to their development & design*. Architectural Press, London (1975).

'Boat World's' Guide Series—

No. 1. Sailing Dinghies

Nos. 2 and 7. Sailing Cruisers

No. 3. Sports Boats

Nos. 4 and 8. Motor Cruisers

No. 5. Inflatables

No. 6. Young People Go Afloat!

Come Sailing (Again) with Peyton

(The above are published by
    Boat World Publications, 39 East Street,
    Epsom, Surrey)

Chaney, Charles A, *Marinas – recommendations for design, construction and maintenance* 2nd ed (1961).

Chaney, Charles A, '*The Modern Marina*'.

Chaney, Charles A, *Boat handling equipment in the modern marina*

(The above are published by the National Assoc. of Engine & Boat Builders Inc., 420 Lexington Ave., New York 17, NY.)

Head, Derek, *Marinas*, Viewpoint Publications Ltd., London

Pleasure-Craft Users Guide to the Tidal Thames, published annually by the Port of London Authority

National Yacht Harbour Association News, Monthly newsletter published by the N.Y.M.A. London

The Ship and Boat Builders National Federation Annual Handbook, S.B.B.N.F.

Webber, N. B. (ed), *Marinas and Small Craft Harbours*, A report on the Proceedings of a Symposium held at the University of Southampton on 19–21 April 1972, Southampton University Press (1974).

'45 weekend cottages at Emsworth Marina', Architects: V. Gibberd Associates, *Design*, 297, pp.56–59 (Sept 1973)

'£12m Marina and Holiday centre at Lodmoor, Weymouth', Architect: D. Burton, *Building*, **223,** 6750 p.73 (Oct 6, 1972)

'£15m Marina and Leisure Centre at St. Leonards-on-Sea, Sussex' *Building*, **224,** 6762, p.39 (Jan 5, 1973)

'£25m centre for the Surrey Docks', Architects: Overton & Partners, *Building*, **223,** 6761, p.25 (Dec 22/29, 1972)

Adie, D., 'Costa Brava comes to Brighton', *A.J.*, **159,** 5, pp.190–3 (Jan 30, 1974)

'Corby Boat House', Architect: J. Stedman, *A.J.*, **158,** 51, p.1510 (Dec 19–26, 1973)

Dower, M., 'Water and Recreation', *Town & Country Planning*, **41,** 4, pp.211–212 (April 1973)

'Hollyburn Sailing Club, West Vancouver, British Columbia, Review', Architect: P. le Mare, *Wood World*, **3,** 1, pp.13–15, (1973)

Hubbard, R. 'Waterside design', *Built Environment*, **3,** 1, pp.564–8 (Nov 1974)

Kaye, S. 'Marine Architecture', *The Architect*, **2,** 8, pp.31–33 (Aug 1972)

'Leisure Centre in Wendtorf Marina', Architect: F. Happ, *Deutsche Bauzeitschrift*, **21,** 7, pp. 1335–8 (July 1973)

Leyland, V., 'The National Water Sports Centre', *Sports, Recreation and Leisure Centres*, **1,** 3, pp.150–156 (Oct 1973)

McNab, A. 'Folly de Grandeur (Brighton)', *Arch. Design*, **45,** 1, pp.31–32 (Jan 1975)

'Marina and Housing in Cubitts Yacht Basin, Chiswick', Architects: B. Engle & Partners, *Building*, **223,** 6755, p.89 (Nov 10, 1972)

'Mariners' Village, Los Angeles', *Arch. Design*, **43,** 9, pp.607–8 (Sept 1973)

'Mayflower Marina, Plymouth', Architects: Marsham, Warren & Taylor, *Building Design*, 122, p.7 (Oct 13, 1972)

'Muizenberg Marina, S. Africa', Architects: L. Falck, M. Lowe & Associates, *Architect & Builder* **23,** 3 pp.14–18 (March 1973)

National Water Sports Centre, Holme Pierrepoint, Notts, Architects: Gelsthorpe & Savidge.
Building, **223,** 6758, p.70 (Dec 1, 1972)
Consulting Engineer, **37,** 4, pp.41–43 (April 1973)
Inst. of Mun Eng. Journal, pp.37–38 (March 1971)
Landscape Design, 104, pp 18–20 (Nov 1973)
A.J., 157, 23, pp.1358–9 (June 6, 1973) and
158, 32, pp.299–316 (Aug 8, 1973)

'Nautical club in Soustons', Architects: A. De Guenin & J. C. Gerard, *L'Architecture Francaise*, **34,** 373/374, pp.46–48 (Sept/Oct 1973)

'Port Deauville, Marina and Residential accommodation', Architects: C. Gondilis and Calleti Architecture, *L'Architecture d'Aujourd'Hui*, **44,** 162, pp.81–83 (June/July 1972)

'Proposals for a Medway Marina near Rochester', Architects, B. Udall, *Building*, **223,** 6758, p.124 (Dec 8, 1972)

'Proposed Marina Complex for Brixham, Devon', Architects: M. Twigg, Brown & Partners.
Architect & Builder, **24,** 5, p.25 (May 1974)
Building, **225,** 6804, p.67 (Oct 26, 1973)
Building Design, **174,** p.13 (Nov 2, 1973)

Roberts, A and Simpson, M, 'Traffic Generated by Coastal Marinas', *Traffic Engineer & Control*, **15,** 7, pp.340–3, (Nov 1973)

Schmitt, Claudine, 'The Marinas of Port Deauville', *La Construction Moderne*, 4, pp.35–41 (July/Aug 1974)

Schräter, Bertram, 'Marinas, Yacht Harbours', *Deutsche Bauzeitschrift* **21,** 11, pp.2211–6, (Nov 1973)

Smart, C. W. W., 'Research associated with water recreation', *Landscape Design*, 104, pp.33–35 (Nov 1973)

'Takapuna Boat Club, New Zealand', Architects: Pepper & Dixon, *Home and Building*, **34,** 12, p.30 (July 1, 1972)

Tanner, M. F., 'Water for Sport & Leisure', *Town & Country Planning* **40,** 9, pp.423–7 (Sept 1972)

'Taupo Marina, New Zealand', Architect: C. Johns, *Nzia Journal*, **40,** 11, pp.320–321 (Nov 1973)

'The Marinas of Port Deauville', *La Technique des Travaux*, **50,** 3/4, pp.93–96 (March/April 1974)

'Training Ship Neptune Sailing and Boat Training Centre, Kingston-on-Thames, Surrey', Architects: Hubbard, Ford & Partners,
A.J., 157, 1, pp.13–15 (Jan 3, 1973)
Building Specification, **3,** 7, pp.39–42 (July 1972)
Concrete Quarterly, 96, pp.26–29 (Jan/March 1973)

'Two-Tree Island, Leigh-on-Sea, Essex', Architects: YRM and Cedric Price, *Building Design*, 210 p. 12 (July 19, 1974) p.12 (July 19, 1974)

'Water Sports Centre of Chalon-sur Saone', Architect: P. O. Fournier, *La Technique des Travaux*, **48,** 338, pp.357–369 (Nov/Dec 1972)

'Water Sports Centre, Lake Motosu, Japan', Architect, K. Mori, *Int. Asbestos Cement Review*, **17,** 3, pp.26–27 (July 1972)

'Waterfront development at Port Dinorivic, North Wales', Architects: Phillips, Cutter, Phillips and Troy, *House Builder*, **33,** 7, p.423, (July 1973)

Wright, M., 'The growth of recreational demands; water under pressure; the future of inland waterways', *Country Life*, **152,** 3933, pp.1194–6 (Nov 9th 1972) and **152,** 3934, pp.1311–3 (Nov 16, 1972)

Stephen Leslie Wagstaffe, *RIBA, M.R.S.H., studied Architecture at the N.E. London Polytechnic, elected corporate member of the RIBA 1971. His RIBA Thesis subject was the redevelopment of St. Katharine's Dock London as a Marina, and included a detailed study of historic drawings of the original buildings. He has been involved in Nautical Buildings, originally in private practice, and later on the staff of the Greater London Council Architects Department. He is an enthusiastic sailor, having raced sailing dinghies and cruised, recently he has developed an interest in inland waterways including fund raising for canal restoration projects.*

9 RIDING SCHOOLS

JOHN M. V. BISHOP, DA (Edin), A.R.I.B.A., M.R.T.P.I.
Architect to The Lee Valley Regional Park Authority
and
M. G. QUINTON
Job Architect to The Lee Valley Regional Park Authority

INTRODUCTION

Riding Schools have in the past grown around existing facilities; for example, adding to the stables of an old house, building an asbestos-clad barn structure over the riding area to provide teaching in all weathers. Some establishments are specially built for breeding or racing, these have different requirements, and are not covered in this article.

There are few completely new riding schools in this country but, in the main, developments have been made in the additions and extensions of existing facilities. The main emphasis has been on improving the lot of the stable girls, introducing wherever possible labour-saving devices and totally enclosing the loose boxes. However, these developments are not without their critics.

SITING

The following are essential requirements of any site:

1. Good vehicular access for lorries as well as cars.
2. Access to open country and/or bridlepaths.
3. Adequate electricity supply.
4. Adequate water supply; possibly including fire hydrants.

The following points should also be considered:

1. Loose boxes should be protected from prevailing winds (especially north winds) to avoid winds blowing directly into doors and windows. Therefore, exposed hill-top sites should be avoided especially with open loose boxes.
2. A well drained site is ideal, preferably chalk or gravel, otherwise drainage must be provided. Low lying sites which catch the water and are usually frosty in the winter should be avoided.
3. Stables should be sited away from adjacent houses, although some residential accommodation should be near or must be provided for the manager and/or head groom, one of whom, should be on hand at any time of the day or night every day of the week.

4. In the external circulation special care should be taken to ensure adequate turning space for horsebox trailers and for lowering ramps both side and rear, with sufficient room to load and unload difficult horses (Fig 9.1). Turning space is also required for the lorry taking away the muck (Fig 9.2).

Access will be required for fire appliances requiring roads at least 3.6 m wide capable of supporting a pumping appliance with a laden weight of approximately 10 tons. Any necessary bends in roads should be able to accommodate an appliance having a minimum turning circle of 17 m diameter. Minimum clearance height should be 3.6 m, for hay lorries 4.5 m will be required. All gate openings should have a minimum width of 3 m in the clear.

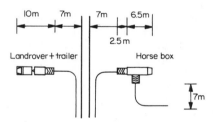

Fig. 9.1   Clearance required for manoeuvring horses into trailer and box

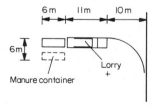

Fig. 9.2   Clearance required for manoeuvring large container lorry

PLANNING

As can be seen from the schedule of accommodation given later, the planning of facilities breaks down into three main groups, Instruction, Horse Management and Administration.

The traditional plan (Fig 9.3) usually arranges the loose boxes looking inwards to a courtyard with only a covered way in front of each box. Later developments totally enclose the loose boxes which are arranged either side of a 3 m corridor enabling them to be serviced by a tractor and trailer circulating through the block (Fig 9.4).

The disadvantages are the extra cost, including extra fire precautions and some people say the horses will become bored without a view. However, in addition to better working conditions for the stable girls, the ventilation can be controlled to eliminate draughts, it is easier to maintain an even temperature, and the quieter conditions can be an advantage if the site is near the road or railways.

Some general principles to be considered are:

1. The stables should be planned so that smells are not carried to the residential accommodation.
2. It is preferable that the school is not so near the stables that the voice of command from the instructors can be heard and may disturb the horses at rest.
3. The risk of fire in stables necessitates special planning consideration. The straw store requires a minimum of 1 hour fire resistance from other parts of the building, or a fire break of at least 4.5 m is recommended.

Although, in the past, timber has been used extensively for loose boxes, it has a limited life and it is accepted that timber boarded linings will require frequent replacing due to damage from kicking. Brick or block walls are preferable but hollow blocks are suspect below 1.5 m and some will not be strong enough to hold a tie-ring should a horse pull hard on it. The internal finish should be rendered or painted with an external hardwearing paint (Sandtex-matt or similar) to facilitate cleaning.

The floors must be impervious, non slip and extremely hardwearing and able to withstand urine attack. Blue engineering brick paviors have been used. They are grooved to provide a non slip surface, but this also provides a tendency to retain the urine and dirt. A dense concrete properly laid and compacted is much cheaper and may be finished with both a carborundum topping and grooves to prevent slipping. The finish between the floor and wall should be coved to facilitate cleaning.

The floor for the indoor school and manage usually consists of approximately 300 mm of a mixture of wood chippings and sand, although other materials (peat or tan) may be used according to availability and cost. There are many opinions of the exact mixture and method of laying the floor. The floor to the indoor school will become dry and will require to be damped. The sub-floor should, therefore, facilitate drainage, and if clay will require at least an extra 300 mm of top soil or a layer of carefully compacted hardcore. Externally, the manage may even require land drains incorporated in the base.

Protrusions generally in the horse areas must be avoided, and all corners of brickwork should be formed with bullnose bricks.

All steelwork should be carefully protected against attack

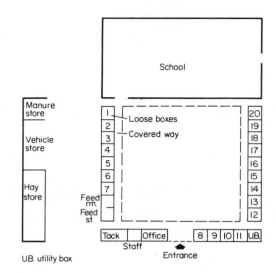

Fig. 9.3 Typical traditional plan for a riding school

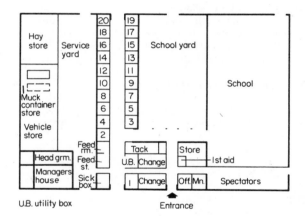

Fig. 9.4 Plan of Lea Bridge riding school

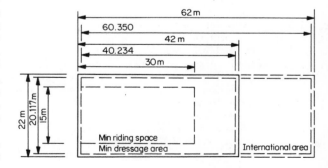

Fig. 9.5 Riding school areas

by the urine laden atmosphere, small items should be gal-
vanized, and structural steelwork should be painted with a
chlorinated rubber based paint.

All timber edges able to be bitten, especially the top edge
of the loose box doors will need to be protected with metal.

SPACE REQUIREMENTS

INDOOR SCHOOL AREA (see Fig 9.5)

Minimum riding space should be 30.5 × 15.3 m.
Minimum area for dressage is 40.2 × 20.2 m with a recommended extra 1 m all round. The total area for minimum
dressage is therefore 42 m × 22 m.
International standard for dressage is 60.3 × 20.3 m with
extra 1 m all round, making a total of 62 m × 22 m.
A full size Military School is 54.9 × 18.3 m (see Fig 9.6).
A minimum height required for jumping is 4 m although at
least 5 m is preferable.
If spectator seating is required this will be additional to the
riding areas outlined above. A judges box will also be
required.

EXTERNALLY

External manage. Areas required as indoor school.

Paddocks. Minimum area required for fine weather riding
is 0.8 ha.

British Show Jumping Association minimum jumping course
is 110 m × 55 m.
Approximate area required for grazing is 0.8 ha per horse.

Loose Boxes (Fig 9.7)
Minimum internal dimensions for:
   Ponies   3 × 3 m.
   Horse below 16hh.   3 × 3.5 m.
   Horse above 16hh.   3.5 × 4 m.
recommended height approximately   3 m.

If there is to be an internal corridor a minimum width of
3 m is recommended for use by servicing vehicles, landrover
and trailer, etc, and in case of fire as means of escape.

Stalls. Minimum length 2.7 m; minimum width 1.8 m;
minimum passageway behind stalls 1.8 m.

Utility box. Used for grooming, clipping, shoeing, washing,
and treatment of cuts, etc. Same size as loose box but without
fittings except tie rings.

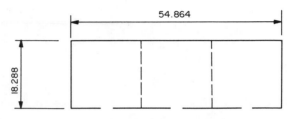

Fig. 9.6 Military school

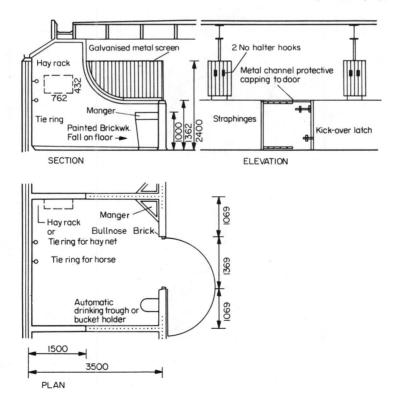

Fig. 9.7 Typical layout for loose box

Could be two stalls with removable central partition. Electric point required.

Sick box. This should be approximately 3.5 × 4.5 m. A completely isolated box for infectious diseases may be required in larger establishments. Otherwise it should be away from the other boxes but within sight of other horses. The door should be in two leaves so that the horse can look out or be enclosed if it requires complete quiet. A sling suspended from a beam with block and chain may be required. 1¼ ton should be taken as maximum loading (for heavy draught horse).

DATA—INSTRUCTIONAL

INDOOR SCHOOL

A kicking board of stout construction is required to a height of at least 1200 mm and should be sloped to an angle of 12–15 degrees on all four sides.

DATA—HORSE MANAGEMENT

LOOSE BOX

Fittings required are manger, hay rack or tie ring for hay net, automatic drinking trough or bucket holder, salt lick holder.

TACK ROOM (Fig 9.8)

Size depends on number of horses it serves. It is normally used for cleaning as well as storing the tack, although in larger establishments a separate cleaning room would be an advantage. The B.H.S. recommend one tack room per 15 horses. Where some horses are kept at livery a separate tack room for their saddlery is advisable. The value of the tack requires that the room is especially secure from burglars. Windows should be barred, etc.

The equipment to be stored in the Tack Room include:

1. *Saddles.* On saddle racks fixed not lower than 700 mm

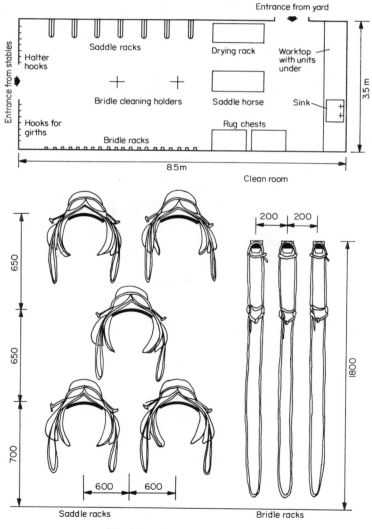

Fig. 9.8 Plan of typical tack room

from floor and not higher than 1.8 m approximately 600 mm centres.

2. *Stirrups and leathers.* Normally hung at the end of the saddle rack with leathers hung, hanging on hooks to one side.
3. *Bridles.* On bridle racks not less than 1.6 m above the floor.
4. *Head collars.* On halter hooks not less than 1.6 m above the floor.
5. *Girths.* On hooks not less than 1.6 m above the floor.
6. *Martingales.* On hooks not less than 1.8 m above the floor.
7. *Blankets, rugs and sheets.* These are usually stored in galvanised steel chests to exclude vermin, moths, etc. A standard chest is $760 \times 560 \times 560$ mm and may be kept in the tack room or the general store.

The Clean room (or part of Tack room) requires:

1. A Butler sink $900 \times 450 \times 250$ mm with draining board/worktop with cupboards under for cleaning materials.
2. Saddle horse—standard 1.4 m long. If more than one is required allow 1.4 m between them or 760 mm if end to end.
3. Drying rack (for blankets and sheets) normally hung from ceiling.
4. Bridle cleaning holder, also hung from ceiling.

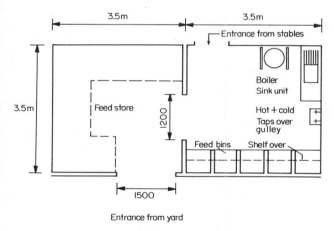

Fig. 9.9   Typical plan of feed store and room

FEED STORE (Fig 9.9)

Normally part of the stables next to feed room. The size depends on number of horses and method of buying feed. Most will buy it in sacks but the larger establishments may have their feed delivered in bulk. The sacks usually weigh as follows:

Oats and Barley	51 kg.
Bran	63.5 kg.
Cubes	31.7 kg.

A horse requires between 3–5 kg per day.

FEED ROOM

Feeds prepared each day vary between horses and establishments. Basic requirements is space for feed bins, sink unit with taps able to fill buckets, boiler racks and shelves.

Bins are $600 \times 600 \times 900$ mm.

Each bin is capable of holding 101 kg of oats, or 76 kg of bran, or 178 kg of cubes.

HAY AND STRAW STORE

This will be a Dutch-barn type structure, the size depends on the number of horses and the method of buying. A year's supply of hay is the most economic way of buying, as the price rises steeply during the winter. The straw price is not affected so much and therefore, the storage is less critical. The following data will be sufficient to determine the size required:

1 horse requires approx	9 kg of hay per day
1 horse requires	½ bale of straw per day
1 bale of hay weighs approx	23 kg.
1 bale of straw weighs approx	18 kg.
1 bale is approx	$900 \times 450 \times 450$ mm = 0.2 m³

approximately 10% extra volume should be allowed on total storage required for air circulation and remaining stock when new load arrives.

VETERINARY STORE

Bandages may be kept in cupboards or pigeon-hole racks. A leg bandage measures 127 mm wide and is approximately 75 mm diameter. Medicines and poisons should be kept in separate cupboards and clearly labelled.

MAIN STORE

Storage of equipment to be used within school, jumps, cavaletti, etc. 5% of school activity area is a recommended size.

TOOL STORE

To store wheelbarrows, yard brooms, forks, racks, shovels, hose, and hay nets.

MUCK STORE

Traditionally open bunkers with brick or block walls on four sides with an opening about 900 mm wide in one side. The concrete floor should drain towards the opening with a gully outside. Size depends on number of horses and management. Allow approximately 5.6 m³ per horse per week. After a month the volume is reduced approximately two-thirds.

Skip-type containers may be used and are recommended. There are various sizes which may be used depending on the number of horses and frequency of removal. The larger ones are 6 m long and 2.5 m wide and are carried on lorries 8.5 m long which off-load the container backwards. Thus, an overall space of 15 m is required for both lorry and container. The method is for the lorry to leave one empty container and then pick up the full one. Thus room must be allowed for two containers side by side and manoeuvring space for the lorry.

DATA—ADMINISTRATION

Size and data on rooms under this section may be obtained with reference to other appropriate building types, e.g. offices (see volume on *Planning: for Habitation, Commerce and Industry*).

ACCOMMODATION

TYPICAL LIST OF ACCOMMODATION

A. *Instructional*

1. Indoor school.
2. Outdoor manage.
3. Grass paddock (minimum 0.8 ha).
4. Access to open countryside or bridlepaths.
5. Cross country training area.
6. Club room/lecture room/canteen.
7. Store for jumps, cavaletti, etc.

B. *Horse Management*

1. Stables (loose boxes and stalls).
2. Feed Store.
3. Feed room.
4. Utility box.
5. Sick box.
6. Tack room.
7. Tool store.
8. Hay and straw store.
9. Muck store.
10. Veterinary store.

C. *Administration*

1. Reception office.
2. Manager's office.
3. Staff room.
4. First aid room.
5. Lavatories.
6. Changing rooms.
7. Garaging for horse boxes, tractors & trailer.
8. Resident accommodation for manager.
9. Resident accommodation for grooms and/or stable girls.
10. Plant rooms (for boilers, electrical switchgear, etc.)
11. Workshop.

SERVICE REQUIREMENTS

Water. Apart from the usual domestic requirements, changing rooms etc., frequent washdown points will be required, in and around the stable block next to the manure store, and in the indoor school. (Check local Water Authority for special requirements regarding possible contamination of supply). Fire hose reel supply may also be required (consult fire brigade).

Electricity. Waterproof switches and socket outlets should be provided in the instructional and horse areas, with no floor outlets. All fittings should be positioned out of reach of horses. Any electrical fires should be permanently fixed at high level. Emergency lighting may be installed (consult fire brigade).

Drainage. The stables have special drainage requirements to prevent straw, etc, passing into mains sewer. Untrapped gullies should be liberally provided in the stable block leading to a drainage run which connects to a straw trap similar to petrol or mud intercepter. A wire tray straw trap may also be provided in each gully, and each run should be constructed so that it is easily rodded.

A similar system should be provided to drain external areas where straw, etc, is likely to collect. Polluted surface water should not be discharged into water courses, and a cess tank may be required.

Communication. Internal telephone or some call system will be required to contact staff in all parts of the building and living accommodation.

A PA system is required in school.
A fire alarm is recommended (consult fire brigade).
BST clocks are required especially in school.

ENVIRONMENTAL REQUIREMENTS

Heating. Is not required in school except possibly for spectator area, if any. No heating required in the stables. The tack room requires a constant temperature of about 13°C. The administration and club room require normal heating.

Ventilation. Ventilation for the indoor school depends on construction. With low insulation and large glazed areas, considerable heat build-up could be expected and therefore, the provision of grills for natural ventilation and/or extract fans may be required.

In the stables minimum of three air changes per hour is required. Maximum velocity of air 2 ft/sec (2.2 km/hr). Draughts should be avoided in loose boxes. Fresh-air inlets, therefore, should not be direct holes through the walls, and must not be at low level.

The tack room should be adequately ventilated to avoid condensation and prevent the leather being attacked by mildew.

Lighting. An even, glare free, illumination is required in the school. Roof-lights should be designed to avoid sunlight drying patches of the floor (windows in walls) should not be low enough to cause a distraction). Light fittings should be easy to replace, waterproof, and provide 100–150 lux at 900 mm level.

The loose boxes should only have windows at high level with adequate lighting for inspection.

*Fig. 9.10   Lea Bridge Riding School—external view
(Figs 9.10 and 9.11 are reproduced by permission of the
Lea Valley Regional Park Authority)*

AUTHORITIES

The Sports Council,
160 Great Portland Street,
London, W1N 5TB

British Horse Society,
35 Belgrave Square,
London, S.W.1.

The National Equestrian Centre,
Stoneleigh,
Kenilworth.

The British Show Jumping Association,
c/o The National Equestrian Centre.

The Riding for the Disabled Association,
c/o The National Equestrian Centre.

The Jockey Club,
42 Portman Square,
London, W.1.

Royal Veterinary College,
Royal College Street,
London, N.W.1.

British Veterinary Society,
7 Mansfield Street,
London, W.1.

Lee Valley Regional Park Authority,
Myddelton House,
Bulls Cross,
Enfield, Middlesex.

LEGISLATION

Attention should be paid to the following relevant Acts:

Riding Establishments Act, 1964.
Means of Escape Regulations.
Fire Regulations.
Clean Air Act.
Petroleum Spirits Act, 1929.
Shops, Offices, Railway Premises Act, 1963.

In addition consideration must be given to any special requirements of the following:

The Insurance Company.
Planning Consents.
Local Authority Building Regulations.
Preservation orders on existing buildings or trees.

EXAMPLES

1   Knightsbridge Barracks (London)   1970

Architects' Journal, p. 992 (28 Oct 1970)
Deutsch Bauzeitschrift No. 11, p. 2261 (1971)

Stabling for 273 horses on two levels, finished to extremely high standard, each troop has its own forage store, feed room and tack room at one end of the line and a dung chute at the other end. The stables are artificially lit and ventilated and linked to the stable yard by ramps which can be heated to prevent ice forming. The only daylight in the school is indirect from a clerestory. The main doors are opened by hydraulic rams.

2   Lea Bridge (Portersfield) Riding School (London)   1973

Architects' Journal, p. 1305 (28 Nov 1973)

Complete establishment for 20 horses, with stables, school, changing rooms, etc., and living accommodation for the manager and grooms. The brick stables are totally enclosed and planned with a corridor wide enough to take a landrover and trailer to serve each loose box. The school, 42 × 22 m has spectator seating for 100 and is clad continuously with white translucent glass fibre sheeting.

Fig. 9.11   Lea Bridge Riding School (above) Indoor school; (below) stables

3   Riding School at Warendorf, Germany   1970

Deutsch Bauzeitschrift, No. 6, p. 11014 (1971)

Stabling for 48 horses with attendant facilities built in two blocks both planned with a central service corridor. Covered links to international size school with offices and spectator gallery for 125 people.

4   Club Hippique de Versaille, France   1966

L'Architecture Francais, No. 303, p. 8–11 (1967)

Stabling for 140 horses in seven blocks. Olympic size school with spectator galleries for 500 people. All ancillary accommodation under the galleries.

5   Turin Hippodrome, Italy   1961

Int. Asbestos-Cement p. 37–9 (Oct, 1964)

School and stables all in one building under an enormous asbestos clad roof. The school, 80 ft × 160 ft is in the centre with stables for 100 horses on the two long sides. Horse entrance and feed stores on one short side and offices, flats, and spectator gallery on the other short side.

6   Le Centre Equestre Lansannois, France   1962

Werk (Zurich) No. 9, p. 350 (1966)

30 loose boxes and 12 stalls linked by food stores and forge, etc., to one end of school. Other end has club rooms and spectator gallery over, linked to separate building containing flats for manager and grooms.

BIBLIOGRAPHY

Basic requirements for a Riding Centre, B.H.S. Publication
Hope, C. E. G., *Teach Yourself Horse Management* (1951)
Stable Management. Magazine of Riding School & Stable Management Limited
Smith, P. C., *The design & construction of stables,* J. A. Allen & Co. Ltd. (1967)

John M. V. Bishop, *Architect to the Authority, Lee Valley Regional Park Authority. Educated in Edinburgh as an Architect and Town Planner. Worked in private practise in Edinburgh then moved into a public office in Coventry under Arthur Ling as Architect/Planner involved in the design of the Town Centre. Worked as Deputy Architect in the new towns of Runcorn and Washington and lectured in Planning at Birmingham and London. At present, Architect to the Authority for the design and construction of the Lee Valley Regional Park. The department covers all architectural, engineering, planning, and landscape architecture aspects for the Park.*

M. G. Quinton *trained at the Bartlett School of Architecture. He joined A.C.P. and was involved in the design of universities, then housing and commercial buildings at T. F. P. Since joining the Lee Valley Regional Park he has designed sports buildings, a leisure pool and many recreational developments including a marina which received a Civic Trust Commendation in 1971 and the Lea Bridge Riding School which was completed in 1973.*

10 SPORTS PAVILIONS AND GOLF CLUBHOUSES

MICHAEL DIXEY, Dip.Arch., A.R.I.B.A.

INTRODUCTION

The growth in leisure activities during the last decade has considerably broadened the choice of activities available to the sportsman and recreationalist. At one time the Pavilion formed the backbone of sports provision in most areas, now there are many other facilities which compete for the limited funds available. Furthermore many of these facilities, such as Local Authority Sports Centres, are new in concept and reflect a demand for a wide variety of sports facilities at a low price on a casual use basis. These developments have had a considerable effect on the role of the Sports Pavilion. The tendency towards the provision of indoor facilities has created a demand for more social accommodation and increasing living standards have resulted in a general upgrading of the sports building; it is no longer the sole preserve of the adult male sportsman. The school building programme has encouraged the provision of more facilities which in many cases are utilised by the public out of school hours and the concept of family recreation is growing in popularity.

It is necessary to take a fresh look at the Sports Pavilion in the light of these new demands if it is to adequately cater for present day needs and fit in with modern concepts of recreational planning. To be financially viable the pavilion should possess the kind of facilities that guarantee its intensive use throughout the week as well as at week-ends. The management of the building will also require greater expertise than has been provided in the past by caretakers and groundsmen.

The emphasis on the provision of indoor sports facilities and their management has in many cases obscured the much wider implications of the design and management of outdoor spaces for leisure and recreation. The upgrading of existing sportsgrounds in many of the urban fringe areas has not taken place. Indeed there are many instances of sportsgrounds in areas of outer London falling into disuse owing to declining interest, unimaginative management and the total absence of attractive outdoor recreational facilities likely to appeal to the family. It is not surprising, in these circumstances, that those organisations seeking to preserve recreational land against the threat of redevelopment have a difficult task if large areas of land remain unused for long periods in order to provide facilities for a declining group of sportsmen. The Pavilion as the servicing element for such areas is therefore likely in many instances to have a somewhat outdated image.

This situation could change dramatically if the philosophy that has encouraged the rapid growth of the indoor Sports Centre (see Section 6) throughout the country is applied to outdoor recreation. If the finance and management resources that have been expended on these centres is focused on the outdoor centre, the role of the Sports Pavilion could change in many fundamental respects. It is therefore important that sponsors of Pavilions and their designers should give serious consideration to the broad pattern of future recreational provision in the surrounding district by investigating a number of factors that are not always considered at present.

Information should be obtained on regional population figures both current and projected over the next ten years, advice should be obtained from all those organisations associated with leisure, sport and recreation in the region. An architect should be appointed with special knowledge to assist with the preparation of the brief and obtain expert management advice on the running of outdoor centres.

At this stage a feasibility study should be carried out in order to assess the viability of the scheme proposed. Research should be undertaken and visits made to existing related projects as appropriate. A check list of items to be considered might include the following:

1. List the possible combinations of facilities.
2. Determine indicative costs of each combination.
3. Assess the viability of the proposals under consideration in terms of: Patterns of use related to known and potential needs; capital costs and apportionments; loan charges and length of repayment period; management alternatives; operational considerations including wages and salaries; revenue and maintenance costs.

These considerations should be discussed with all interested parties. Time should be allowed for consultations with interested authorities and organisations. Agreement should then be reached on whether or not to proceed.

Steps to be taken following the decision to proceed with

an initial study should include:

1. The selection of site and appropriate alternative in terms of building type.
2. Consider nature of facilities to be provided including possible outline plan forms.
3. Consider possible relationship with similar existing facilities in the locality.
4. Prepare cost plan.
5. Present feasibility study to interested parties with preferred alternative, allow time for further consultations.
6. Establish firm commitment on whether or not to proceed.
7. Appoint Architect to commence design work.
8. Establish steering committee as appropriate with representatives of different organisations involved.
9. Prepare overall timetable.
10. Prepare detailed programme with the Architect for the design and constructional processess.

TYPES OF SPONSOR

In the past, three main types of sponsor have predominated:

1. The Private Club.
2. The Local Authority.
3. Firms' Sports Clubs.

More recently sponsorship by a voluntary organisation, such as a charitable trust, have developed. These have certain advantages, e.g. the benefit of any tax concessions that may be available and it is possible that this might be the more appropriate arrangement where local support is particularly strong and only limited facilities are required.

THE PRIVATE CLUB

One of the most significant trends in recent years has been the trend towards co-operative effort as many individual clubs are finding it difficult to survive or develop alone. The Walker Cricket Ground Trust, the Redbridge Sports Centre and the Harlow Sports Centre are examples of clubs grouping together under an umbrella organisation. These centres are run on the lines of charitable trusts.

THE LOCAL AUTHORITY

Many local authority pavilions tend to concentrate on the more basic kind of pavilion accommodation, such as changing rooms, showers and groundsman's storage space. The social accommodation is often more limited than is the case with the private club or charitable trust.

Recently the bulk of Local Authority resources have been devoted to the Indoor Sports Centre; the Pavilion as a building type has not developed significantly in this sector. (See also Section 6).

FIRMS' PAVILIONS

Many industrial and commercial enterprises have long recognised that good industrial relations depend to a large extent on the social and recreational facilities that are available to their employees. In many cases the facilities are run by a Sports and Social Club to which employees and their families can belong.

A considerable number of pavilions catering for this type of user have been built in recent years. In many instances this has been due to the relocation of sports grounds away from the firm's offices or factory so that this accommodation might be extended. Road improvement schemes and motorways are often sited across sportsgrounds in order to reduce the compensation payments, this has resulted in the formation of new grounds in outer suburban areas.

OTHER FORMS OF SPONSORSHIP

There are many other types of organisation who promote sports pavilions. These include; Schools (dual-provision facilities attached to schools available to the public out of school hours); University and Polytechnic pavilions; Pavilions for the armed services.

SPECIALIST PAVILIONS

Many Pavilions have been designed to serve one or two particular games some examples are as follows:
Tennis pavilions
Bowls pavilions
Cricket pavilions
Soccer pavilions
Rugby pavilions
Hockey pavilions
Athletics pavilions
There is, however, a trend towards more multi-purpose pavilions that are equipped with facilities for indoor games such as squash, badminton and combat sports. The planning of these facilities will be dealt with later.

SITING

There are a number of factors which require consideration when siting a pavilion these include:
Means of access for vehicles
Main services (particularly the sewer)
Availability of public utilities (water, electricity and gas)
The choice of fuel will have a considerable effect on running costs.
The pavilion will need to be sited in order to retain the largest land area for playing purposes but at the same time allowing space for future expansion.

ASPECT

Aspect becomes an important consideration if it is the intention to use the pavilion as a base for spectators. A low setting sun can seriously effect the viewing of games where the spectator facilities are positioned to face the geographical arc south-west to north-west. Table 10.1 provides an indication as to the correct orientation for pavilions serving four typical outdoor games.

Table 10.1 ORIENTATION OF PAVILIONS

Activity	Time of day	Pitch axis	Pavilion orientation (facing)
Football, rugby, netball, hockey	early p.m.	North/south	East
Cricket	11.00–20.00	NW to SE	South East
Tennis	p.m.	North/south	East
Running tracks	p.m.	NNW to SSE	West

In the case of certain games, in particular; football, rugby, netball, hockey, the increasing popularity of all-weather surfaces and reinforced grass surfaces will permit the surfaces to be more intensively used. It is probable that the greater intensity of use will result in the use of these pitches throughout the day, in fact it is economically desirable that this occurs in order to justify the high capital cost of the surface.

Having minimised the effects of solar glare by orientation residual glare factors can be examined by reference to a stereographic sun-path diagram as indicated in Fig. 10.1 which relates to latitude 52°N. The diagram requires amendment for each degree of latitude, north or south of the value quoted (London lies mid-way between latitudes 51° and 52°N) for such fine adjustments an infinitely variable sky vault elevation indicator is required, but the sun path diagram may give the designer an adequate grasp of the sun angles with which he has to contend.

In practice such close examination of sun angles will be required only for precise placing of canopies which need to act as solar louvres.

Another important consideration is the direction of the prevailing wind; sheltered viewing should be provided if possible. Sports Pavilions are often located on exposed sites and natural shelter should be considered wherever possible. In many cases architectural detailing related to weather protection should be carefully considered to prevent the penetration of damp through doors windows and junctions. Increased thermal insulation may also need to be provided.

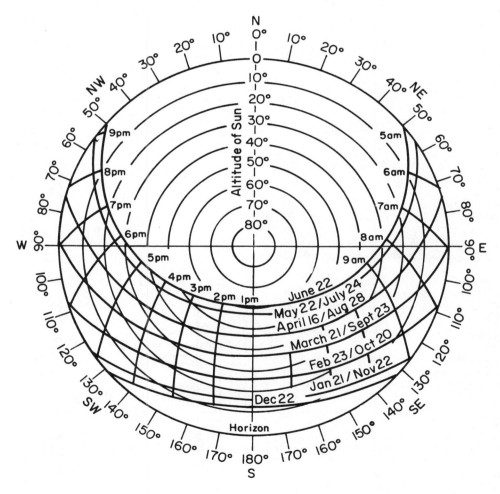

Fig. 10.1 Sun-path diagram

PLANNING

The design of sports pavilions differs little in method from that adopted for all buildings. Factors affecting the brief and site location have already been mentioned, but before starting, all information needed regarding the site and the building requirements must be collected, including an accurate site survey, facilities for access, availability of services, planning limitations and accommodation requirements. Reference has been made to the types of sponsor and it is likely that the range of accommodation to be provided will vary considerably with the type of user, however the basic accommodation is likely to remain the same with differences in emphasis. For example the premises of a private or industrial club are likely to include more extensive social facilities than perhaps a local authority pavilion serving a municipal ground. Non playing members will require to be accommodated in the former and more generous lounge and catering facilities will be required as well as children's play facilities.

Listed below are the kinds of accommodation required in most medium sized sports pavilions serving private and industrial clubs:

> Entrance hall
> Clubroom, terrace
> Lounge
> Dining-room
> Games room
> Billiard room
> Bar, bar service area, bar stores and access yard with crate store
> Administrative office
> Committee room
> Kitchen servery
> Kitchen, preparation area, storage, cold room
> Men members' changing rooms, men visitor's changing rooms
> Men's showers and toilets
> Women members' changing rooms, women visitors changing rooms
> Women's showers and toilets, powder room
> Referee's changing room, Coach's room, First aid room
> Laundry
> Public toilets and cloakroom off the entrance hall
> Staff room with facilities for making light refreshments
> Professional shop, internal store for sports equipment (sports gear shop)
> Boiler room, fuel store, electrical intake room, calorifier room
> Battery room for emergency lighting equipment
> Resident officer's living quarters including; living room, dining space, kitchen, bedrooms, bathroom and w.c.

Outside facilities

> Score box and board (cricket) flagmast
> Store for field equipment, gang mowers, tractor and other items
> Fertiliser store
> Groundsman's yard for maintenance
> Workshop

10–4

Circulation, dealing as it does with the position and placing of individual rooms and their relationship to each other, is vital to the efficiency of any building. Regardless of size, circulation is a factor of prime importance in the design of all sports buildings, including pavilions, because users are frequently moving from one part of the building to another, or passing to and from the playing fields.

Once the basic circulation requirements have been established, it may be equally possible to implement them in buildings with one, two or more storeys. This is particularly the case on the open sites which are usually available for pavilions. The smaller types are almost always single-storeyed structures but larger buildings may require additional storeys to ensure compactness, or to provide adequate prospect conditions or even to ensure that the mass of the building will be imposing. In cases where the site is restricted and the building large, more than one storey may be unavoidable even if desirable on all other counts.

Circulation diagrams relating to small, medium and large pavilions are shown in Figs. 10.2, 10.3 and 10.4.

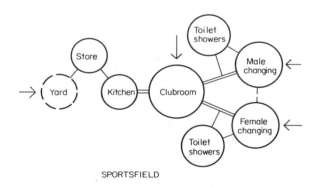

SPORTSFIELD

Fig. 10.2   Circulation diagram for small pavilion

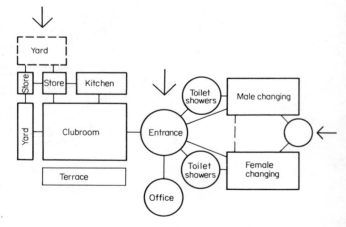

Fig. 10.3   Medium pavilion

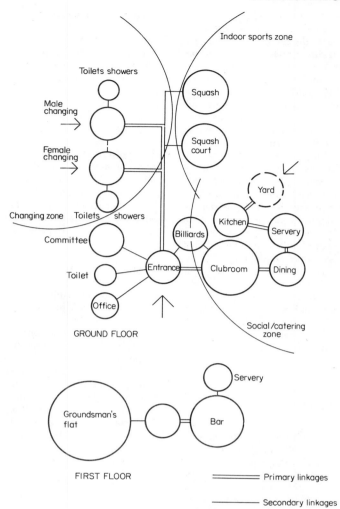

Fig. 10.4   Large pavilion

ENTRANCE HALL

An entrance hall can either be an introductory space to one of the larger rooms, probably the clubroom itself, or it can serve as the circulation centre, linking the various rooms and areas together.

In practice it is likely that it will perform both of these functions.

The entrance hall is likely to play an important role in determining the success of the social facilities that are provided. It should encourage social interchange and a relaxed atmosphere. Social facilities such as the bar, clubroom and cafeteria are more highly utilised if they communicate directly with the entrance hall.

In the larger pavilions public toilets should be readily accessible from the entrance hall, their size will depend upon the nature of the accommodation to be provided in the pavilion. A sports shop is another facility for which the entrance hall provides an ideal location.

Where squash courts are incorporated into the pavilion a display court can, by means of the glass back wall, be located off the entrance hall where it will promote interest in the game and add to the attraction of the entrance hall. Plenty of space should be allowed for notice boards with strip lights to provide information on club activities and hanging space for club photographs and trophies. Provision should be made for a public telephone.

CLUBROOM

In small pavilions the clubroom has to serve a multitude of purposes. Its nominal function is that of providing for the social life of the club, but this can be extended if facilities for refreshment, drinks, administration and indoor games, such as table tennis, are included. In larger buildings it is probable that the clubroom will have a more defined and specific function more closely related to social activities. Ideally the clubroom should overlook the sportsfield and provide viewing for spectators of the outside sports.

The sports pavilion is essentially an outward looking building and access to an outside terrace and external facilities should be easy. It is difficult to establish a rational method of determining the area of a clubroom and the circumstances will differ in each design problem. In the case of small pavilions, critical dimensions are likely to be governed by the minimum area required to accommodate two cricket teams for refreshments and the occasional sit-down tea. In the larger pavilion, considerations such as the minimum area for a dance floor with space for tables around the perimeter will apply. If funds permit, the clubroom could relate to the minimum dimensions required for a singles badminton court (16.5 × 9 × 6.7 m high).

A clubroom that is to be used for dances must not be less than 6 m wide to function effectively. The guide to the number of dancers is 2–2.50 m² of space per couple. Refreshment service is essential; even if a separate dining-room or lounge is included in the plan service is usually best provided by means of a hatch directly from the kitchen or a service area and counter.

The bar usually forms a part of the clubroom in the smaller building, and for some clubs this is satisfactory. Where families are likely to use the building, as is increasingly the case, a separate room is better. The bar may be effectively incorporated with the refreshment service in some cases.

In larger buildings, space for a band will be required with provision for a stage which may be 450 mm high. An amplification or record room adjoining the stage area is an advantage (1.8 × 1.5 m) with a countertop and space for storage of records.

LOUNGE

The lounge, as distinct from the clubroom, can be entirely separate, or a part of the clubroom itself with dividing doors, to enable the larger space to be used when required.

It is difficult to assess the number of persons likely to use the lounge at any particular time. At least 1.86 m² per person allows for comfortable seating, with space for tables and service of teas and light refreshments. If it is decided to provide an entirely separate room it might be appropriate to position it well away from the clubroom, in a quiet part of the building and with a different and more intimate outlook.

The lounge is likely to be used by lady members, or for card games and as a supplementary committee room.

DINING ROOM

Few sports pavilions need a special dining-room as the clubroom will serve this purpose when meals are required for such functions as evening dinners and on special occasions. A combined social centre and pavilion may in certain circumstances need a dining-room, but as with the lounge, this may be a part of the large social area separated by sliding folding doors.

If a considerable number of social functions are certain to take place, an independent dining-room with efficient servery from the kitchen is needed. Guidance for the size of room required is 1.2 m² per diner. Small tables for two or four persons can be used and stored when bench or long tables are needed for team teas or evening dinners.

LADY MEMBERS' ROOM

Lady members' rooms are less common in pavilions than in golf clubhouses, but in many ways this is a useful element, providing a quiet lounge and rest room. If a separate lounge is provided, this might well be combined and used as a lady members' room.

GAMES ROOM

It is a considerable advantage in a large building to have a separate games room in addition to a clubroom, which may itself be used for indoor games. Generally sufficient space should be allowed for table tennis and measure 8 × 4.5 m.

A smaller room might do for card games and darts, but would not make a good general games room. Direct sunlight is undesirable as glare in the player's eyes must be avoided.

BILLIARD ROOM

The provision of a full sized billiard table is advantageous in the majority of clubs. The table itself is 3.86 m × 2.03 m × 750 mm high but a floor area of 7.62 × 5.48 m is required for cueing. If more than one table is required, there should be a space of 1.8 m between the tables. If seats are required around the walls, 450 mm will be required in addition to the cueing space. Marking board and cue racks are fixed to the walls in convenient positions.

A reasonable height for the room is 3–3.6 m to permit adequate ventilation as well as space for lights and shades. Flat surfaces for drinks and ash trays are required in the form of fitted units. If ceiling heights are lower than recommended additional ventilation will be required in the form of mechanical extractors.

BAR

The bar will consist of a room used by members for taking alcoholic drinks in company with their fellows, together with a bar service space. The design of the service area is particularly important and is frequently overlooked as service areas are often complicated.

It is recommended that discussions should take place with the licensing authority as early as possible in the design process so as to establish the form and position of the bar. It will need to be separated from other catering areas in order to allow children and juveniles to obtain snacks and refreshments during licensing hours.

The bar counter requires special consideration and the advice of a local brewery should be sought as early as possible in the design programme so as to ascertain the provision that should be made for equipment and display. The length of the counter is a critical factor. A long counter enables more staff to be employed at peak periods and facilitates service to the customer.

Adequate provision behind the counter will be required for CO_2 bottles, beer kegs wash up sinks and glass storage. Behind the bar ample provision should be made for the display of bottled beer, spirits and minerals.

The bar room will govern the size of the service area. For

comfort, at least 0.74 m² of space per member is required, but it is difficult in practice to determine how many members at a time are likely to use the room. If two rooms are provided, each should be adjacent to a single service area, and only one opened unless a large number of users occupy the premises at one time, or an evening function is in progress. This arrangement prevents the unsatisfactory atmosphere created by only one or two people drinking in a large cold room.

BEER STORE

The size of this area will vary according to the frequency of beer deliveries. The store should be situated either at the back or under the bar area.

Spirit store. A separate lock-up spirit store should adjoin the beer store.

Crate store—open yard. Ample space should be allowed for the storage of crates, part of this area might be covered with lean-to roofs for unused crates. Recommended minimum area, for medium sized pavilion, 36 m². The floor surface should be laid to fall to a gully for washdown purposes.

ADMINISTRATIVE OFFICE

This room is primarily for the use of the resident officer in the pavilion. The area may be between 7.4 m² and 14.8 m². Good daylight is essential and a pleasant prospect desirable, if possible the office should be located to facilitate supervision of the sports ground and pavilion accommodation.

It is probable that provision will be required for a small safe containing money, confidential documents and members' valuables. The office should be near the entrance hall so that an enquiry counter or hatch is immediately accessible to persons entering the building. A telephone will be needed in the office, together with a master clock, serving slave clocks located where necessary throughout the building.

COMMITTEE ROOM

Ideally, every club should have small rooms where committees controlling the various activities can meet. Reference has already been made to the use of the lounge as a supplementary committee room but, in the larger pavilions a separate committee room might be considered necessary.

The committee room should be easily accessible from the main circulation areas and might adjoin the bar or cafeteria from which it might be divided by a sliding folding partition. In a room designed solely for committee use the only furniture required is a large central table and a small table near one wall, with some chairs.

KITCHEN

The size of the pavilion and the nature of the catering likely to be required will determine the size and complexity of the kitchen. Smaller buildings with only one room for social activities will require direct service to this area through a hatch with a counter.

The kitchen area should meet the requirements of the Food and Hygiene Regulations 1955 and the latest requirements of the Public Health Authority. It is essential to decide initially on the type of catering that it is the intention to provide, by ascertaining certain basic requirements relating firstly to equipment and accommodation and secondly by arranging the various items of equipment in the correct sequence with adequate space for access.

The amount of equipment and accommodation will relate principally to the following:

Number of meals to be served
Length of the dining period
Form of service
Type of meal and range of menu
Staff available.

The arrangement of equipment and accommodation will be decided by the correct analysis and an understanding of the sequence of operations taking place in the area. A wash hand basin provided with hot and cold running water should be installed in addition to the sinks in any pavilion kitchen, this is a public health requirement.

Where space available for catering is limited and the maximum amount of space is required for dining, savings of space in the kitchen area can be achieved by the use of food which has been prepared before delivery to the premises. These are commonly known as 'convenience foods' which range from washed peeled vegetables to fully prepared precooked frozen foods requiring only to be reheated or regenerated to form the basis of a meal. The use of these foods can enable storage accommodation and preparation areas to be reduced, although the volume of refrigerated storage will need to be increased.

KITCHEN/SERVERY

The design of a servery or service area is very important in a pavilion, regardless of its size. In many cases this area has to serve as a bar, and for snacks and beverages, but this arrangement is not ideal.

CHANGING ROOMS

One major difficulty in designing changing rooms is to estimate how many of each sex will be likely to attend at any particular time. Generally men predominate. Some clubs, such as tennis clubs may need accommodation for equal numbers of men and women, while larger pavilions may be designed to provide separate changing rooms for visitors. Flexibility of planning is desirable, allowing the allocation of space to vary according to the number of each sex likely to predominate at any time. When it is possible to estimate accurately a definite ratio, two independent plan areas may be incorporated without considering flexibility. (See diagrams in Fig. 10.5 which show the plans of the Sports Pavilion at Merton College Oxford).

Changing space can be either in one large room, or in a series of cells or smaller rooms served by passages. The latter method is preferable in terms of amenity control and safety of clothes and valuables. Each changing room should be big enough to accommodate about twelve persons at the recom-

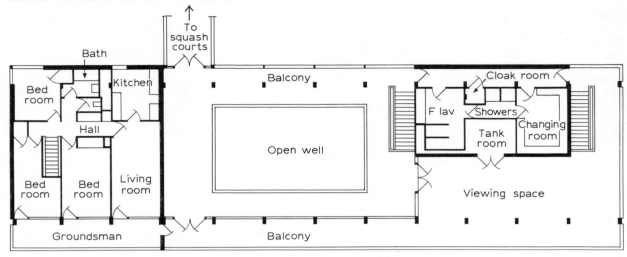

First floor plan

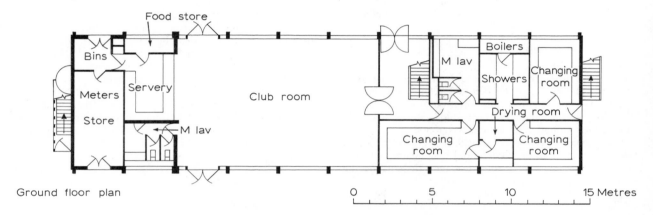

Ground floor plan

Fig. 10.5   Plans of the Sports Pavilion, Merton College, Oxford

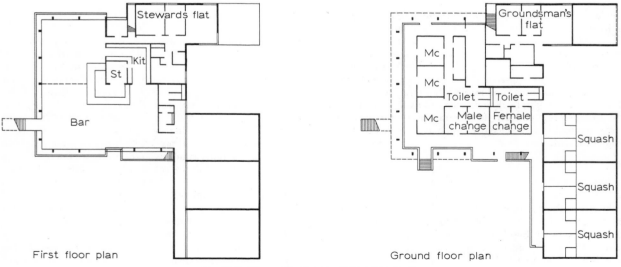

First floor plan

Ground floor plan

Fig. 10.6   Plans of the Uxbridge Cricket Club Pavilion

Fig. 10.7   Sports Pavilion, Merton College, Oxford
(Photographer: Thomas-Photos)

Fig. 10.8   Sports Pavilion, Old Dean Common, Camberley
(Photographer: Richard Sharpe Studios Ltd.)

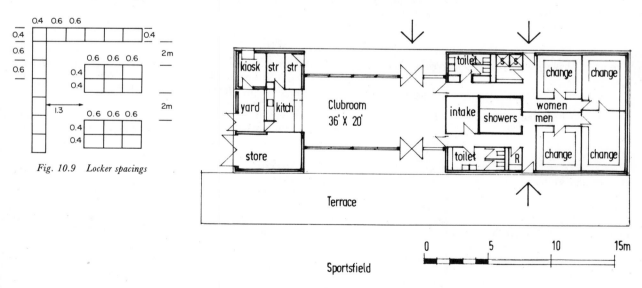

Fig. 10.9   Locker spacings

Fig. 10.10   Plan of the Sports Pavilion, Old Dean Common, Camberley

mended figure of 0·7–0·84 m². Large changing rooms may be subdivided into manageable units of approximately 10 m² by seats and clothes-storage fittings. This is economic in use of the space and provides an amenity standard comparable with individual rooms, excepting for the protection of clothes and valuables from pilfering. This latter factor is likely to be a particular problem in local authority pavilions and in the large social centre where several teams play and use the building simultaneously.

The provision of individual lockers (Fig. 10.9) is an ideal solution in all changing rooms, but the expense involved usually precludes this solution. Changing rooms approached from passages may be locked up separately to enable one team to use each room and this reduces the need for locker accommodation. If indoor sports, such as squash and badminton, are played some lockers will be required and the same applies to outdoor games such as tennis.

Increasing building costs will undoubtedly lead to the examination of the increased use of changing rooms. This can be achieved by staggering the start of games and the provision of more lockers to facilitate greater intensity of use. Another recent method is the provision of wardrobe units, each unit being large enough to accommodate the clothes storage requirements of a team. Two wardrobes are provided in each changing room thus enabling two teams to utilise the same room provided the period between the commencement of the games is at least 15 minutes.

Changing rooms should be sited to give direct access, via a corridor, to the outside playing areas. The corridor should have a hard floor finish such as quarry tiles or a granolithic floor finish. The number of changing spaces will relate to the maximum utilisation of the playing spaces, plus an allowance for overlap. The extent of the changing accommodation will depend on the maximum number of players passing through the changing rooms within a given period multiplied by a factor of between two and three for overlap, dependent on demand. This is particularly the case where games such as tennis, badminton and squash are played.

For example, if there are two tennis courts and two squash courts, assuming a one hour play period for tennis and a half-hour play period for squash, the number of changing spaces will be as follows:

Tennis
2 courts × 4 players playing × 2 (overlap) = 16

Squash
2 × 2 courts × 2 players playing × 2 (overlap) = 16

Total number of changing spaces = 32

SHOWERS

It is considered that three to four showers per 12 players, are adequate to meet present day requirements for outdoor games. In the case of indoor games, there should be at least one shower provided per seven changing spaces with a minimum of two showers for each sex. For squash, the number of showers should be increased to provide one shower per five changing spaces. Separate shower cubicles are preferred by women.

All shower areas should be fitted with high level extract fans. Air change rates per hour should be between eight and ten. Shower areas should, if possible, directly adjoin the changing rooms. Cross circulation between changing rooms and showers should be avoided. Elimination of corridors between changing and showers is to be preferred, by placing showering and drying areas as an integral part of the changing room. If corridors are necessary they should serve as linkages between changing rooms and showers with as few other functions as possible.

The high coincidence of demand for showers in pavilions necessitates the provision of large capacity cold water storage tanks and larger than average calorifiers. Adequate space should therefore be allowed for a calorifier room or an enlarged boiler room in the case of larger pavilions. In some smaller pavilions, instantaneous gas water heaters have been used, provided adequate pressure can be obtained from high level storage tanks. If the Water authority permits these appliances to be connected direct to the mains, considerable savings in cost can be obtained. It is probable, however, that heaters will be required in the ratio of one to each shower.

PLUNGE BATHS

These are still preferred by most rugby clubs and many soccer players and can be considered where the finance is available as an additional feature to the shower provision, which may be reduced accordingly.

Plunge baths do, however, require a much more generous water supply and boiler capacity than can generally be afforded by most sponsors.

TOILETS AND WASH BASINS

WCs (2 minimum)	1 per team or 15 persons.
	2 per team or 15 persons female.
Urinals	1 per team or 15 persons.
Lavatory basins	1 per 15 males.
	1 per 15 females.

REFEREE'S/COACH'S ROOM

It is often advantageous to provide a small separate referee's room in the changing room area to permit the referee to be away from the players.

For a small pavilion providing for a single referee, a room 6 m² would be sufficient. Larger rooms can be provided to the same space standards as the changing accommodation.

DRYING ROOM

A small drying room is sometimes required, where players have no laundry facilities of their own, as in universities. This will adjoin a small laundry room with a double bowl sink unit and space for a washing machine.

STAFF ROOM

This room should be located away from the primary activity

spaces with, if possible, a pleasant outlook. A sink with cupboard space should be provided together with facilities for making teas and light refreshments.

PROFESSIONAL SHOP

Unlike golf clubhouses, pavilions rarely incorporate a shop for marketing sports equipment and clothes. The pavilion with extensive indoor sports such as squash and badminton, however, would benefit considerably from such a service.

The shop may be simply a room with shelving for display and cupboard storage at one extreme or a miniature shop in the accepted sense of the word with counter and plate glass window. In some cases, separate lock-up display cabinets are provided, with the equipment being sold from the office.

INTERNAL STORE FOR SPORTS EQUIPMENT

In addition to the normal storage related to the functions of the building i.e. cleaners' cupboards, chair and table stores adjoining the social areas and kitchen and bar stores, provision should be made for the storage of sports equipment. If possible the store should adjoin the office so that balls, rackets and other sports equipment can be hired out to members.

Stores for the larger items of equipment such as table tennis tables and nets and posts for indoor games such as badminton and volleyball (if larger halls are provided), should be located directly adjoining the space where the equipment is required.

STORES FOR EXTERNAL EQUIPMENT

Storage for the various items of groundsman's equipment including; gang mowers, tractors, markers and items such as goal posts, can be accommodated in the pavilion or in a separate groundsman's compound which might adjoin his house.

It is probable that most medium sized pavilions will require an area equivalent to at least three lock-up garages. In addition a small store will be required for fertiliser.

A garage will be required for the groundsman's car. This is often overlooked and valuable space in the equipment store has to be used for this purpose.

SCORER'S BOX

Space will be required for two or three scorers with a wide prospect of the whole field. Space should be provided for a table or fitted unit with a desk top and seats. The score board should be sited conveniently near the scorers so that it can be seen from all parts of the field.

In some cases scorers can be accommodated on the pavilion balcony but difficulties can arise if the score board is manually operated as it is difficult for the scorers to see the board and for the score to be registered on the board.

BATTERY ROOM

This room is only needed when a building is to be licensed for public entertainment and when, in consequence, a secondary system of electric lighting is necessary. It houses the batteries which are charged by the mains supply and which function in the event of the mains supply failing.

The size, dependent on number of batteries, is generally 2.3–2.8 m² in area. The floor must be tanked to a depth of 150–225 mm and covered with acid resisting compound or tiles in order to contain liquid in the event of breakage or a leak from any of the units.

EXAMPLES

Esher Cricket Club Pavilion
    Architect: Colin Stansfield Smith, of Emberton Tardrew & Partners.

University of Essex Pavilion
    Architects: Gasson and Meunier.

Merton College Oxford Pavilion (Figs 10.5 and 10.7)
    Architect: Michael Dixey in association with R Sudell and Partners.

Old Dean Sports Pavilion, Camberley (Figs 10.8 and 10.10)
    Architect: Michael Dixey in association with R Sudell and Partners.

Uxbridge Cricket Club Pavilion (Fig. 10.6)
    Architect: Jaques Muir and Johnson.

BIBLIOGRAPHY

Ackroyd, P. *Sports Pavilions,* National Playing Fields Association (Jan 1970).
Dixey, Michael, *Local Recreation Centres,* National Playing Fields Association (Feb 1974).
Sports Halls: a new approach to their dimensions and use, Sports Council.
Facilities for Squash Rackets, TUS Bulletin 2. Sports Council
Sudell, R. and Waters, D. Tennyson, *Sports Buildings and Playing Fields,* Batsford (1957).
Sudell, R. and Dixey, M. G. D. 'Suitable sport buildings for local Authorities', *Municipal Journal* (Nov 1963).

GOLF CLUBHOUSES

INTRODUCTION

The popularity of Golf is growing rapidly and there is a considerable shortage of courses. The Golf Foundation estimate that the number of golfers in Britain doubled between 1954 and 1967. In both national surveys golf ranked in the top three active pursuits for men in the age groups 30–44 and 45–60. The game has many advantages which suggest further growth. It requires little organisation and is played throughout the year by both sexes over a wide range of skill and age.

The current level of provision in England and Wales is one 18-hole course per 50 000 population. The Sports Council estimate that there will be a requirement for one course per 36 000 by 1981.

The Sports Council's assessment of requirements suggest that future provision should be concentrated principally on the provision of municipal courses. The regional assessments suggest that the equivalent of 485 new 18-hole golf courses will be required by 1981. Present evidence suggests that municipal courses are best for achieving a high usage rate and a more flexible management policy.

There is increasing evidence that there is a need for a more professional approach to the management and design of golf clubhouses perhaps based on American practice.

The selection of an appropriate site for courses will follow on the same lines as those outlined for pavilions, a similar check list might be appropriate.

TYPES OF SPONSOR

There are two principal types of sponsor;

1. The private club.
2. The Local Authority municipal clubhouse.

The basic requirement of both types are similar, but it is probable that the private club will develop along the lines of the Country Club.

THE PRIVATE CLUB

The tendency to broaden the choice of facilities is perhaps one of the most important developments. As with pavilions, squash courts, swimming pools and facilities for children are being included in many new golf club developments.

The proposed major golf/sports complex at Ragley Hall near Stratford by Roger Dyer Associates illustrates the sort of facility that might develop in the private sector in the future. The complex includes; 12 squash courts, a conference centre, sports hall, sleeping accommodation, a leisure pool, restaurant together with facilities for children, etc. This sort of complex is common in the USA and requires expert management for its efficient operation, (see Figs 10.10, 10.11 and 10.12).

MUNICIPAL GOLF COURSES

There is a tendency for municipal courses to investigate the possibility of permanent membership in order to stabilise the operating costs and encourage social membership. There is therefore the probability that private and public courses will come closer both in the provision of facilities and in the type of management in the future.

SITING OF CLUBHOUSE

The clubhouse should not be so sited that defects in the layouts of holes are introduced. A good starting and finishing hole, two or more starting points, views of play, especially the 18th green and 1st tees, should receive consideration, together with consideration of such questions as access and services.

Clubhouse sites in the corner of a course or at the end of a narrow neck of land may cause difficulties in general layout. A central situation is easier, but might involve increased road costs. The careful investigation of the problem is therefore of paramount importance.

Most clubhouses function throughout the year and are continuously in operation. It is therefore essential that provision is made for a steward's flat.

ACCOMMODATION

The basic accommodation required for an 18 hole golf course is likely to be as follows:

> Men's changing room with lockers (including drying area, showers and toilets)
> Ladies' changing room with lockers (including drying area, showers and toilets)
> A large professional Shop and workshop
> A Committee room
> A flat for a Steward
> A Manager's office
> Lounge
> Kitchen/stores
> Clubroom with bar (in some cases the committee room will adjoin the clubroom)
> Beer store with separate lock up spirit store
> Toilets

Additional accommodation might include:

> A trolley store
> A Professional's flat or house
> Multi-purpose room

CIRCULATION

It is important that the locker rooms and professional's accommodation have easy access to the 1st tee and 18th green and also, preferably, the 9th green and 10th tee.

The main entrance to the clubhouse from the car park is generally separate from the golfer's access to the course. The changing rooms and locker rooms should be arranged to facilitate the changing of wet clothes and footwear prior to entry into the social areas.

The secretary's room and manager's office will need to control the main public entrance from the car park and will provide supervision and green fee payments. The social accommodation is often provided at first floor level with views over the course. The Steward's flat will need to adjoin the bar, lounge and clubroom areas.

A basic circulation diagram is shown in Fig. 10.11.

MEN'S CHANGING ROOM

The area of the locker room will depend upon the capacity of the course. An 18 hole course will be saturated at about 120 players based on four balls every six minutes for three hours. If allowance is made for evening players, the course will support 150 players.

The maximum number of people likely to be using the locker/changing room at any one time will probably not exceed 40–50. An allowance of 0.93 m² per person will therefore give a minimum area of 46.45 m². An extra allowance should be made for lockers. If clubs are kept in lockers, each locker, with seat, will occupy approximately 0.46 m²; an area of 92 m² should therefore be allowed for lockers. Access to the course from the changing/locker room should be supervised by the professional's shop.

Extra space, preferably not enclosed, should be allowed for a drying area.

MEN'S TOILET AND SHOWERS

It is possible that 50 players will require to use the sanitary accommodation at any one time. It is therefore necessary to double the normal standards, one urinal and w.c. for 25 men and one basin for 15 men; e.g. 3–4 w.c.'s, 4 urinals and 4.5 basins for 50 people. At least 2 showers should be provided.

LADIES' LOCKER ROOM

Slightly less space will be required for the ladies' locker room owing to the smaller number of players. The ratio of male to female players will need to be ascertained as far as possible at the design stage. Similar space requirements, per player, will be required to those provided in the men's locker rooms, but an increased proportion of hanging space and hand lockers will be required.

Toilet accommodation will be similar in proportion to numbers to that provided in the men's locker room, based on normal standards.

PROFESSIONAL'S SHOP

As the Professional is likely to control starting times and collect green fees the Shop should be located with views over the course, particularly the 1st tee. Recommended area is

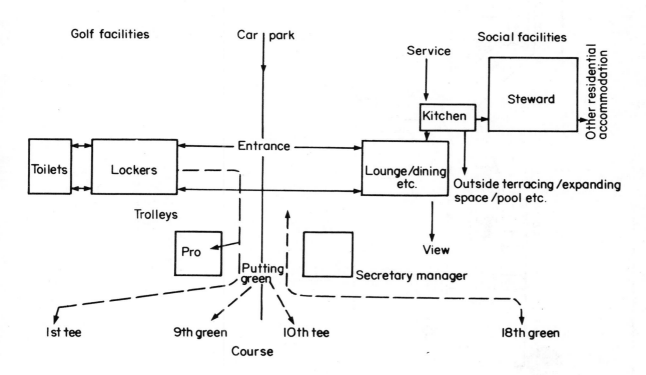

Fig. 10.11 *Typical circulation diagram—single storey building*
The circulation for a two-storey building would be similar.

10–13

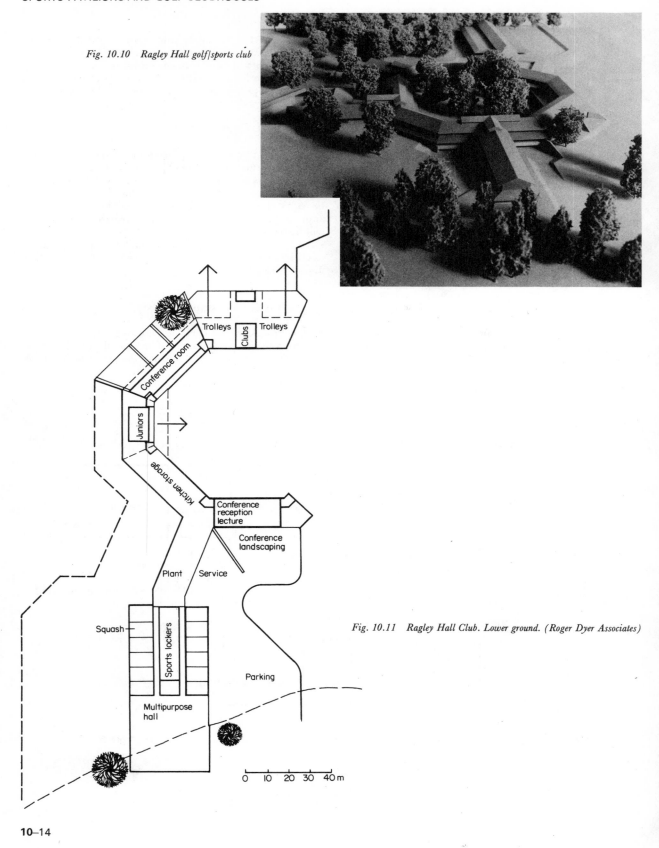

Fig. 10.10   Ragley Hall golf/sports club

Trolleys

Clubs

Trolleys

Conference room

Juniors

Kitchen storage

Conference
reception
lecture

Conference
landscaping

Plant   Service

Squash

Sports lockers

Parking

Multipurpose
hall

0   10   20   30   40 m

Fig. 10.11   Ragley Hall Club. Lower ground. (Roger Dyer Associates)

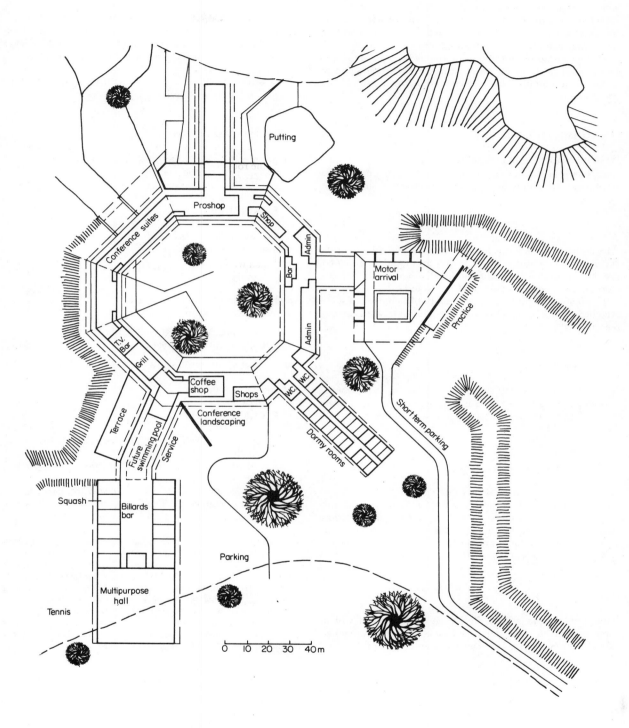

Fig. 10.12   Ragley Hall Club. Ground floor plan (Roger Dyer Associates)

55.75 m². Adequate space for display should be provided as well as height to swing a club, if the shop is not linked to an undercover practice area. The workroom should be of sufficient size to accommodate a vice bench. Office and trolley storage can also be incorporated into this complex.

If clubs are to be stored outside the locker area space will be required in this area, more clubs can be accommodated if stored horizontally, but less wear and tear will result if they are stored vertically.

COMMITTEE ROOM

As in the Sports Pavilion, a space large enough to accommodate a table tennis table would be an advantage. A space 8 × 4.5 m is recommended, but a smaller room would suffice.

STEWARD'S FLAT

The position of the flat is important and it should adjoin the social and bar facilities. Three bedrooms should be provided, to enable a family to be accommodated, otherwise the accommodation should be to Parker Morris standards.

This facility might be omitted on a Public course but some attached living accommodation is desirable for security reasons.

MANAGER'S OFFICE

This room should supervise all points of access to the course, should be capable of accommodating permanent records, day to day papers as well as a typist. Recommended area is between 13.94 and 23.23 m².

LOUNGE/CLUBROOM

The area of this room may be from 55.74–111.48 m². Views over the finishing hole are essential. This room will only accommodate day-to-day use unless linked to other rooms, perhaps the committee room, when it may accommodate competitions. The room may be integrated with a snack bar or bar in the smaller clubs.

KITCHEN/STORES

This room should adjoin the lounge and bar and will be large enough to serve bar type snacks if of minimum size. Area recommended is between 18.58 and 37.16 m².

MULTI-PURPOSE ROOM/BAR

Area recommended may vary between 32.52 m² and 80 m². This will provide a snug bar at the minimum area. If extended the room might be used for TV viewing, golf societies and committee meetings, if no separate accommodation is provided.

The service facilities to the bar will be similar to those suitable for the Sports Pavilion.

PROFESSIONAL'S FLAT

If required will be to similar standards to those of the steward but perhaps better appointed.

EXAMPLES

Bentley Golf and Country Club
  Roger Dyer Associates

Lilley Brook Golf Club Cheltenham
  Roger Dyer Associates

Kenilworth Golf Club, Kenilworth
  Roger Dyer Associates

Hatchford Brook Municipal Golf Club, Birmingham
  Birmingham City Architect

Ragley Hall Golf/Sports Club Stratford (see Figures 10.10, 10.11 and 10.12)
  Roger Dyer Associates

BIBLIOGRAPHY

Dyer, Roger, *Golf Clubhouses—a planning guide*, Golf Development Council.
Provision for Sport. Indoor Swimming Pools. Indoor Sports Centres. Golf Courses, Sports Council.
Public Golf Courses: provision and management, Sports Council.
Sudell, R and Waters, D. Tennyson, 'Sports Buildings and Playing Fields', Batsford (1957).

Michael Dixey, *Dip. Arch. RIBA, Educated at the Northern Polytechnic School of Architecture. Joined Playne and Lacey in 1955 and Sudell and Partners in 1958. He formed his own practice in 1968 and is currently with the Department of the Environment. Michael Dixey has been responsible for a number of sports pavilions and recreation centres including the new sports pavilion for Merton College, Oxford. Researcher for the National Playing Fields Association and spent 2½ years with the Technical Unit for Sport at The Sports Council. He has conducted research into most types of recreational buildings including facilities for Squash. Author of 'Local Recreation Centres' published by The National Playing Fields Association.*

INDEX

INDEX

INDEX